THE TREASURY OF THE
AUTOMOBILE
BY RALPH STEIN

SPECIAL PHOTOGRAPHY BY
THOMAS H. BURNSIDE

A RIDGE PRESS BOOK
GOLDEN PRESS / NEW YORK

THE TREASURY OF THE
AUTOMOBILE
BY RALPH STEIN

SPECIAL PHOTOGRAPHY BY
THOMAS H. BURNSIDE

A RIDGE PRESS BOOK
GOLDEN PRESS / NEW YORK

PREPARED AND PRODUCED BY
THE RIDGE PRESS, INC.
PRINTED IN THE UNITED STATES
OF AMERICA BY WESTERN PRINTING
AND LITHOGRAPHING COMPANY.
PUBLISHED BY GOLDEN PRESS, INC.,
ROCKEFELLER CENTER,
NEW YORK 20, NEW YORK

EDITOR-IN-CHIEF: JERRY MASON
EDITOR: ADOLPH SUEHSDORF
ART DIRECTOR: ALBERT A. SQUILLACE
PROJECT EDITOR: EVELYN HANNON
ASSOCIATE EDITOR: RUTH BIRNKRANT
ASSOCIATE EDITOR: EDWINA HAZARD GLEN
ART ASSOCIATE: LEON BOLOGNESE

CONTENTS

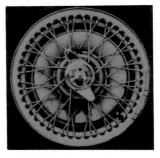

PREFACE

This is a book for people who like the automobile. Any kind of automobile. New cars, old cars, sports cars, steam cars, racing cars, good cars, even bad cars.

These are the years of the renaissance of the motor car. After decades of disinterest, the rebirth of excitement about automobiles has not only brought forth new and wondrous road vehicles and new clubs devoted to motor sport or the collecting of antiques, but has set people to reading (and writing) about anything and everything to do with cars.

For years, during the 1920's and 1930's, it was hard to find much to read about cars. Those few of us who were daft about automobiles depended on foreign magazines like the British *Autocar* and *Motor*. For information about sporting and racing cars we read *Motor Sport*, also from England. The few American magazines about automobiles had ceased, long before, to direct much of their contents toward the car owner. They were almost entirely devoted to trade matters; their advertising tried to sell things like greasing racks and cylinder-grinding machines.

To satisfy our craving for books about cars, we found it necessary to go to the Public Library and read what was published between 1900 and 1914—years when automobiles still engrossed people enough to be written about. In the library we first discovered such wonders as W. Worby Beaumont's *Motor Vehicles and Motors* (1902), Gerald Rose's *Record of Motor Racing* (1909), Charles Jarrott's *Ten Years of Motors and Motor Racing* (1906), *Motors and Motor Driving* (1902), one of the Badminton Library's series on sporting subjects, and many others, almost all of them published in England. Of course, we feasted, too, in the reading room of the Public Library, on the bound volumes of foreign and early American automobile magazines like *The Horseless Age*.

One evening, in about 1932, as my brother and I sat enchanted over a dusty volume of the British *Motor* of the Twenties, looking at the pictures in an article about Morgan Three-Wheelers, a young man next to us nudged me. He held up a dog-eared snapshot of a Morgan Three-Wheeler, similar to the ones we were admiring, and motioned toward the door of the reading room. We followed eagerly and went outside to talk cars for the next few hours.

No, he didn't own a Three-Wheeler, but he *did* own a 1914 Stutz Bearcat and his name was Smith Hempstone Oliver. Finding someone who had even *heard* about sports cars in those benighted times was a memorable event. Within the next few days we sampled his Stutz, he our Alfa Romeo. Years later, Oliver became Curator of Land Transportation at the Smithsonian Institution, and I have used photographs of cars he had in his charge in this book.

Nowadays, happily, there is much lovely stuff to read: American magazines like *Road and Track* and *Car and Driver,* and so many new books about cars that the interested reader can wallow in automotive lore if he wishes. There are books devoted exclusively to racing cars, to antique cars, to sports cars, to racing drivers, books full of mathematical formulae about cylinder heads, books specializing in the cabals of roll centers and slip angles. They are fine. I love them all. Many people who palpitate with enthusiasm about the innermost minutiae of motor cars love them, too.

But this book is not specialized. It covers a long period and a large canvas and the brush strokes are necessarily broad. But not so broad, I hope, that the car lover who is intrigued by interesting detail will not find enough of it here to pique his curiosity. I think, too, that most will enjoy the pictures, as I do—especially Tom Burnside's, which were taken for this book.

Starting with the earliest vehicles which were not yet cars, but were at least horseless, I have endeavored to evoke the romantic aspects of the earliest steam coaches and the first faltering excursions of the automobile on the public highway. I have tried to recall some of the fierceness of racing, from the early, dusty days to the present. I have even hazarded a strained look into the future.

The core of this volume, I think, is the long chapter on the Grand Marques, those cars that are the nobility of automobilia. These great machines have been dealt with in considerable detail and it was this part of the book that I most enjoyed doing. I regret that I couldn't have included a few more of these important automobiles. Surely, I have left vital things out and I have certainly made mistakes. I bow to the greater knowledge of such experts as find me out.

Many people have helped me with this task. Briggs S. Cunningham furthered the book by allowing Tom Burnside to photograph his notable collection of vintage sporting machinery. Henry Austin Clark, Jr., who owns the Long Island Automotive Museum, opened his bulging files of photographs and other material to us and gave much valuable counsel. In Paris, M. Charles Dollfus allowed us to use material from his extraordinary collection of steam-coach prints. Leslie Saalburg permitted us to reprint his fine water color of the Hispano-Suiza. We are also indebted to his son, Philippe, for his efforts in tracking down material in France. L. Scott Bailey, Ralph Buckley, René Dreyfus, Jerry Foley, and Bob Grier, among many others, helped us photographically. Publications helped us, too: *Autosport, The Autocar, The Motor* in London; *Road and Track* and *Car and Driver* in this country. We owe thanks also to the Smithsonian Institution, the Henry Ford Museum, the *Conservatoire National des Arts et Métiers* in Paris, and the B.B.C. picture library in London, as well as to those car manufacturers who aided us with photographs and information. There are many others, I am sure, whom I have neglected to mention here, but whose names will occur to me, conscience-stricken, after this has gone to press. I thank them, too.
"Tumbrils' End" Westbrook, Conn.   R.S.

Good Ales

LONDON AND BATH

G. MORTON. Del.

Published by Tho.s M

The Guide or Engineer is seated in front, having a lever rod from the two guide wheels to turn & direct the Carr
hind part of the Coach contains the machinery for producing the Steam, on a novel & secure principle, which is con
contains about 00 Gallons of water, is placed under the body of the Coach & is its full length & breadth — the Chir

THE FIRE CHARIOTS

CHAPTER 1

nother at his right hand connecting with the main Steam Pipe by which he regulates the motion of the Vehicle — the
Pipes to the Cylinders beneath & by its action on the hind wheels sets the Carriage in motion — The Tank which
fixed on the top of the hind boot & as Coke is used for fuel, there will be no smoke while any hot or purified air
of fuel & water, the full length of the Carriage is from 15 to 20 feet its weight about 2 Tons. The rate of

Haymarket. London.

PYALL. Sculp.t

As far as we know, Nicolas Joseph Cugnot, a French army engineer, was the first man to sit behind the controls of a self-propelled road vehicle. Remember this the next time you are stuck in traffic. There, far down the road, at the very head of the line, in space and time, sits M. Cugnot.

Cugnot designed his steam carriage for hauling field artillery. It was constructed in the 1760's by a man named Brezin, but the King's Minister of War, apparently not too satisfied with his first machine, ordered another one built at the royal arsenal. It is this second machine (of 1771?) that you can see if you should go to the *Conservatoire National des Arts et Métiers* in Paris.

French politics during the dizzy reign of Louis XV and the Seven Years' War prevented this second machine from being run, but Cugnot's first machine did run, and conflicting reports say that it was capable of carrying four passengers at two to six miles an hour. Its steam-making capabilities were not much; every fifteen minutes it had to stop and boil water.

Cugnot's car was a three-wheeler with a chassis built of heavy timbers. Its great pear-shaped copper boiler and the two monstrous cylinders of 50 liters capacity to which it fed steam, plus the primitive driving mechanism, all hung from and turned with the single front wheel that steered the beast. It evidently didn't steer too well, nor was its stopping power very good, for it is said that Cugnot once knocked over the wall of the courtyard where it was being tested and another time upset it on a Paris street.

Certainly there had been earlier attempts to improve upon the horse. Eccentric European monarchs in the Sixteenth Century even resorted to faking horseless carriages by putting some of their hapless subjects to work on treadmills inside of elaborately carved and gilded structures on wheels. About 1600, Prince Maurice of Nassau had built for himself, by one Simon Stevin, a four-wheeled, two-masted affair to sail on the beach near Scheveningen, Holland. It was big enough to carry his entourage of twenty-eight frightened Dutchmen plus a possibly even more frightened Spanish admiral, Mendoza by name, who was at the time the good Prince's prisoner of war. An early automotive expert of the time, named Howell, wrote in a road-test report: "This engine that

hath wheels and sails, will hold above twenty people, and goes with the wind, being drawn or mov'd by nothing else, and will run, the wind being good, and the sails hois'd up, above fifteen miles an hour upon the even hard sands."

In the late 1700's steam power began to change the world. It powered the industrial revolution of the Nineteenth Century and the new ships and railways that would shrink the globe. But after Cugnot's brief success in Paris, it was not to be France that would lead the way to mechanical road locomotion. France was too busy with other interesting projects, like storming the Bastille and getting rid of the Bourbon kings. The tumbrils had no engines. For years afterward the French were too involved with Napoleon to do much about steam wagons. Come to think of it, however, Napoleon, although he didn't dream of it, did do quite a lot toward helping the French become the leading automobilists of a century later. He built their wonderful road system.

It was in England (although God knows they were busy enough themselves with rebellious American colonials and later with Bonaparte) that the idea of hooking a steam cylinder to a wheel next appeared.

In 1784, in Redruth, a village in Cornwall, William Murdock built a small, three-wheeled, non-passenger-carrying model, which ran away from him after dark one night, throwing out sparks and making an unholy row. It is said to be the first self-powered vehicle to terrify a pedestrian—the village parson, who must have thought that Beelzebub himself was abroad on the roads. But Murdock did not continue his experiments with road vehicles for long. His boss was the great James Watt, who, jealous of his assistant, gave him so much other work to do that he had no time for such frivolities as horseless steam carriages.

About this same time, Richard Trevithick, another English steam engineer, was also working on a model steam carriage—which was really the first locomotive, too—and by 1801 he had become so successful with it that he started with his cousin, Andrew Vivian, the construction of a full-sized machine. Describing a trial trip on Christmas Eve of that year, a witness said that Trevithick drove his machine up a hill half a mile, carrying eight people "faster than a man could walk." But Trevithick could get no one interested enough to invest money in development and finally scrapped the machine, selling its engine to a man who used it to power a mill.

In the United States in 1805, Oliver Evans, a mechanic born in Newport, Delaware, built his famous amphibious steam-powered dredge, the Orukter Amphibolus, which waddled from the workshop in which

Preceding pages: Goldsworthy Gurney's Steam Carriage of 1827-28. This machine could carry twenty-one passengers at speeds upwards of 15 mph. If you look closely, just forward of the rear wheels, you can see the "legs" Gurney fitted "to help upon hills."

M. Cugnot's Steam Tractor of 1771 (upper left), second model
by the man credited with building the first self-propelled vehicle, is
now in the Conservatoire National des Arts et Métiers.
Two 50-liter cylinders, its boiler, and its primitive drive mechanism
(upper right) all turned with the single front wheel. Steering was
obviously almost impossible. An early print (center, right)
purports to portray the world's first car accident when Cugnot's
machine struck a courtyard wall. Stephen Farffler (center, left)
employs a more primitive method of propulsion in his one-man power
sports-wagen of 1670. Albrecht Dürer engraving (lower right) shows
a mechanical carriage built for Emperor Maximilian I, in 1520.

Steam locomotion was a subject for hilarity and sarcasm in the 1820's. The satirical English cartoon at right takes a dim view of the future of such transport, investing the movement with a boisterous, chaotic character, and presenting the vehicles in ridiculous, fanciful forms. The machines which took to the English roads in this period were gaily painted and Gargantuan. Typical was F. Hill's passenger-carrying steam carriage of 1839 (below). The huge boiler on the back is reminiscent of those seen on early locomotives and required just as much tending. Also notable is the similarity of the suspension of this machine to the type used on railway carriages. Murdock's model steam carriage of 1784 (bottom, right) is a non-passenger-carrying device and now can be seen at The Science Museum in London.

he built it, through the streets of Philadelphia, and into the Schuylkill River under its own power. It was hardly a steam automobile for it weighed some twenty tons, and in addition to wheels it was liberally festooned with chain buckets, digging devices, and paddles to move it through the water. Still, it *was* a self-propelled vehicle and as such a biological ancestor of the automobile.

Men in places as far apart as Hartford, Connecticut, and Prague, and Halifax, Nova Scotia, were building steam carriages. But suddenly in England in the 1820's there was a boom in such road locomotives, a boom—oddly enough—caused by horse-drawn coaches. For coaching had increased tremendously in England owing to the new need for mobility in its rapidly expanding economy after the Napoleonic Wars. And more coaching meant that better roads were needed. Two road-building geniuses, Telford and Macadam, whose name still clings to our tar-surfaced roads today, revolutionized methods of highway construction and within a short time Eng-

land had wonderful roads eminently suitable for mechanical transport, steam transport.

Starting in the 1820's, there took to the roads of England as wild looking, gaily painted, and oddly designed a lot of vehicles as has ever existed. It seemed for a while that every engineer in Britain was designing boilers and furnaces and running gear for the new steam carriages. These were not for the use of individual owners, however. These were giant pantechnicons, as big as Greyhound buses, to carry paying passengers.

Burstall & Hill, Maceroni & Squire, James & Anderson, Scott Russell were just a few of the host of engineers at work. And David Gordon. We must not forget Gordon, for he was the genius who, convinced that mere wheels could not propel his carriage, fitted it with six steam-powered, jointed legs and feet to push it along.

Even the great Goldsworthy Gurney, whose steam buses were later among the most successful, fitted his first machine in 1827 with similar steam-driven legs,

"To help when starting up and upon hills." This first carriage of Gurney's was capable of carrying twenty-one passengers. It had a water-tube boiler and was fitted with separators to insure dry steam for the cylinders. This machine was often seen chuffing about in the London area and was capable, when everything was working right, of reaching 15 miles an hour.

As if it weren't dangerous enough just to ride in these carriages with their primitive boilers, shaky steering, and laughable brakes, the passengers had to be continually on guard against angry citizens. Filson Young, in his book, *The Complete Motorist* (London, 1904), tells of one of Gurney's trial trips:

"On one journey which he made to Bath with a number of guests, his carriage was attacked at Melksham where there happened to be a fair. The people formed such a dense mass that it was impossible to move the carriage through them; the crowd, being mainly composed of agricultural laborers, considered all machinery directly injurious to their interests, and with a cry of 'Down with all machinery,' they set upon the carriage and its occupants, seriously injuring Mr. Gurney and his assistant engineer, who had to be taken to Bath in an unconscious condition."

The "assistant engineer" was what we would call the fireman. This poor wight stood on a rear platform in some carriages, or inside, among the hot fireboxes, flailing rods, and leaping chains in others, shoveling coal and coke (liquid petroleum fuels were some forty years in the future), greasing the machinery with a brush dipped in lard or palm oil and apprehensively checking the safety valve to see that it wasn't stuck.

A daring entrepreneur of the time, Sir Charles Dance, bought three of Gurney's coaches and operated a sort of bus line between Gloucester and Cheltenham for four months from February to June, 1831, during which time he made no less than 396 trips and traveled 3,644 miles.

But it was Walter Hancock who was the most successful builder of steam carriages. He built nine machines with wonderful names: Infant, Autopsy, Automaton, Era, and the like. In 1834, from mid-August until November, he ran the Autopsy and the Era between the City, Moorgate, and Paddington, carrying in all some 4,000 passengers. He was perhaps the first builder to use high-pressure steam. Where others were satisfied to use it at, say, fifty pounds per square inch, Hancock used over two hundred pounds. This could sometimes be a disadvantage. W. Worby Beaumont, in his *Motor Vehicles and Motors* (London, 1902), reports drily about Hancock's Enterprise of 1832: "The engine attendant had fastened the safety valve lever down with copper wire, and had started the engines and blower while the coach was standing. The effect of the forced draught was that intended, but the steam not being used as fast as made, nor free to escape at the safety valve, it got out elsewhere, and at the inquest which followed, the evidence was more complimentary to the boiler than its attendant."

The charming qualities of these early steam diligences and the character of their inventors, who left little to chance, is shown by the illustration of Gordon's steam carriage of 1824 (top, left). Gordon, unwilling to believe that his road locomotive could climb hills or even start from rest without wheelslip, designed a delightful system of mechanical legs to help his creation along. Above are part of the fleet of steam carriages built by Walter Hancock. He made nine in all and engaged in a successful passenger-carrying service for several months —from August to November, 1834—transporting approximately 4,000 passengers during that period. The Enterprise (below) was involved in one of the few serious accidents suffered by the company. Her engine attendant fastened the safety valve closed with a piece of copper wire while the coach was standing at rest, then developed a fine head of steam in the boiler, which blew up with interesting results.

H. Alken's Illustration of Modern Prophecy, or Novelty for the Year 1829.

I say Fellow, give my Buggy a charge of Coke, your Charcoal is so D__d dear.

THE PROGRESS OF STEAM.

London Pub.d Jan.y 1828 by S & J Fuller, 34 Rathbone Pla...

Two men were required to operate these private
steam road-carriages—one to steer and another to feed
the fire and tend the boiler. Such especially built
contrivances were restricted to a few wealthy and venturesome
gentlemen. The one at left was built by Thomas Rickett
for the Marquis of Stafford in 1858 in England.
The one at far left was built by Cecil Rhodes, also in England,
but the lucky owner remains unknown. The fanciful
French design (right) is almost prophetic of the tail-finned
extravagances of Detroit. Two cartoonists of
the 1820's (below) poke fun at the future of such vehicles.
H. Alken (lower left) forsees the advent of service
stations and "gas wars" to cut prices, while the illustrator at
right sums up his feelings about mechanical locomotion
with his nonsensical teapot fitted with wheels.

There is but one other recorded case of such a mishap, for although it must have been miserably uncomfortable, the steam carriage does not seem to have been generally dangerous. In 1834, one of Scott Russell's machines, running between Glasgow and Paisley, burst its boiler and killed three people.

But it was not its dangerous aspects or its discomfort that pushed the steam carriage off the roads of England. It was, rather, the ferocious antagonism of the new railways and the coaching interests, and the savage tolls levied against them. For example, between Prescot and Liverpool, where a four-horse coach would pay 4s. (about the equivalent of a dollar), a steam carriage would pay £2-8-0 (about $12). Bucolic locals vented their spleen against the new machines by continual sabotage. For instance, Summers and Ogle's eighteen-passenger carriage of 1831 (which, by the way, could better 30 mph), originally had six-foot driving wheels. But these were reduced to five feet, six inches after hirelings of the anti-steam-carriage faction sawed the spokes three inches from the rim, so that the wheels fractured and gave way on the road.

The steam carriages were not entirely blameless either, for they blew sparks and smoke into farmyards, and the noise of their passing must have been frightful. Nor was a little device like that fitted to one of Hancock's machines likely to engender the friendship of other road users. This feature was a

trap door under the firebox which slid open to deposit the ashes or, if the operator wished, even the whole fire onto the road.

In 1831, a committee had held hearings and reported to the Houses of Parliament in favor of steam coaches and a reduction in tolls, but it was to no avail. The powerful forces against steam on the roads finally won out and by 1840 the steam carriages had almost disappeared from the king's highway. Not a one of them was preserved. A pity. What a prize one would be today for an antique-car restorer.

In England, a few hardy types persisted in building road steamers for individuals, notably Thomas Rickett of Buckingham, who made them for eccentric milords like the Marquis of Stafford (in 1858) and the Earl of Caithness (in 1860). But in 1865 came the notorious "Red Flag Act" which lasted until 1896. This ridiculous ordinance prevented any self-powered vehicle from traveling faster than four miles an hour in the country, or two miles an hour in towns. And in both instances a man was to walk ahead of such a machine, carrying a red flag.

So, although the British had been the first to operate self-propelled vehicles successfully, they took to the roads only by stealth until 1896. Other men in other countries would develop the automobile.

For a time they continued to concern themselves with steam. In the United States, Richard Dudgeon built steam vehicles not too different from those of

Richard Dudgeon of New York built his steam wagon (upper left) in 1867. Not quite the thing for a ride on a hot summer's day, the carriage was so designed that the passengers sat draped about the steaming boiler. It provided its riders with little comfort compared to a French-designed carriage—"L'Obéissante" (above)—of only a few years later. The latter was Amédée Bollée, père's steam omnibus. He built it in 1873. It was one of the first vehicles to have pivoting front wheels (Lankensperger steering). The front wheels were independently sprung, and each rear wheel was driven individually by its own two-cylinder, "V" engine. The boiler was coal-fired. It weighed 8000 pounds and its 20 hp engines propelled it at 25 mph. It is still in existence at the Conservatoire National des Arts et Métiers in Paris. At the left is a handbill advertising Sylvester Roper's steam vehicles.

Rickett: small, horizontally boilered locomotives, coal-fired, with seats arranged about the boiler, just the thing for a ride on a hot summer's day. Dudgeon built his first machine in 1853, but a late Dudgeon steamer of about 1867 still exists in the museum of the Veteran Motor Car Club of America in Brookline, Massachusetts.

In 1869, Sylvester H. Roper, of Roxbury, built a steam velocipede in which he astounded the peasantry at county fairs in New England. A later four-wheeled steam carriage of Roper's can be seen today in the Henry Ford Museum in Dearborn, Michigan.

In 1884, Lucius D. Copeland fitted a high-wheeled "Penny-farthing" bicycle with a beautifully delicate

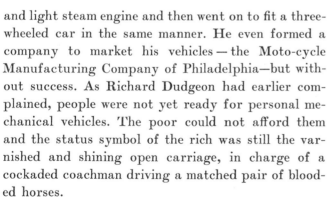

PHAETON MOTO-CYCLE

WEIGHT, 220 POUNDS.
SPEED, 10 MILES PER HOUR.
POWER, 2 HORSE.

MOTO-CYCLE MANUFACTURING COMPANY,

J. E. WATKINS, President.
W. H. TRAVIS, Secretary.
E. F. SMITH, Treasurer.

1529 Arch Street, Philadelphia, Pa.

Lucius D. Copeland (left) sits aboard his wonderful steam tricycle outside the Smithsonian Institution in 1888. Copeland, unlike so many of his predecessors, succeeded in building marvelously light and delicate steam engines, one of which still exists in the Arizona Museum, Phoenix. Only a few years had passed since Copeland posed with his steam high-wheeler (above), an earlier and more experimental design which made the phaeton possible. The circular advertising his vehicle (above, left) was distributed by the Northrup Manufacturing Company of Camden, New Jersey, which formed the Moto-Cycle Manufacturing Company to market the Copeland design. But, alas, without success.

and light steam engine and then went on to fit a three-wheeled car in the same manner. He even formed a company to market his vehicles — the Moto-cycle Manufacturing Company of Philadelphia — but without success. As Richard Dudgeon had earlier complained, people were not yet ready for personal mechanical vehicles. The poor could not afford them and the status symbol of the rich was still the varnished and shining open carriage, in charge of a cockaded coachman driving a matched pair of blooded horses.

In France, Amédée Bollée, the elder, was building successful steamers (his L'Obéissante of 1873 is still preserved in France), as were the Count de Dion (in 1887) and Leon Serpollet, who in 1890 was among the first to use liquid fuel in a flash-steam boiler. Serpollet was destined to keep steam important well into the Twentieth Century.

In any case, although steam cars would be built in America until the 1920's, the age of the road locomotive was ending. The gasoline automobile was almost ready to appear.

Yet even the first crude automobiles could never have appeared on the roads of Europe and America without a host of inventions, discoveries, and new techniques, which were the fruits of the Nineteenth Century's mechanical investigations. A few of the more important were:

1. The ability to bore an (almost) truly round hole or turn an (almost) truly round shaft.

2. Metals with predictable and uniform properties.

3. Petroleum (for lubrication and fuel).

4. The vulcanizing of rubber and the invention of the rubber tire.

5. The application of electricity (the battery, the induction coil).

6. The Lankensperger (or Ackermann) steering system, whereby each front wheel turns on its own pivot, or king-pin, as opposed to the method of pivoting the whole front axle at its center, as on a horse-drawn carriage.

7. The differential gear.

8. The internal combustion engine—of course!

Who invented the internal combustion engine? Who first put the fire inside a cylinder and used its expansive force to drive a piston directly, instead of using the fire first to boil water and make steam, and then to pipe the steam to the cylinder to move the piston?

There were many, each of them making advances—and mistakes—from which others learned. The first people to put the fire inside the cylinder seem to have used too much fire. They tried gunpowder—with uncomfortable results. It wasn't until combustible gases became available that combustion inside a cylinder was possible. In 1804, a Swiss, Isaac De Rivaz, succeeded in building an internal combustion engine of sorts, using hydrogen. In fact, he even mounted it on a wheeled chassis which is said to have moved. Although De Rivaz was granted a patent for this vehicle on January 30, 1807, he did not succeed in developing his invention.

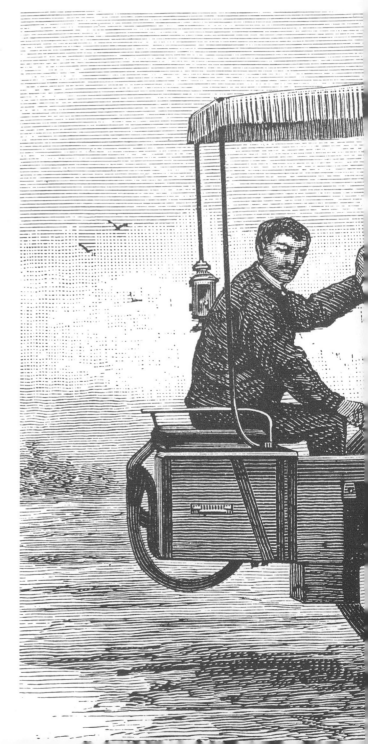

Before setting forth on a run from Paris to Lyons in 1890, Leon Serpollet (above) poses for a moment with his friend, Ernest Archdeacon. Serpollet was both a pioneer in the use of liquid fuel and, in 1888, the inventor of the "flash" steam generator. His machine, like that of his American contemporary, Lucius Copeland, was light and handy compared to the cumbersome road vehicles of the day. Messieurs de Dion, Bouton, and Trepardoux (right) are transported by a far more weighty conveyance. However, this steam phaeton was built in 1885, pre-dating the Serpollet machine. Count Albert de Dion, a wealthy boulevardier, became interested in the Eighties in building a "horseless." To this end he enlisted the services of two penurious model makers, Bouton and Trepardoux. Trepardoux quit, but the firm of de Dion et Bouton, after building many types of steam vehicles, went on to fame as one of the great gasoline automobile manufacturers.

In 1860, in France, however, Etienne Lenoir built what must be considered the first practical gas engine. He used illuminating gas for fuel and an electric spark from a Ruhmkorff coil for ignition. This first engine of Lenoir's was not much smaller than a bungalow and about as light. He must have had to feed many francs into the gas meter to keep it running, for it swallowed a hundred cubic feet of cooking gas to develop each brake-horsepower. Lenoir is said to have experimented with liquid fuels, too, and even to have installed one of his later engines in a road vehicle he drove in the environs of Paris as early as May, 1862. He also used it to run a motorboat at about

the time the *Monitor* and the *Merrimac* were fighting it out at Hampton Roads. These later experiments came to nought, but Lenoir must be acknowledged the creator of the first internal combustion engine that really worked. Further, Lenoir's efforts attracted other inventors to the possibilities of internal combustion. In 1862, the Frenchman, Beau De Rochas patented, but never built, a four-cycle engine. In 1878, N. A. Otto, in the town of Deutz, Germany, actually constructed a four-cycle engine that is the direct granddaddy of the engine in the car you are driving today. Otto never tried to put one of his engines in a vehicle. He and his partner, Langen,

were interested in stationary engines, not horseless carriages. One of their employees, Gottlieb **Daimler**, was interested in horseless carriages, however.

The first gasoline automobile is popping and grinding just around the corner now. Who is in the driver's seat? Was it that erratic genius, Siegfried Marcus? The work of Marcus was until recent years so unrecognized that the 1946 edition of the Encyclopaedia Britannica even spells his name wrong. It calls him Narkus. He was born in Malchin, Germany, in 1831 and from the age of twelve, when he was apprenticed to a machinist, until he died, poor and worn out by sickness in 1898, he lived and worked in a frenzy of engineering excitement. He restlessly dabbled in chemistry, electricity, even dentistry. He once pulled out one of his own teeth, but in his excitement made a great wound in his cheek; he treated that himself, too. When he was seventeen he was hired by the then

newly organized firm of Siemens and Halske, for whom, two years later, he invented an electrical relay system for telegraphy. When he was twenty he left them and went to Vienna. There he worked for the court mechanic, the Imperial Medical Academy, the Royal Chemical Laboratory. In 1860, when he was twenty-nine, he rented some rooms at 107 Mariahilferstrasse, Vienna, and set up his own engineering laboratory. Here he secretively worked on all manner of inventions, in his own dilettante way, seldom finishing anything once he had got it to the point where he was satisfied it could work.

He was fascinated by the idea of electric lighting and got the idea that perhaps benzene vapor ignited by an electric spark would make a beautiful light. It didn't. It made a beautiful explosion. From there he jumped to the thought that a benzene-vapor explosion in a cylinder might make an engine run.

Siegfried Marcus may have invented the world's first gasoline automobile. He built his first car in 1865, his second (upper left) in 1874. The first man to build a "usable" gas engine was Etienne Lenoir, who as early as 1860 used "cooking gas" to run his engine (left). By 1879, George B. Selden was applying for a patent for an automobile (see page 60). He submitted the model (above) to the United States Patent Office.

By 1865, he was driving a car—a handcart powered by a two-cycle engine coupled directly to the rear wheels, *sans* clutch. It was necessary to lift the rear wheels off the ground to start the engine; when they were dropped the handcart took off. In addition to no clutch, it had no brakes. But it ran well enough to suit Marcus, and he therefore abandoned it. Anyhow, what sense was there in using benzene imported in bottles from Germany at three marks a liter!

For the next ten years or so, Marcus turned to other ideas and projects and even prospered a little. He tutored the Austrian Crown Prince in science, installed an electric-bell system in the royal palace (during which he horrified the courtiers and amused the Empress by leaping on the silken royal bed to mark the spot on the wall for the button) and was even grudgingly recognized by the Royal Academy of Sciences.

In 1874, he was involved with automobiles again. This time he made three cars—one in his own shop, the other two were done by an outside firm under his direction. One of these still exists in the *Technisches Museum* of Vienna, and is still capable of running under its own power. This car has a single cylinder four-stroke engine (very likely built before Otto's) with low-tension magneto ignition and a carburetor fitted with an internal revolving brush to assist vaporization of the fuel. It is of 1570 cc and develops ¾ hp, which is capable of driving the car at about four miles an hour. The chassis is of wood, has half-elliptic springs, a steering wheel, iron tires, a steel-cone clutch, but no gearshift (for the simple reason that it has but one speed).

Marcus had a car, all right. He called it a *strassenwagen*. Anyone but he would have pushed to get backing to go on and improve it, to build more and

31

better cars. But the police fussed about the noise and Marcus was bored with his new gadget, anyhow, so he just said the hell with it and went on to other, more exciting experiments.

In 1924, the Viennese put up a statue to Marcus, and the *Technisches Museum* exhibited his car and even had a booklet about the inventor available until 1938, when Hitler's troops marched in. The Germans tried to destroy the car, but the museum people had stashed it away. The Nazis did manage to burn most of the booklets. They didn't like people thinking that a Jew might have invented the automobile before Gottlieb Daimler and Carl Benz.

The Nazis, as usual, were being wrongheaded. Marcus's accomplishment did not detract from the glory Gottlieb Daimler and Carl Benz had so rightfully earned. For while Marcus had drifted away from his idea, Daimler and Benz nourished and developed their weakling, putt-putting, single-cylindered, brain children. From them, directly, grew the giant automobile industry of our day.

In 1885, when Daimler and Benz, each unknown

to the other, first wheeled explosion-engined vehicles out of their workshops, Europe was just about ready for the automobile. People—at least the upper classes—felt secure and prosperous. The long peace after the Napoleonic Wars had been broken but once by the almost farcical Franco-Prussian War. In half a century, the railways had changed from a frightening new means of rapid travel for the adventurous to a commonplace which spread its tracks across the continents. Every town had its factories and foundries; things mechanical were no longer a fearful mystery.

It was the efforts of Carl Benz and Gottlieb Daimler which made commercially practicable, gasoline-engined motor vehicles possible. Daimler constructed a "motorcycle" in 1885 with a single-cylinder engine using "hot-tube" ignition. The photograph (below) shows a reproduction of the original machine. In that same year, 1885 —and quite unknown to Daimler—Carl Benz, as fascinated as his countryman by the prospects of internal combustion, powered his three-wheeled design (left) with a one-cylinder engine which employed an electric ignition system. Within a decade, Benz had developed his primitive design into a highly saleable carriage, such as the 1898 Benz (bottom).

Now, too, people were just about to get their first taste of the delicious freedom of fast personal travel on the road aboard the newly invented safety bicycle.

Gottlieb Daimler was fifty-one by the time he had his first roadable machine running. He had spent most of his working life with engines, first with steam which convinced him that for many purposes the steam engine was outmoded, and then, in 1872, with gas engines as technical director of the Deutz Engine Works owned by Otto and Langen. Otto and Langen were well satisfied with the ponderous, slow-speed, stationary gas engines they built, but Daimler was not, although he had made many improvements in them. Daimler's dream was a light, high-speed engine that could be run on benzene (*not* named after Carl Benz, by the way). In 1882, after much hassling with Otto and Langen, he left, taking with him Wilhelm Maybach, who had worked closely with Daimler, and opened his own experimental shop in Cannstatt. By 1883, Daimler had perfected his system of hot-tube ignition, based on earlier experiments by a man named Funk, and soon afterward he had a neat, compact, high-speed (750 rpm) engine. This is as good a place as any to explain hot-tube ignition.

Nowadays an electric spark ignites the charge in the cylinder. Old Lenoir also used an electric spark, but his apparatus was huge and clumsy. Otto's engine used an open gas flame which was exposed to a gas-air mixture at just the right instant by a sliding valve which then clapped shut again. Daimler's device was a small platinum tube which screwed into the side of the cylinder much like a modern spark plug. A Bunsen burner, fed from its own little tank of benzene or gasoline, heated this tube red hot. When the rising piston compressed the mixture in the cylinder, some of it rushed into the tube and was ignited. Simple! I once saw the late Joe Tracy—of Vanderbilt Cup fame—diddling with hot-tube ignition on a Bollée tri-car. It worked pretty well. Of course, he had to light the burner with a match before cranking the engine. And there were other nuisances, such as having the burners blow out in a high wind or the whole business catch fire if the car upset. But Tracy showed me how it was even possible to vary the ignition timing by changing the position of the flame along the tube. The further away from the cylinder, the later the timing.

In 1885, Daimler installed one of his engines in a bicycle of his own design—a primitive motorcycle of wood, with iron-shod tires and outrigger wheels, like the training wheels children use. A great leather saddle covered the single-cylinder of the ½-hp engine. The benzene tank for the burner was practically in

Emile Levassor was the first designer to put the engine up front. Behind it, logically, he placed the clutch and gearbox. By so doing he set a fashion which persists into our time. The diagram (upper right) from Worby Beaumont's "Motor Vehicles and Motors" (1902) shows Levassor's Daimler-engined car of 1894. But Levassor didn't place the engine up front immediately. The photograph (lower right) of an 1890 Panhard-Levassor shows that earlier he had built at least one vehicle with the engine amidships. The Panhard-Levassor of 1895 (top of the page) is fitted with what must be one of the very first attempts at closed coachwork. The Renault below it, built in 1900, five years later, doesn't show any great advance in the art of building sedan bodies.

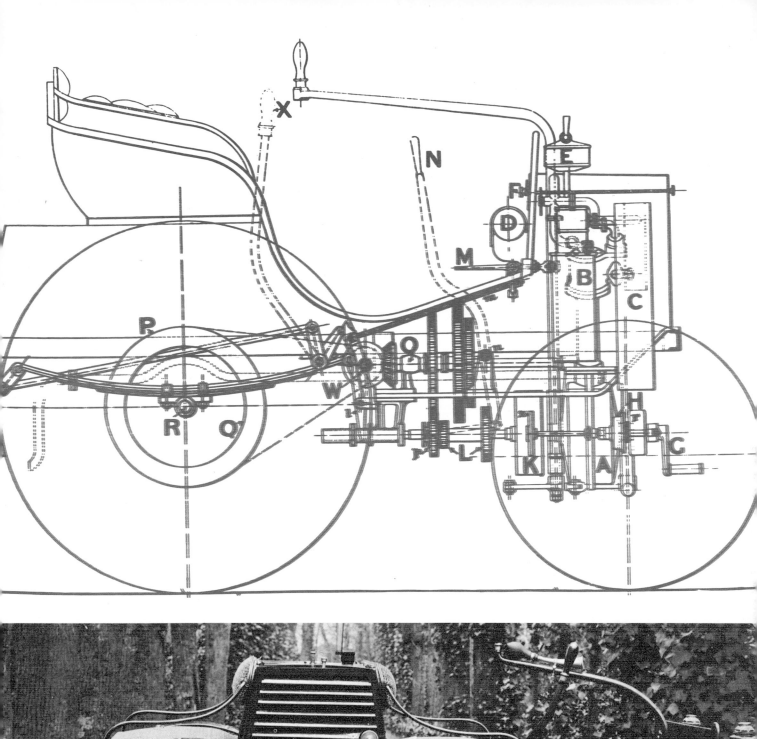

the rider's back pocket, while the burner itself warmed the crook of his right knee.

But the thing ran. On November 10, 1885, Daimler's son, Paul, drove it the three kilometers from Cannstatt to Unterturkheim and back. Later, when Lake Cannstatt froze over, this early motor bike, fitted with studs on its rear wheel and a sort of ski in front, amazed the local skaters as it did figure eights on the ice.

Daimler was really more interested in engines than in automobiles. He installed them in boats, in tramcars, and even in a dirigible built by a local genius. Certainly he saw that his engines would be wonderful for propelling road vehicles, but, at first, he looked upon them as accessories people might buy and install, instead of the horse, on the family carriage. He tried it himself in 1886 and Daimler's first four-wheeled car was no more than a beefed-up horse carriage with an engine sticking up out of the rear floor. Nor did he use swiveling front wheels to steer. The whole front axle still swung on a center pivot. Still, this car ran pleasantly enough, attaining some 10 mph from its 1½-hp engine which drove the rear wheels by means of belts. There was no differential and the two speeds were selected by tightening and loosening the belts.

Daimler rapidly improved his cars, but it was his engines, exported to and licensed in other countries, especially France, that gave automobilism its great push forward.

At about the same time that Daimler's son was riding his father's motorcycle, Carl Benz was trying out his first car, a spidery three-wheeler. Benz, like Daimler, was fascinated by small internal combustion engines, but while Daimler had been an important engineer, employed by a successful gas-engine company, Benz was starting small engine factories, going broke, taking in partners with capital, and being cheated by financial backers. Eventually, with new backers, he founded a company styling itself Benz & Cie., in Mannheim, to manufacture stationary gas engines using an electric ignition system he had devised. It was almost exactly like the one we use today, with storage battery, coil, and spark plug. Business was fine, but Benz had the itch to build a car using one of his small engines and in the spring of 1885 he succeeded.

Benz's car was three-wheeled. He had either not heard about Lankensperger steering, or perhaps considered it too fussy to build. Rightly, he dismissed the horse-carriage steering that had satisfied Daimler. The car had a single-cylinder, ¾-hp (at 250-300 rpm), water-cooled engine in the rear. The connecting-rod stuck nakedly out of the horizontally mounted cylinder and drove, by way of a similarly unenclosed crankshaft, a huge, horizontal, spoked flywheel which

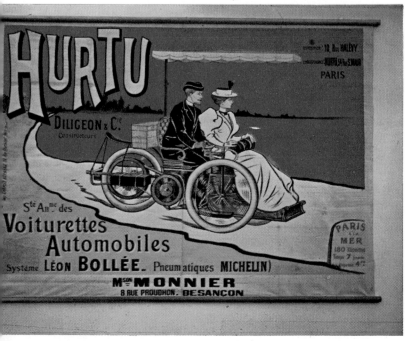

America's first mass-produced car was the Curved Dash Olds of 1901 (above, a 1902 model). Built by Ransom E. Olds (whose initials also formed the name of a car), it had a rugged simplicity typical of American cars of that period. Powered by a single-cylinder, 5 hp engine, it was capable of 20 mph. Note the tiller for steering. Comparatively sophisticated machines like the Peugeot quadricycles of 1893 (far left) and 1896 (left center) were already gaily chuffing down the grands boulevards of Paris when American machines were still in their early, experimental stages. Note the front seat in the 1896 car, which could make a bumper of your mother-in-law. At left is a poster for the Hurtu Tri-car, another European marque.

A typical "horseless" of 1895 stands at right. This German-built Lutzmann had a 4 hp, single-cylindered engine in the rear and a belt clutch like a modern lawn mower. Seated in it are H. J. Lawson and early motorist J. A. Koosey. Lawson later tried to form a monopoly of the infant British auto industry. Above is the ingenious and advanced English Lanchester of 1903. With its two-cylinder-opposed engine and twin crankshafts, it successfully eliminated the bone-shaking vibration which was the bane of early motorcars. It had an epicycle transmission and a worm-drive rear axle. The Duryea brothers' car of 1903 (below) was first successful American automobile.

had to be pulled around to start the engine. Like Daimler's machine—which, of course, he hadn't seen—it was driven with belts and pulleys. But unlike Daimler, he devised a differential of his own for the rear axle.

To the detriment of his gas-engine business, Benz kept fussing and fiddling with his baby and constantly improving it. And running down his battery, too. Nights he'd lug the battery home and hook it up to a generator driven by the foot treadle of his wife's sewing machine. So, while Herr Benz studied blueprints under the gaslight, Frau Benz pumped away for hours to charge the battery for tomorrow's experiments. It was Frau Benz, also, who went on one of the first long trips in an automobile. At five o'clock one morning, while Benz lay fast asleep, she took her two older boys and set off in the car (a slightly later model) from Mannheim to Pforzheim. Eugen, the eldest, steered. On hills they all got out and pushed. But they made it. The first person to pilot a car on a longish road journey was a middle-aged German hausfrau!

Although at first Benz had a terrible time selling his cars, the time came when he couldn't make them fast enough. For the first fifteen years of automobilism Benz did very well. But Benz was a stubborn old Teuton and, although his later cars had four wheels, he still clung to his belt drive and his slow-speed rear engines. It was not until 1903, when he hired a Frenchman named Marius Barbaroux, who designed a front-engined car for him, that Benz began to catch up with the automotive parade he had done so much to start.

It was the French who made the gasoline automobile popular. De Dion and Bollée and Serpollet had done wonders with steam cars, but it was not until the French got their hands on Daimler's (and Maybach's) wonderful engine that their auto industry blossomed. And no one had more to do with that than Émile Levassor. Levassor was a partner of René Panhard in the firm of Panhard & Levassor, which still builds excellent automobiles, although in those days they were in the business of making band saws. Daimler and Levassor had a mutual friend, Édouard Sarazin,

a Belgian who had acquired the rights to sell Daimler's engines in France. Sarazin talked Levassor into making them there, as well, and when he died, Mme. Sarazin not only continued the business arrangement with Levassor, but eventually married him — complete with the license to build Daimler engines.

Naturally, Levassor had seen the latest model of Daimler's car, which had been built for the Paris Exhibition of 1889. He was unimpressed by the quadricycle, which looked like two bicycles side-by-side with the passengers and machinery slung between them, but he was much taken by its motive power: a two-cylinder, 15-degree V-engine which turned at what was considered in those days to be the very high speed of 750 rpm.

When Levassor designed his own car, it was the archtype of almost every machine which would be built for the next fifty years. Levassor put the engine in the front (where it belongs?). Behind it he put a clutch and behind that the gearbox. Between the rear wheels was a differential.

At last the car as we know it today had appeared. **39**

France was ready. And no wonder, for the French loved cars and France was the one country in Europe with long, straight, smooth Napoleonic roads. It also had a Gallicly logical officialdom that wasn't against everything new (as were the British) and an upper class with plenty of money to spend.

The Panhard & Levassor was not the only car buzzing along the *grands boulevards*. Peugeot, a manufacturer of coffee grinders and bicycles, soon brought out its own model—also with Daimler engines, under license from Levassor. French-licensed Benz cars (the Roger-Benz and the Hurtu-Benz) were popular, as were the Bollée and the de Dion-Bouton. And don't forget the Renault Brothers;

we'll hear from them again, too.

Eventually, the British woke up. Daimler had licensed his engines to the company which still uses his name, and the remarkable Frederick Lanchester was building the first gasoline-engined, four-wheeled cars made in England.

Almost immediately, American millionaires began importing the fashionable new toys from Europe. But Yankee tinkerers in Connecticut and machinists from the railroad shops in the Midwest were but vaguely aware of this latest craze of Newport society. They weren't part of Newport. They were hammering and filing away at their own kinds of horseless carriages. Hiram Percy Maxim, Ransom E. Olds, Elwood

Haynes, the Apperson brothers, Henry Ford, the Duryea brothers—any of these or a score of others could have been first, but in 1893 Frank Duryea drove the first gasoline-powered American automobile in Springfield, Massachusetts.

In design it was years behind the Europeans. They were already building cars. This was still a buggy with an engine attached to it. But while the European car would for years be the plaything of the privileged, this piece of machinery, almost as crudely agricultural as an iron plough, was the true precursor of the especially American type of rough-and-tough automobile that was to change the way Americans lived and worked and thought.

Preceding pages: In this 1901 Columbia, Hiram Percy Maxim, following the lead of Émile Levassor, placed the engine up front. Mounted on springs, it jiggled nervously as it ran. This Columbia was also the first American car to sport a steering wheel instead of a tiller. Built by the Pope Manufacturing Company, of Hartford, Connecticut, its design was well ahead of most other American cars. At left: The Leon Bollée tri-car of 1897. This engaging little beast was the sports car of its day. Its air-cooled, hot-tube-ignited, 3 hp engine could make it scoot along at over 30 mph. No wonder young sportsmen like C. S. Rolls, later of Rolls-Royce, here seen at the midship controls, loved driving it. People who have driven these Bollées claim that the piston going down its square-finned cylinder sounds like a subway train in a tunnel. Bottom: An 1896 Delahaye. The French Delahaye of this period was inspired by the Benz. Note the radiator made of bent tubing. The 1901 two-cylinder Autocar (below) was built in Ardmore, Pennsylvania. These cars already had shaft drive and left-hand steering (by tiller).

STUFF FOR S

2

THE YEARS OF FULFILLMENT

During the 1890's America's towns were tied to each other by the railroad, not the highway. At the edges of the cities the pavements suddenly disappeared and gave way to mere scratches across the landscape. These were the roads. Elongated mudholes in winter, dusty, sandy tracks lacking signposts in summer, they were used mainly by farmers to haul their produce to the towns or to take their families to the village church on Sundays in the family buggy. Unhappily, the village doctor used these miserable byways, too, as he forced his horse and buggy toward some winter midnight's childbirth.

The farmer would have snorted with derision had anyone told him that the new-fangled horseless carriage was about to change his life, that he was about to be rescued from his kerosene-lit isolation.

But the village doctor could hardly wait. He wanted an automobile more than almost anything else in the world. The townsman, too, wanted a car. The bicycle had on Sundays freed him from the trolley car. With his friends of the bicycle club or with his girl friend aboard a tandem, he had discovered a new way of personal travel outside the iron-bound routes of the transit companies. Cycling was delightful, but he wanted a motor to keep his legs from getting so tired. And then, of course, there were the

Preceding pages: This Welch touring car of 1907 was a typical, high-priced ($5,500) luxury car of its time. Its seven-passenger "Roi des Belges" coachwork was upholstered in diamond-pleated leather, and it was possible to buy a "hardtop" to keep its passengers cozy behind plate glass in wintry weather. Built in Pontiac, Michigan, the Welch had a four-cylinder, 50 hp engine, and a multiple-clutch transmission. In the early 1900's, when the American motorist ventured into the countryside, he was entirely on his own. Paved roads were luxuries of the future. There were no gas stations, motels, or even route markers. Help was always distant. Those who owned these early machines had to be dedicated, willing to suffer for their sport, unafraid to dirty their hands in caring for their cars' innards. The owner of the 1904 White Steamer (below) has run into luck and found a source of water to refill his car's thirsty flash steam boiler.

Bearing a strong resemblance to a handsome buggy, the 1905 Pierce Stanhope (far left) was also sometimes known as the "doctor's car." It was powered by a one-cylinder, French, de Dion engine. Its gearshift was attached to the steering column. The auto saved the physician the expense of keeping horses and eliminated "the bother and disagreeable features of drivers." As an added attraction, the Pierce had a fold-away front seat that stowed neatly beneath its dummy hood. Another device of the times was used in the 1903 Model A Ford (lower left). A tonneau to hold two more passengers could be fitted to its rear deck. As late as 1902, the Napier at left had larger wheels in the rear which, with its chain drive, necessitated a rear-entrance body.

rich; they just had to have a motor car. Didn't the papers say Mrs. Vanderbilt had one?

The automobile of the Nineties was a horror on wheels. The brave eccentric who owned one happily put up with its crankiness if the beastly thing would only run. It was unbelievably difficult to operate and control, and when it wouldn't run nobody knew how to fix it.

By 1914 the automobile was, in almost every respect as good as the car standing in your driveway right now—and in some ways it was better. In those few years since the Nineties the automobile advanced more than anytime before or since.

Let us pretend that it is, say, April of 1898 and that you are your own grandfather. Last fall you started a campaign to convince your dear wife that a horseless carriage was exactly what you needed:

"Look how much we'll save on oats for the mare. An automotor (even the word 'automobile' wasn't common usage yet) doesn't eat when it isn't actually running," you said, "and there isn't all that cleaning up after it, or harnessing, or those bills from the veterinarian."

Your logic finally prevails and on this fine spring morning there stands before your house a sparkling, black horseless carriage, cautiously tied to the hitching post by the man who dragged it, behind a horse, from the freight station.

Your new car is a pretty little thing not too different in appearance from the buggy in your stable. It has a patent leather dashboard and patent leather mudguards over its tall, nickel-plated wire wheels and rides on sausage-thin pneumatic tires. Its 5-hp, one-cylinder engine is cleverly hidden under the seat, but unlike a buggy it has a tiller on top of a column

sticking out of the floor. Also affixed to the column are some little handles and knobs. A few pedals grow out of the floor, too. It doesn't, naturally, have any shafts for a horse but, strangely, it has a whip socket. Furthermore, a metal bar a yard long is hinged below the chassis, its free end pointing rearward. This is a sprag, which can be quickly let down to dig into the road should the brakes fail and the car start rolling backward down a hill.

You'll have to teach yourself to drive it; nobody in town can show you how. Nobody has even seen a horseless carriage, let alone drive one. But luckily an instruction book has come with the machine.

"Charge the tanks with water and gasoline," it reads, "and make sure that the crankcase is filled with lubricating oil."

The water part is easy, but you rush Junior down to the paint store on the corner for the gasoline, which he brings back in gallon bottles. Meanwhile you have crawled under the car to, as the book says, "Open the petcock in the side of the crankcase and watch for some oil to drip out." It drips; you have enough oil. You also check various grease cups on the chassis; they have been filled at the factory.

Now to start the engine!

Luckily, this automobile of yours has electric ignition unlike some of the old-fashioned machines which used a hot tube. "Set the spark back to preclude breaking your wrist," says the book. "Also put the gears into their neutral position by means of the lever on the steering column; then set the brakes."

You insert the plug which turns on the ignition.

"Now vigorously turn the handle which protrudes from the right side of the body and the engine will start," says the book optimistically.

Before the days of the sports car, it was not unusual for well-fixed young gentlemen to take to the road
in out-and-out racing cars, like this 1902, 40 hp Mors (below, left). The huge sprocket upon which the chain
runs shows that it is a racing machine. Note, however, that it was equipped with a headlamp for night
driving. Charles S. Rolls, who is here shown at the controls, was still several years away
from his epic collaboration with Henry Royce. The 1907 Cadillac (left and above) was the model that would make
Henry M. Leland famous. It was similar to those which were torn to bits, scrambled, then reassembled to show
how completely its parts interchanged. It had a single-cylinder, 9 hp engine and a planetary transmission.

You do this. Nothing happens.

You do this some more. Much more. Still nothing happens. Your wife, your son, your neighbors stand around expressionless as you crank. Nothing. A man driving a wagon goes by. "Get a horse," he yells. It's a brand new expression he's picked up from a drover in the next town where there is also an automobile.

You crank some more.

Suddenly, happily, the engine is running. Everybody has backed away from your car which is vibrating like a mechanical jelly. Everything shakes, the mudguards, the kerosene lamps. You yell, "She runs, she runs," but no one can hear you over the wild barking of the exhaust and the howling of gears.

Fearfully, you mount to the seat, release the hand brake and step on the clutch pedal which also applies the foot brake. You put the gear lever into its lowest speed and very s-l-o-w-l-y, as the book advises, let out the clutch! With a neck-snapping jerk you're going down the street at four miles an hour. To slow down you fiddle with the spark control or slip the clutch. To speed up you must go into a higher gear. Control of engine speed by means of a foot throttle—or even a hand throttle—is still in the future. True, one of the pedals on the floor is called an accelerator, but that is only for momentarily cutting out a governor which keeps the speed of the engine down to 750 rpm. A higher speed will certainly break something. As the book says: "Continued use of the accelerator will cause the engine to 'run away' and seriously damage it." But today you are satisfied to go chuffing around the block in your low gear. When you've learned better how to control that tricky tiller, so you don't swerve from one side of the road to the other, there will be time enough to learn about shifting gears.

Within the week you succeed in shifting the gears, but it is a noisy, crunchy, operation, since it is difficult to slow the engine down in neutral no matter how much you set back the spark control. But it is worth the risk, for, while you could do but four mph in first gear, you find that you can go up to nine mph

A pair of 1902 four-cylinder "cross-engined" Franklins (right) pause at the roadside to allow a nervous horse to be led past them. This was required by law in some parts of the country if the oncoming brute seemed at all restive. The Earl of Dudley's 1902 Panhard-Levassor stands far right. This expensive Edwardian had a rear entrance to the tonneau which spread voluptuously out over the rear fenders, and a typical gilled-tube radiator. Compare its suave design with that of the crude two-cylinder Winton (bottom, right) in which H. Nelson Jackson crossed the North American continent in 1903. Jackson's trip took sixty-three days.

in second, and a thrilling 17 mph in top gear.

But things aren't really going smoothly between you and your car. Your wife doesn't think you should have paid out that hard-earned $900 on it. Especially since you spend as much time under it as in it. For one thing, there's that awful vibration that keeps shaking bits loose. You're forever tightening loose nuts, if you're lucky enough to find them still on their bolts. Otherwise you have to put a new one on from that big toolbox you carry about with you. Another thing that gives you trouble is road dirt getting into moving parts. The exposed gears, for instance, just grind themselves away in a paste of grit and grease and road filth, and the factory takes ages to send new ones, which you have learned to put in by yourself. Tires last no time at all. Your hands become a bleeding mess from continually tearing tires off the rims to patch them or to throw them away and put on new ones. Nor has the car been able to take you on those wonderful little trips into the country that you promised the family. At the edge of town the paved roads suddenly end. And you find that your 7 hp are not enough to push those thin tires through hub-deep sand or mud.

Did you give up automobiles? You did not! In spite of your dear wife, you bought another car, a better car. Cars had to get better fast in those days. Or the new little companies that rushed into the business of making automobiles would go right out of business. Which most of them did, anyhow.

Doctors were the first people to buy automobiles in any quantity. Brave men, they tried every type: electrics, steamers, and "hydro-carbon wagons." At first the steam cars were more popular. Electrics were too slow and gasoline cars too complicated and mys-

terious for those steam-oriented men of the Nineteenth Century.

Early auto magazines, such as *The Horseless Age*, are filled with accounts of the experiences of automobilists, most of them doctors. In the issue of November 6, 1901, there are a pair of typical accounts:

"After having used horses in my medical practice for ten years I became interested in the automobile as doing away with the great expense of keeping teams, the bother and disagreeable features of drivers, etc. I subscribed for the three leading automobile journals, sent for a catalogue of every vehicle I saw advertised, attended every automobile show I could get to, and finally pinned my faith to steam as the best power for my business. The first of April finally saw me in possession of a steam carriage of the latest construction. Ready for anything and on the point of selling my teams — so sure was I that the automobile was the proper means of locomotion for a doctor. My experience with steam had all been on paper, my knowledge of it being derived entirely from catalogues and journals. So after fixing up after a fashion I started out and ran quite a distance very successfully. Then, wishing to appear before my family as a full-blown chauffeur, I started for my residence, just in front of which I began to smell gasoline for five minutes. Without stopping to think, I pulled out a match and attempted to relight the fire. Piff! Bang! And the whole thing was ablaze. I retained presence of mind enough to turn off the main gasoline supply and to throw out the cushions and throw mud and dirty water from the street at it until I had subdued the flames, but my $800 auto looked like a bad case of delirium tremens: the paint was scorched and the machine covered with mud, my clothing was dirty

The car at top is not a phaeton without its team or a horseless carriage of the Nineties, but a Kiblinger auto buggy built in 1907. It had tiller steering and a two-cylinder engine, and was perfect for farmers, who needed plenty of road clearance. Built in a different idiom is the four-cylinder 1910 Buick (left). Above: The engine of the 1907 Welch. This car had an overhead camshaft engine with hemispherical combustion chambers as early as 1904. It was unique in its day.

and soiled and my reputation as an expert shattered the first day among all the neighbors, who, as usual, witnessed the accident.

"This first experience rather put a damper on my enthusiasm, at least for two or three days, but when the machine had been washed up it looked somewhat better, and after much persuasion I induced my wife to accompany me on a short spin. After we had ridden out about a mile I suddenly missed the water. The fusible plug blew out and my boiler was burned. Now I was simply going to shine! I explained how this could easily be overcome, for (according to the catalogue) all that is necessary is to insert a key where the fusible plug was, pump up the water by hand, and go rejoicing on your way. Spreading a robe on the ground I proceeded to put my printed instructions into practice; but, alas! I found the key would not fit in the opening, as the babbitt metal stuck to the sides and the tubes were leaking badly. So with fingers burned and clothes soiled and disordered I was again towed home in disgrace, and here I learned my two first lessons in automobiling: First, don't believe over one-half you read in the printed catalogue; second, never wear a silk hat, frock coat and white linen on an auto trip; they don't look well after an accident."

Another cautiously enthusiastic doctor wrote:

"Many object to the steam type of machine on the ground that there are so many important matters to keep in mind. I personally think this is one of the advantages, for it gives one a great deal of personal satisfaction to master a beautiful piece of mechanism and keeps his faculties alert while utilizing the same. We do not go fishing for pleasure with a net, and spirited horses are still in demand. As I have never had two machines at one time I cannot really decide on my preference for use. I intend to have both styles next year, and shall be curious to find out which one I really get the most use out of. I am sure the beginner will usually have more luck with the steam machine, for its main points can be appreciated in fifteen minutes' time. I have seen an expert work on a gasoline machine all day, and then after it got to running be unable to tell which of his various adjustments had accomplished the end in view. There

At a time when most machines still steered from the right, Autocar already had moved the tiller to the left. Its position is clearly visible in this 1903, two-cylinder model (below). It was a natty car with a rear entrance and a gigantic "glass front" which ran from the dash to the top. The side baskets could have been designed to hold hero sandwiches for lunch.

is no question that the gasoline machine is far ahead as to economy of fuel, though the repairs of batteries and cost of oil used are somewhat amazing. The usual repair shop would hardly care to tackle the mechanism of a gasoline engine, and if the carriage is purchased from a manufacturer some hundreds of miles away the element of time and expense involved is rather appalling. Another trouble with the heavy gasoline machines is the very weight which enables them to obtain the high speeds and be properly steered. Many of them cannot be pulled by a single horse and offer a severe strain to the ordinary harness. If one gets down into a ditch it is practically impossible to do anything without the assistance of quite a gang of men."

But the doctors never did go back to the horse and buggy, and it was their example, perhaps more than anything else, that encouraged the more progressive small-town types and farmers to think about owning a horseless carriage.

In 1900, Americans bought 4,192 automobiles. By then the American motorist had a choice of makes. Some were destined to become famous; some to last even until our day: Oldsmobile, Packard, Winton, Autocar, Peerless, and a dozen makes of steamers and electrics.

Elegant and moneyed Easterners sneered at native machinery. They imported Panhards and Mercedes and almost until World War I would continue to look down their noses at even the best American autos. But these American machines had something. They were cheaper and, if cruder, they had a certain agricultural simplicity which made every blacksmith an automobile repairman. Furthermore, they were light and not quite so likely to subside into the inevitable knee-deep mud as the heavier, more luxurious European machines. True, Europe, especially France, made light cars, too, like the Decauville and the de Dion-Bouton. But the American machines of the early 1900's had another advantage which made them singularly suitable over here. They had a four-foot, eight-inch tread and would fit the ruts made by farm wagons. (Roman chariots made four-foot, eight-inch ruts, too.) European cars running over decent roads had no trouble with ruts and were narrower.

Ransom E. Olds was the first man to provide just the kind of automobile most Americans wanted: the Curved Dash Oldsmobile, the first quantity-produced car, in 1901. Olds had built a steam car as far back as 1887, when he was twenty-seven and working for his father, Pliny F. Olds, who owned a gas-engine works in Lansing, Michigan. But Olds was more interested in "hydro-carbon" carriages and by 1897 he had built a quite good machine (now in the Smithsonian). Although he now owned his father's old company, he didn't have enough capital to launch an automobile factory. On a visit to Detroit, he met a retired gentleman named Smith, who was loaded with millions from copper mining and who was crazy enough to put up $199,600 to build horseless carriages — with the understanding that his two sons would get jobs. The new company was the Olds Motor Works, and it lost its shirt ($80,000) on the first car it put on the market. It was too fancy and cost too much—$1,250. This was big money for 1899, when you could buy a quart of whiskey for a dollar, a suit

for $12, and a nice, comfortable house for $2,500.

So Olds decided to add cheaper cars to the line, one of them the Curved Dash Oldsmobile for $650. Even this might not have saved the company, but Olds was lucky. His factory burned down. The only car saved was the pilot model of the new little "Merry Oldsmobile" which happened to be standing near the door. Somebody started cranking the thing, but it wouldn't start (naturally) and they pushed it out.

Everything else, fortunately, burned up, blueprints, patterns, molds. Only the Curved Dash Oldsmobile remained. Olds had no choice. Using the surviving prototype, he started production. In 1901 he sold 425; in 1902, 2,100. By 1903 he was selling 3,750, a third of all the cars sold in this country. No wonder there are still so many nicely restored examples of this model still around.

The Curved Dash Oldsmobile was a simple enough machine and is fun to drive even today, as I discovered when I recently went out in one owned by a

friend. It is perhaps the shortest car I've ever ridden in. Its wheelbase is a mere sixty-seven inches, although its tread is a full fifty-six inches wide. It has one long spring on each side with the front axle attached to the forward eyes, while the rear axle is gripped by the rearward ends. Additionally, a small transverse, full-elliptic spring keeps the front axle from getting too lively. Mounted on this grasshopper-like structure is a pair of seats with a box behind, while the famous curved dash curls toward one's ankles. From the floor a graceful tiller arches toward the driver's hand.

The machinery, consisting of a single cylinder of about 1500 cc, which turns a huge flywheel, a planetary two-speed transmission, and the single chain drive to the rear axle, is all nicely hidden under the seat and the box.

My friend cranked for a few turns and I was surprised at how easily the engine started and how quietly it ran. There was only a subdued puffing sound **57**

In 1910, when most big cars were doing, say, 60 mph, the Simplex "Speed Car" (left) was booming along at better than 80. Its four-cylinder, T-head engine, although rated at 50 hp, developed considerably more power. It was to be expected, therefore, that this muscular Simplex, and its bigger brother, the 90 hp model, were favorites among America's wealthy young sporting set. These Simplexes, among the last American machines to be chain driven, were built right on Manhattan Island and were tested on the then open roads of Long Island. The cheap and popular four-cylinder 1911 Hupmobile (right) was exactly the opposite kind of car. Henry Ford's six-cylinder Model K of 1907 (lower left) was one of the few high-priced cars to bear his name.

from the exhaust and the vibration was just about enough to set the brass kerosene side-lamps gently jiggling.

If you've ever climbed aboard a light buggy, you'll know the feeling as I set foot on the step plate of the Olds. There was no denying its springy horse-carriage ancestry. On the road the absence of any structure in front made for slight unease at first as the road surface seemed to streak right beneath me. There was no problem with wind, nor did I feel the need for goggles as I have in windshieldless cars of just a few years later. For flat-out on a level road we couldn't have been doing more than 20 mph. The slightest rise meant shifting down to the lower of the two gears and just crawling while the engine behind gave vocal notice that it was working. But remember, the Oldsmobile was only a 5-hp car.

Until about 1904 the Oldsmobile was typical of American cars. Most of them (except perhaps Hiram Maxim's Pope-built Columbia) had a one- or two-cylinder engine under the seat, a planetary transmission, single-chain drive, and a rudimentary cooling system utilizing a few yards of finned pipe as a radiator, which hung almost any place on the car where there was room.

Except for individual idiosyncrasies on the part of their builders — like Alexander Winton's compressed-air system of governing engine speed—the Cadillac, the Ford, the Pope Hartford, the Packard, and a dozen others were all built in the same American idiom, although some of them had wheel steering instead of a tiller.

But times were good in the early 1900's—until 1907, anyhow. People wanted cars big enough to carry the whole family, cars that looked like those fancy foreign machines New York swells owned. They could, very early, have bought a detachable tonneau, which device, containing some back seats, was hooked on aft of the usual two front buggy seats and into which the passengers inserted themselves by way of a high and tiny back door. Once in, they sat facing each other, playing kneesies, while their feet were entangled in a greasy stew of tools, chains, punctured tires, cans of oil, and filthy rags.

The earlier European cars had offered their rear passengers no better amenities, rear entrances being necessary until wheelbases grew longer and the sprocket and chain moved far enough back so that a side door became feasible.

By 1904 or so, European machines, led by Mercedes, already had honeycomb radiators, gate gearshifts, four-cylinder engines up front, good acetylene headlamps and, above all, comfortable, commodious, side-entrance *Roi des Belges* coachwork. This type of tulip-shaped body, with its after quarters swelling voluptuously out above the rear wheels, was named after the one which the King of Belgium had built to be mounted on his "Sixty" Mercedes in 1901. He was said to have been given this idea by his great and good friend, the actress Cleo De Merode, who, hearing that he was having a car body built, pushed together two of the lavishly upholstered tub chairs in her boudoir and suggested that the body be based on their combined shape.

59

George Baldwin Selden, of Rochester, New York, was a sharp young lawyer farsighted enough to realize that someday somebody would build and try to sell a gasoline automobile. When that day came he wanted to hold the patents on it. He got his idea after seeing a Brayton stationary engine at the Philadelphia Centennial in 1876. By 1877, he had come up with an idea for a car, a crude vehicle in which a Brayton engine, the gearbox, and the clutch were attached to the front axle and turned with the front wheels. Crude as his proposal was, the U.S. Patent Office allowed him to file it in 1879. But Selden was too canny to allow the Patent Office to grant him a patent. He didn't want a patent, which was valid for only seventeen years, until somebody started building cars. He kept his application alive by changes and legalisms until 1895, when he finally permitted the papers to be issued.

At about that time, Colonel Albert A. Pope, the bicycle tycoon who had had Hiram Percy Maxim design and build various electric and gas autos for him, learned with horror that somebody besides himself had a right to monopolize the budding gas-car industry. The good Colonel, therefore, rounded up some of the millionaires who were his pals and partners in an outfit called the Electric Vehicle Company and got Selden to join them in a cozy plan to control the gasoline-car industry.

To this end they formed the Association of Licensed Automobile Manufacturers. If you wanted to sell cars, you paid these gentry five per cent of the retail price—of which percentage Selden got a tidy share—and got a Selden-patent plaque to stick on your product. If you wouldn't play ball, they sued you and also threatened to sue anybody who bought an "unlicensed" car.

Most manufacturers fell for this, but Henry Ford told the A.L.A.M. to go to hell.

After years of legal pettifogging, Ford won. In 1911, when the patent had almost expired, the courts deciding that Selden's patent applied only to vehicles driven by the Brayton engine. The car shown here was built in 1905 to prove to the courts that a Selden machine would actually go. Fourteen hundred feet was the farthest it could ever be persuaded to run.

By 1907, the *Roi des Belges* type of touring body on a chassis long enough to accommodate it was commonplace not only in Europe, but in America as well. And now, too, tall structures of beveled glass and wood rose over the back portions of the body to enclose the passengers in luxurious silken privacy and to protect them from the weather. By now, too, the four-cylinder engine sitting up front behind a brass-bound radiator was usual even in cheap cars. In England, Napier and Rolls-Royce were already building six-cylinder-engined cars of a magnificence which has never been surpassed. In this country Packard, Peerless, and Pierce, the great "three P's" were making superlative automobiles, hardly inferior to the best Europeans and better suited to American conditions. For although American roads were getting slightly better, they still were rough and rutted enough to require a simpler, more rugged type of car with a higher ground clearance than the European machines.

I drive a lesser-known make of this period, a Welch made in Pontiac, Michigan—a car which cost $5,500, a fortune in its day. It is quite a large machine with a wheelbase of 128 inches and weighing some 4,000 pounds ready for the road. Its four-cylinder engine develops about 50 hp at 1,500 rpm, but is somewhat unusual for its day in having an overhead camshaft and hemispherical combustion chambers. Its transmission, however, although no longer of the planetary type common five years earlier, is not yet the sliding-gear selective gearbox for which Mercedes had set the fashion. The Welch gears are in constant mesh, but rotating freely on their shaft until the one the driver wishes to use is locked to its shaft by means of a multi-plate, steel-and-bronze clutch which is selected by a long, bronze hand lever. There is, of course, a separate clutch for each of the three speeds, but no foot-operated declutching mechanism.

These are but minor differences from other cars of its era. The road-feel and handling are no different from any other large and expensive car of 1907; the Welch is a true child of its time. Although it is only eight years or so younger than the first cars people bought in America, it is no longer a temperamental beast. True, it must be hand cranked, but cranking is an easily acquired knack, even with such a large and heavy engine as the Welch's.

After flooding the carburetor, the crank is turned a few times with the switch off to suck gasoline vapor into the cylinders. Very often when the ignition is switched on the engine will start itself; otherwise, a single, sharp, upward pull on the crank will usually cause it to burst into full song. And full song it is,

for a 1907 engine is a virtual symphony of sounds: a tympanic clatter from the valve mechanism, a healthy whirring sound from the gears, and a solid boom of exhaust. Though there is some vibration, it is nothing compared to the stamping-mill pounding of a car of, say, 1899. But this is still an American engine. By comparison to an English Rolls-Royce, or a French De Dietrich, or Panhard of 1907, it sounds like a threshing machine.

On the road it is a delight. Seated behind the mahogany-rimmed steering wheel on the end of its brass column, the driver has an almost dangerous feeling of omnipotence. He feels superior to anything on the road beneath him. Yes, beneath him, for the roofs of modern cars are at the level of his knees. Once in high gear the sound of the slow-turning engine is left behind and the car glides along quite as silently as any modern machine, with an easy, springy motion from its full-elliptic rear suspension—helped, no doubt, by its great, three-foot diameter wheels which don't fall into every little hole in the road as modern, caster-sized wheels do.

To a modern driver, the Welch's steering would feel odd. The diameter of its steering wheel is small and even a tiny movement puts the car into a terrifying swoop. The steering transmits a considerable amount of movement from the front wheels, and gripping the wheel hard enough to make the knuckles white does not control it. So the driver must allow the wheel to jiggle gently in his hands, taking firm measures only when disaster is imminent.

This Welch has no windshield, although many 1907 cars did, and at speeds over 40 mph (it is capable of 55) the wind of its going becomes uncomfortable, even with goggles. It's a good idea to keep your mouth shut unless you like the taste of bees.

This Welch also has the commodious *Roi des Belges* body. The driver and his passenger sit in deeply tufted, horsehair-stuffed, diamond-pleated, red-leather armchairs. The rear seat in the tonneau is similarly upholstered, but is as wide as a sofa and seats three. Also in the tonneau are a pair of leather jump seats which can be faced forward or sideways, or can be removed altogether if luggage is to be carried on the rear floor.

The fancy Welch catalogue describes a "convertible" limousine body:

"Our limousine bodies, seating five inside, possess the unique feature of having removable tops giving the standard open, dustless body when taken off, thus giving either a summer car or the ideal winter car when the top is on. The car is electrically lighted and heated from the muffler when desired. The top

The 1906 Pierce "Great Arrow" (above) was one of America's greatly respected "Three P's"—Pierce, Peerless, and Packard. With its lushly upholstered "tonneau" and a chauffeur up front, it was perfect for touring "de grande luxe." In spite of the numerous drawbacks of rough dirt roads and blacksmith-mechanics, the nation was now on the roll. A 1907 Franklin (top of the page) nosed a somewhat unusual "barrel hood" into the American auto picture. Its engine was air-cooled by fins on its cylinders. The more refined designs of the period—such as the 1905 Italian F.I.A.T. at right—still came from Europe. With its four-cylinder engine rated at 24 hp, it had low-tension, "make-and-break" ignition that used interrupters in the cylinders. Upon breaking contact, they created the spark to explode the charge. No spark plugs were used. Very much under the influence of Mercedes, the F.I.A.T. of the first decade used a honeycomb radiator almost identical in shape to that of the German marque. F.I.A.T. also produced a 60 hp, six-cylinder version similar to the four-cylinder model. A major difference between the two models was an early self-starting device which worked by compressed air. Only the six-cylinder car offered this innovation.

is trimmed in richest satin and seats in Morocco or first quality hand buffed leather. Toilet articles, speaking tubes, etc., are provided. Side windows open and tonneau front and door glass are removable giving a semi-open car for Spring and Fall; in fact, it is the only ideal all-the-year-around car thus far produced. The richness of the combined mahogany, bevel plate glass, satin, leather, and brass finishings cannot be described . . . large luggage apartment under rear seats, locker and tool drawer under front seat, both under lock and key."

But it wasn't all roses for the automobilists of 1907. They struggled with unreliable tires and an afternoon's trip almost always meant that there would be some bother with patches and pumping. If the casing was damaged as well as the tube, there was a little leather corset in the tool kit that could be

laced to the wheel over the wound. Dust was the terrible enemy. Every car trailed a great cloud of it, part of which was sucked forward to settle on the muffled and duster-clad unfortunates in the tonneau. Blindly passing another car in its almost opaque dust cloud was no joke. By modern standards the two-wheel brakes were laughable, but the roads were free of the suicidal traffic of today. They didn't need the neck-snapping brakes we must have to stay alive.

The first cars lit their way with candles in coach lamps. Next came kerosene lamps, feeble but better. In the early 1900's acetylene lamps came into use, with each lamp containing its own means of making gas from carbide and water. By 1907 the acetylene generators lived on the running boards, and copper tubing carried the gas to the lamps. About this time, too, it became popular to buy compressed acetylene gas in cylinders, which were less of a nuisance than generators. Since they had to be filled with water and lumps of calcium carbide, the generators, like the self-generating headlamps before them, required constant cleaning out.

These match-lit gas lights were not too bad considering the lack of traffic and the low speeds of cars at night. In fact, people even complained of being blinded by what we would consider dim light, giving head-lamp manufacturers a chance to market dimming devices—little shields which were pivoted to hide the fearsome glare of the gas flame.

In 1907 the bottom dropped out of the market for expensive cars. The United States suffered a financial panic and depression that would not be equalled for twenty-two years. Still, unlike 1929, production went up from 43,000 cars in 1907 to 63,500 cars in 1908.

63

The cheaper, mass-produced car was beginning to rear its ugly little hood.

Most people believe that Henry Ford was the first man to think of mass production; some are even convinced that he invented the automobile. Ford was perhaps the first to adopt assembly line production to automobiles, but assembly line production required interchangeable parts so precisely made that any part of any car of the same model would fit any of its mass-produced brothers.

The first man to have this revolutionary concept of interchangeable parts for mass production was Eli Whitney, of Connecticut, inventor of the cotton gin. He first used his idea in 1798 to make muskets for the young United States Government. He first tooled up, made dies, jigs, and then put each man in his small factory to work on one specialized bit of each gun.

The idea of interchangeable parts took hold in New England and by the mid-Nineteenth Century Yankee factories were turning out everything from watches to sewing machines by assembly line methods. And it was a Vermont Yankee named Henry M. Leland who first applied real standards of precision and interchangeability to car manufacturing in quantity. Born in 1843, he had worked during the Civil War for the Springfield Arsenal and later for Colt's Patent Firearms Manufacturing Company, where guns were made according to Whitney's ideas. After the war, he went to Detroit where, with a partner named Faulconor, he built Oldsmobile engines. In 1902 he became one of the organizers of the Cadillac Automobile Company and in 1908 he showed the world what true interchangeability of parts meant.

He sent three Cadillacs to Brooklands in England. There, officials of the Royal Automobile Club had the cars disassembled and their parts scrambled like so much scrap iron. Then Cadillac mechanics, using hand tools only, rebuilt this clutter of metal into three Cadillacs. Officials of the R.A.C. then had the

A brace of four-cylinder 1908 Corbins (upper left). Corbin was a quality car built in New Britain, Connecticut, and advertised itself as: "The Car of Destiny, the Repairman's Dream." The Stevens Duryea (upper right), also built in America in 1908, was another fine car of the day. It was one of the first machines equipped with an all-aluminum body. Its engine had six cylinders instead of the more usual four. It sold for $3,500 and was marketed just in time to ride the crest of a new enthusiasm for giant six-cylinder engines. The movement had begun in 1907 and was led by Napier and Rolls-Royce. A favorite gimmick to gain publicity for such cars was to run them tremendous distances with their transmissions locked in high gear to show that their power was sufficient to preclude shifting gears. The 1907 French Darracq (right), also with a six-cylinder engine, is a portrait in Edwardian elegance before a Motor Club run to Brighton in England.

Famed English racing driver Charles Jarrott (left) takes his 1908 Crossley across the channel to motor in France. This car was not dissimilar from staff cars of the same marque used by the British Army in World War I. It had a 4½-liter engine of some 50 hp. Before the first World War, the 1913 model (top) and the 1911 model Loziers (like that above) were among the most powerful and greatly desired American sporting machines. The 50 hp Lozier engines were remarkable among the domestic machines for having roller-bearing crankshafts in their six-cylinder engines.

cars driven for 500 miles on the track. The cars behaved perfectly. The amazed and delighted Britishers awarded Cadillac the Thomas Dewar Trophy for the outstanding motoring feat of that year.

By the time of the Kaiser war, the automobile had almost ceased to be an instrument of adventure and a mark of wealth; true, Henry Ford had much to do with this. By 1914 he was selling 248,307 cars a year at the fantastically low price of $490 for a tourer.

But it wasn't only interchangeable parts, mass production, and low prices that made the automobile the household appliance it is today. It was the woman driver. Certainly there had been lady drivers from the very beginning, even lady racing drivers like Mme. Du Gast, who had driven in the great Paris-Madrid race of 1903, or Mrs. Joan Newton Cuneo, who drove in the Glidden Tours. And, of course, lady drivers sat behind most of the tillers of the crawling electric cars that were blocking traffic on the shopping streets of every American city. But women stayed out of the driver's seats of gasoline cars for a very obvious reason. Hand cranking an engine was just too hard and dangerous a job for them.

Manufacturers had from the beginning come up with all kinds of laughable devices to eliminate the crank, or "starting handle," as the English call it. One consisted of a giant spring which was attached to the engine where the crank normally lived. This spring was wound up by the engine while it ran. Theoretically, the next time you wanted to start the engine, you had but to release a lever and, presto, the unwinding spring would whir it into life. Unfortunately if your engine was suffering a slight malaise your spring would unwind itself to no avail, and you'd had it, sister! Pushing the car was your only remedy.

Another crank-eliminator offered by some manufacturers, including even staid Renault, also stored the power of the engine, but in the form of compressed air and a cat's cradle of piping to the cylinders. The driver opened a valve and air rushed in to the cylinders and rotated the engine. If it felt like it, it started. The Winton, from 1907 on, had saved exhaust gas under pressure to start its engine, and the Prest-O-Lite Company, which was supplying tanks of acetylene for lighting, tried for a while to sell a zany system of piping and valves which would fill the cylinders with acetylene gas whose explosion, it was hoped, would start the engine.

In 1912, Cadillac offered an electric self-starter and electric lights. A lady could now start a car just by touching a button with the toe of her high-button shoe. In America, at least, the rough, tough open

67

car built for male drivers was doomed. Henceforward, women would have as much, if not more, to say than men about the kind of car that would be built. From now on cars would be glass-enclosed rooms on wheels, softly sprung to insulate ladies' delicate bottoms from the realities of rough roads. And steering would became lower geared to make it easier for women to turn and park.

But it took years to complete the undoing of the motor car. A quality car of 1913 or 1914 was still a delicious mechanism to take out on the road.

By 1914, a Sunday afternoon's excursion in the family car was no longer the near-desperate adventure of ten years before. Roads were much improved, tires were better, and with the advent of the quick demountable rim, hardly more difficult to change than they are today. Mechanically, a high-grade car was as reliable as a contemporary car. Engines were more flexible, and gear shifting was necessary only for hills and starting from rest. The six-cylinder engine was a commonplace on higher-priced cars. A V-8—copied from de Dion in France—was available on the 1914 Cadillac and a year later Packard came out with its famous twelve-cylinder Twin-Six.

The Locomobile catalogue of 1912 gives a mouth-watering glimpse of the wonderful construction and luxury a man could buy in those spacious days: "... The rear seat cushion and back in our six-cylinder models are provided with upholstering *ten inches thick*.... This detail alone permits any one regardless of age, figure, or constitution to enjoy the same restful ease when riding in the car as when seated in the most luxurious library chair....The Locomobile crankcase is *government bronze*.... The crankshaft has seven main bearings, one between each connecting rod...." But there is a disturbing note too: "Passengers are seated low in the car, giving a sense of security," says the catalogue. The days when a motorist sat on a car rather than in it were ending. The

The 1910 Chadwick (below) was called "the speediest stock car in the world." It was a thrilling mechanism to look at—and to hear—when the exhaust boomed from the big ports in the side of her hood. A Chadwick practicing for the Vanderbilt Cup once reached 107 mph. As far back as 1907, Lee Chadwick, its creator, built the first supercharged engine. Another high-quality big car was the 1907 Thomas Flyer (upper right). It was the Thomas that won the New York to Paris Race in 1908. An extravagance of Latin magnificence—the 50 hp Itala (lower right) was constructed for the Queen of Italy in 1906. Note the three rows of richly upholstered seats for her court, and the bucket seat over the tool box—for the King.

delights of sitting high and mighty with a commanding view of the countryside were nearly gone. Since around 1910 there had been front doors, too. The occupants of an automobile were destined to be enveloped by more and more sheet-metal bodywork until a nadir would be reached in the Thirties, when they would see the passing world through glass slits in tank-like bodies.

However, almost all cars of this period still had the one serious flaw that would make them useless on the roads of our era: two-wheel brakes. Fast—70 or better for powerful types—a joy to handle, they took forever to come to a stop. Argyll in Scotland and Isotta-Fraschini in Italy already had early forms of four-wheel brakes, but not until after the World War would most cars have an anchor on each wheel.

Not everybody wanted a car capable of carrying the whole family. Young bloods wanted machines that were more like the racing cars of the day: rakish two-seaters with bodywork consisting of bucket seats with a bolster-shaped gas tank and a pile of spare tires behind them. Light and windshieldless, these first sports cars (although the term didn't come into general use until many years later, in England) were

Quite different from the loftily built Stoddard Dayton of 1910 (right) was the 1911 American Underslung (above). Its chassis frame hung below the axles and made it one of the lowest, most stable machines of the period. Its four-cylinder engine developed 50 hp, and the car sat on huge wheels which wore tires 41 inches in diameter. The six-cylinder, 50 hp Napier (far right) in 1912 was the rival of the other great British-built, six-cylinder car, the Rolls-Royce. The Napier's engine was so long that it was necessary to extend the hood ungracefully forward beyond the axle. Note that its radiator is wider than the hood.

fast, surprisingly stable and maneuverable, and a joy to drive. Almost every manufacturer built cars that looked like this, but only a few built cars that had the exhilarating performance to match their looks: Stutz and Mercer, Marmon, Lozier, and Simplex. Some of these lasted until the early Twenties, but their heyday was during those few happy years before the first German war.

I had a wonderful ride in a Simplex "Speed Car" once, a 50-hp model of 1912. For some reason, which I disremember, it had been necessary to follow in a Rolls-Royce a friend of mine, Austin Clark, who owned this machine. We were on an open stretch of the Montauk Highway on Long Island and to my surprise I had found that I had to do 80 even to keep the Simplex in sight. When we reached our destination I climbed out of the Rolls and expressed my amazement at the manner of the Simplex's going.

"Want to drive it?" asked my friend.

"Oh, no—thanks. I might bend it," I said insincerely as I moved to climb behind the wheel.

Clark turned the ignition switch, then walked up front, and after one quick, practiced flick of the crank, aided by a decompression device, he had the

In 1909, Peerless built its runabouts, like the one shown at left, with cambered and dished rear wheels that, at the time, were thought to be stronger than previous designs. If you look closely, the slightly concave appearance of the rear wheel can be seen. Before 1912, when electric lighting brought vast changes to auto history, the automobile gloried in its sparkling brass gaslights, bulb horns, and other gleaming accoutrements. People who didn't have chauffeurs or diligent wives to polish these decorative—but necessary—accessories, welcomed the coming of nickel and, eventually, chromium.

engine singing its healthy basso-profundo song. An open cut-out contributed to this, of course. Clark climbed in on my left and handed me a pair of goggles. We were sitting in minuscule, leather-upholstered, bucket seats set low on the chassis, with our legs stretched out toward a mahogany dashboard so distant that I could read neither the speedometer nor the gas-pressure gauge mounted upon it. There was, of course, no windshield. I could see before me a great, red, dog-house-shaped hood, a pair of brass headlamps, and the front mudguards. I could also see both front wheels. (Visibility was hardly a problem in those days.) I must have looked worried as I sat there gripping the mahogany steering wheel on the end of its impossibly long, brass tube.

"Go ahead. Put her in gear and let's go," said Clark callously. "She has four speeds, you know. When you want to stop, put on the hand and the foot brake at once."

This really gave me pause, but I grasped the outside gear lever and put it into the first speed notch in the big brass gate, let in the clutch, and we were off. I was hardly giving her any gas at all with the foot throttle (there's another on the steering column), but even in first gear, the Simplex seemed to surge away. I shifted, double-clutching, into second. "No need to double-clutch on upward shifts," Clark yelled into my ear. He was right. On these early gearboxes with their big, coarse teeth transmitting power from low-speed engines, shifting is far easier than on cars of twenty years later.

I was in third gear now and we were flying. The engine just burbled and didn't seem to be working at all. But there was noise all right from the big chains driving the rear wheels. In the tradition of the early

Mercedes, which it resembled more than somewhat, this Simplex was one of the last of the chain-driven monsters, like the Mack trucks of my youth.

I put my foot down as we charged along. "Ha!" I thought, "I bet Clark thought I couldn't drive this beast of his."

But Clark deflated me. "Shift," he screamed in my ear, "Shift into high." The Simplex surged ahead. Never has a car felt so fast to me. A modern sports car at 120 seems dull by comparison. My cheeks were pulled out in the gale. My hair was being yanked by the wind. The back of my jacket was a balloon trying to lift me out of my seat.

"Turn left at the next crossroads," Clark bellowed.

I stamped on the foot brake, shifted into third, pulled at the hand brake—Clark was right; the brakes were lousy—I was still going far too fast to make that corner! Foolishly I wrenched the wheel hard left. The big Simplex just sailed around, no squeal, no sway, no sweat!

Sobered, I drove slowly back to Clark's place. "Sorry I drove so fast," I said trying to forestall any sharp remarks about my high-speed cornering. "Not at all," said the ever-polite Clark. "But you don't have to slow down that much for a turn."

Even before the war in 1914, the United States was building more cars than all of the countries in Europe combined. By 1920, the United States was making, with a few exceptions, 2,000,000 of the stodgiest, most uninteresting cars the world had ever seen. When Europe got back on its feet we would see exciting automobiles again, but meantime most Americans lost interest in automobiles except as prosaic means of transport. It would be thirty years before Americans really fell in love with cars again.

Famous to almost every American is the name "Stutz Bearcat."
The 1914 version (above) had a four-cylinder, T-head engine which could
develop some 60 hp and, although it weighed about 4,000 pounds,
it was capable of 80 mph. The car sold for $2,000. In those days,
the Stutz and the Mercer owners were great rivals on the road and off.
The Stutz owners composed and chanted this derisive measure: "There
never was a worser car than a Mercer." Not to be outdone, the Mercer
contingent countered: "You have to be nuts to drive a Stutz." By
1906, when the French Darracq Landaulet (left) was built, automobiling in
Europe was commonplace—even the ladies had caught the fever.

By 1911, when this English Vauxhall (above) was built, the torpedo-style, flush-sided, four-door body was beginning to bring the motorist down from his high perch in the fresh air. This type of body first appeared during the Prince Henry trials of the preceding year. Note, too, that the flat dashboard is starting to curve into the hood. Before long the break between the hood and the body was to disappear altogether. In the 1916 Locomobile "Sportif" (below) the line from radiator cap to tail is unbroken. Compare its sleekness to that of the 1910 Stoddard Dayton (right) which, although built only six years earlier, looks like a machine from another century.

EARLY RACES

The earliest racing was done in France and it began almost as soon as the machines were invented. Théry aboard the Richard-Brasier (preceding pages) leaves his competitors in a cloud of dust as he hurries home to win the 1905 race for the Gordon-Bennett Cup. The first official auto competition was organized by "Le Petit Journal" of Paris in 1894 and ran from Paris to Rouen. Some of the competing cars are, left to right from top: A Panhard-Levassor two-seater and a sister Panhard model, two early Peugeots, the de Dion-Bouton Steam Tractor—seen again at right with a carriage attached, trailer fashion—and M. Maurice Le Blant's nine-passenger steam omnibus.

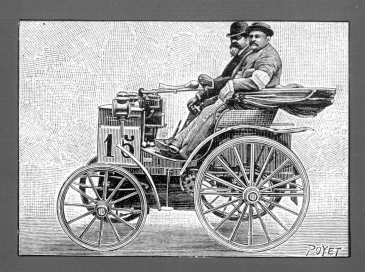

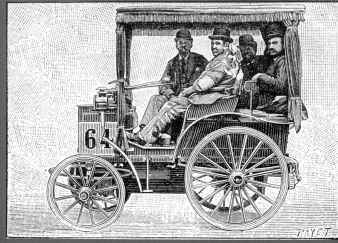

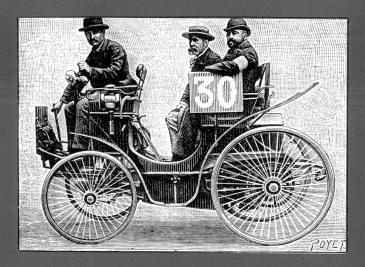

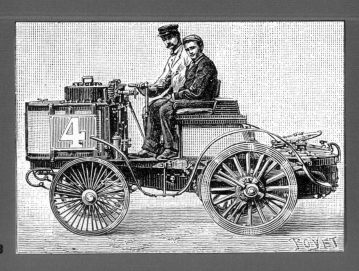

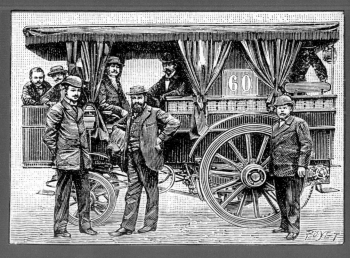

o sooner did an early builder of a "horseless" succeed in actually making it run, no matter how painfully and haltingly, than he looked around for other such machines against which he might pit his darling in a contest of speed.

It was, naturally, in France that motor racing first started, for only there did enough machines exist; only there, in any case, were the roads good enough. Motor racing has always done much to develop the speed, road holding, and stamina of automobiles, and it was these races, perhaps, that did as much as anything else to enable France to lead the world in *l'automobilisme* in this period.

The first such contest, the Paris-Rouen Trial of 1894, was not strictly a race, for as the organizers, *Le Petit Journal* of Paris, pointed out, the winning car would be that which was: "Without danger, easily handled and of low running cost." One-hundred-and-two entries were received, but each car had to undergo a preliminary trial to prove that it could do fifty kilometers in three hours. This was later changed to four hours when the competitors claimed that ten miles an hour was a dangerously high speed. Considering the odd vehicles that were entered, who could blame them? For some of these early sporting gentlemen spurned such prosaic means of propulsion as steam, electricity, or gasoline. One, Monsieur Rousselet of Paris, insisted that his *voiture* ran by gravity. A Monsieur Victor Popp contemplated running under compressed air and a Monsieur Laval entered a machine he called a Baricycle that "moved by the weight of the passengers." Others had such delightful propellants as "a system of pendulums," "automatic," and "combination of animate and mechanical motor."

On July 22, 1894, nineteen cars, the very first group of racing automobiles ever to leave a starting line, departed the Porte Maillot in Paris for Rouen, 126 kilometers away, accompanied by an industrious reporter from Mr. James Gordon Bennett's *New York Herald* aboard a bicycle.

The start was not without incident. For a Monsieur Etienne Le Blant, described at the time as "a person of good intentions but insufficient automobile experience," ran a big steam van belonging to the Parisian shop *La Belle Jardiniere* up on the sidewalk, demolishing a bench and frightening the whiskers off a Monsieur Cassignol, the official observer riding with him. His more experienced brother, Maurice Le Blant, had entered a nine-passenger omnibus which was to perform a most useful service during the run; it picked up the crews of such cars as became disabled. At one point the Maurice Le Blant steamer itself got stuck among the loose stones of a road under construction and forty or fifty of the wildly enthusiastic spectators started hauling on ropes to drag the fuming monster clear. Suddenly its wheels became unstuck and the machine bounded away amid a shower of stones and fleeing rescuers.

But Maurice Le Blant's steamer finished in the money, anyhow. *Le Petit Journal* announced on July 24, 1894:

FIRST PRIZE 5000 FRANCS [$1000] Awarded equally to Messrs. Panhard and Levassor, of Ivry, Seine, and Le fils de Peugeot Fréres, of Valentigny, Doubs, "Both employing the petrol motor invented by Herr Daimler, of Wurtemburg."

SECOND PRIZE 2000 FRANCS [$400]
Awarded to Messrs. de Dion, Bouton et Cie.,
"For their interesting steam tractor which
draws a carriage like a horse, and develops
(though with a powerful engine it must be
admitted) a speed absolutely beyond comparison, especially uphill."

THIRD PRIZE 1500 FRANCS [$300]
Awarded to M. Maurice Le Blant, of Paris,
"For his nine-seated car on the Serpollet
system."

For the 78.75 miles from Paris to Rouen, the de Dion
had averaged 11.6 miles per hour. (Although fastest,
it did not comply with regulations, since it carried a
steam engineer in addition to the driver.) The fastest
Peugeot (five finished) averaged 11.5 mph; the fastest
Panhard (four finished) 11.1 mph. Le Blant's steam
bus averaged 7.3 mph; even his clumsy brother was
among the twenty finishers, averaging 6.9 mph.

They could hardly wait, these Frenchmen, to do it
again in 1895. But this time it would be a proper
race, from Paris to Bordeaux and back to Paris, an
astronomical distance for those days of 732 miles.
Drivers could be changed en route; repairs made only
by such means as could be carried on the car. Nothing
outside was to be procured except, as the regulations

Manuel Roble's impressionistic aquatint (preceding pages) was
engraved after the 1903 Paris-Madrid Race, the last of such country-to-country
competitions. Marcel Renault (above, before the race) was among the many
drivers and spectators who were killed. Lady-driver Mme. du Gast
(upper left) appears confident at the controls of her de Dietrich. She and the
chevalier René de Knyff in a 90 hp Panhard-Levassor (bottom, left)
were among the other competitors in that fatal 1903 run. A year earlier,
de Knyff's mount had been the 75 hp model Panhard (center, left).

said, "entertainment for man and machine."

At noon on June 11, 1895, twenty-two racers
started from the Place d'Armes at Versailles: thirteen
gas cars, six steamers, one electric (a Jeantaud), and
two motor tricycles.

Troubles started early, as Mr. Gerald Rose re-
counts in his monumental *Record of Motor Racing*,
published in 1909: "It appears that one of the big
ends [of a Bollée steam bus] heated and M. Bollée
wrapped a pad of wet rags round it during a stoppage
for supplies. Unfortunately, the pad was forgotten,
and, on re-starting, the rags were drawn into the machinery and played havoc with the engine...."

It is the great Émile Levassor's run that still ex-
cites us most after sixty-odd years. Levassor knew
he couldn't win from the start. Only four-passenger
cars were qualified for prizes. Levassor was on a solid-
tired two-seater of his own make, a Panhard with a
2-cylinder, 4-hp Phenix engine of 1,206 cc, which
ran at 750 rpm.

Not long after leaving Versailles, Levassor succeeded in passing the fast steam cars that had been
sent off ahead of him. By the time he reached Ruffec,
the town where a relief driver was waiting, he was
well in the lead, even though he had by then driven
for over six hours in darkness, his road ahead lit
only by guttering candle lamps. At Ruffec, his relief
was still abed. Rather than waste time waiting for

him to get up and dress, Levassor pressed on to Bordeaux. It was easier now. In that latitude the summer
sun rises early. By 10:30 in the morning Levassor
was in Bordeaux making his turn back to Paris, fighting his way over streets crammed with excitedly cheering Bordelais. He had reached Bordeaux in the im-
pressive time of twenty-two hours.

This time his man in Ruffec was all set to take his
seat on the Panhard. Levassor waved him off and
pushed on for Paris non-stop except for halts to take
on fuel and perhaps a quick drink. Not long after
noon on June 13, Levassor pulled up at the Porte
Maillot, two days and forty-eight minutes after he
had set out for Bordeaux.

In an account printed in the "North American
Review" in September, 1899, the Marquis De Chas-
seloup-Laubat, himself a formidable early automo-
bilist, wrote of Levassor:

"M. Levassor remained on his machine about fifty-
three hours, and nearly forty-nine of these on the run.
Yet he did not appear to be over-fatigued; he wrote
his signature at the finish with a firm hand; we lunched
together at Gillet's, at the Porte Maillot; he was quite
calm; he took with relish a cup of bouillon, a couple
of poached eggs, and two glasses of champagne; but
he said that racing at night was dangerous, adding
that having won [?] he had the right to say such a
race was not to be run another time at night.

"The general mean of his velocity was 14.91 miles an hour; the maximum was eighteen-and-a-half miles an hour between Orleans and Tours."

Of the twenty-two machines that started, nine finished. Among these only one was a steamer. Five steamers had fallen out, as had the Jeantaud electric. Second and third places had been taken by Peugeots, respectively, six hours and eleven hours behind Levassor's Panhard. It was one of the Peugeots that actually collected first prize, for it was a four-seater.

In 1894, right after the Paris-Rouen trial, a brash young newspaperman named Francis Upham Adams, who worked for the *Chicago Times-Herald*, sold his boss, H. H. Kohlsatt, the publisher, the idea of running an automobile race. After all, what Paris could do, couldn't Chicago do better? Adams must have been a great salesman for he got Kohlsatt to put up $5,000 as a purse, with $2,000 for the winner.

Applications poured in, almost ninety of them, from every crossroads mechanic who ever dreamed of building a horseless carriage. *Two* entries were even received from a place called Pine Bluff, Arkansas. But as race day approached, Adams and Kohlsatt came to the horrifying realization that most of the automobiles entered were still but dizzy dreams in the heads of their inventors. The race, originally set for the Fourth of July, 1895, was postponed and postponed again, finally to Thanksgiving Day while the opposition papers in Chicago, which had jeered at the venture from the beginning, howled with glee.

To stir up some interest in the race as the months went by, Adams announced a prize contest for a new name other than "horseless carriage" for the new mechanical marvel.

When Thanksgiving Day dawned there were eight inches of snow and slush on the ground, and merely getting to the starting line at the Midway Plaisance was quite a feat. The cars that ploughed their way to the start were: an Electrobat electric built by Morris and Salom, a Duryea gasoline machine, two Benz gasoline machines, a Roger-Benz gasoline machine entered by R. H. Macy, a Sturges electric.

At 8:55, the Duryea got the flag and slithered off with Frank Duryea at the helm and an umpire in the seat beside him. The other machines were sent off at one-minute intervals, most of them requiring a push by the happy spectators before their macaroni-thin tires could get a grip on the slushy snow.

Meanwhile, Frank Duryea's brother, Charles, took a train to the Loop where he had a light horse-drawn sleigh waiting. Driving this he met his brother by taking a short-cut to Van Buren Street where he fell in behind him.

The course followed the lake shore to Evansville where, after a control check, it was to return via Roscoe and through Humboldt Park to the start. The gasoline wagon, as the Duryeas called it, ran well until it crossed the Rush Street Bridge. There the steering gear suddenly let go, but Frank managed to stop without hitting anything.

Frank couldn't fix the broken part with the tools he had on the car; he needed a workshop. So Charles, in the sleigh, charged around frantically until he found one open on the holiday. There Frank repaired the part, but he had lost fifty-five minutes. Macy's Roger-Benz was now thirty-five minutes ahead of him.

Deep snow now slowed the car down, and Charles in the sleigh got bored and hungry. He stopped for a leisurely lunch for himself and oats for the horses, while poor Frank went ahead through the slush on an empty stomach. Charles took a short cut and caught Frank, who was now back in the lead. This business of Charles stopping for refreshment and then taking short cuts to meet his brother went on for a while, until Frank finally failed to show up at a relay station where Charles was waiting.

Frank had not only lost his way, but had broken down with ignition trouble. By the time Charles, who had been dashing up and down back streets, found him, Frank was squatting over a little charcoal fire heating an electrical part, so that he might bend it enough to refit it.

Even though he had lost a whole hour this time, Frank Duryea was still in the lead, and though he

had further mechanical trouble—a chipped tooth wedged in the gears—his drive back was almost a lark. (We hope Charles got him a sandwich along the way.) It was a holiday, remember, and the Duryea, its noisy engine popping and its warning bell ringing, was followed through the darkening November afternoon by a cavalcade of cheering young bloods and their girls in sleighs to the finish line at 7:18 p.m. It had covered the fifty-four-mile course in eight hours and twenty-three minutes.

The only other car to finish was a Benz entered by Oscar Müller, but Müller wasn't at the tiller. Overwrought and dead tired, he had collapsed. Charles King, his umpire, who would later make a great name for himself in the automotive world, brought the Benz to the finish line at 8:53.

The contest for a new name for horseless carriages? The name that won was "motocycle."

Now began a golden time of road racing from town to town, country to country. Bewhiskered, begoggled giants, the like of whom disappeared, perhaps forever, at Verdun or on the Marne, raised clouds of choking dust on the highroads of Europe as they raced their monstrous, almost unmanageable machines from Paris to Amsterdam, Paris to Berlin, Paris to Vienna, and, finally, tragically, from Paris toward Madrid. Soon, too, the world would see the Vanderbilt Cup Races in America and the beginnings of the French Grand Prix.

Typical of these almost legendary country-to-country contests was the Paris-Vienna Race of 1902. In the six short years since Levassor's epic run on his Panhard in 1895, racing cars had changed out of all recognition. Where Levassor's machine had been hardly more than a gas buggy and was in no way different from the touring cars of its day, the machines of 1902 had, during the frenzy for motor racing which suddenly gripped Europe, developed into road monsters almost utterly useless for touring purposes. Where Levassor's Panhard had developed 4 hp, some of the Panhards in the Paris-Vienna were of no less than 70 hp! To develop such power in those days, their four-cylinder engines had to be, by our stand-

Early racing was a spectacle of monstrous cars and superhuman driving. Drivers struggled with mechanical troubles and unreliable tires. Christian Werner (below) changes a tire on his Mercedes during the Gordon-Bennett Race in 1905. Villemain, on a Clement-Bayard, corners in the 1906 French Grand Prix. A 120 hp Panhard-Levassor (bottom) shows Henri Farman up. In the 1903 Paris-Madrid, he drove a 90 hp model (left). Mme. du Gast (far left) checks her route-card box before a race. Charles Jarrott—well-known to early racing fans—poses (above) in his Gordon-Bennett Napier.

Once as popular as the World Series, the Vanderbilt Cup Race was in its day the great annual American road brannigan. Important foreign drivers brought their European machines to the United States each year to pit them against the best drivers and cars this country had to offer. In 1908, it was "Old 16" (preceding pages) that took the cup for the Americans. George Robertson drove the 120 hp, 1906 Locomobile racer home. Crossing the finish line (above), he seems far ahead of the field. In 1906 (right), the crowd cheered another hero: Vincenzo Lancia, the colorful daredevil whose bravado spelled a speedy end to his Italian F.I.A.T.'s chances. The damage he caused to another entry, the front-drive Christie, nearly earned him a pummeling from excited onlookers. But he escaped to later build a fine automobile under his own name.

ards, gigantic, with cylinders of 160 x 170 mm and a total capacity of 13.7 liters. These huge and heavy engines were mounted in wood-framed chassis, hardly strong enough to bear their great weight, let alone the racking strains of racing over the rough road across the Alps to Vienna. Nor was it only the Panhards that had such over-powered light chassis. The Mors cars had 60-hp engines, the Mercedes 40 hp.

The 615.4-mile Paris-Vienna race started on June 26, 1902. Before dawn, the competitors were sent off at two-minute intervals. The race was divided into classes: heavy cars, light cars (under 24 hp), voiturettes (under 12 hp), and even a class of motorcycles and tricycles.

The scene at the start, at Champigny on the outskirts of Paris, must have been fantastic. Thousands of spectators had come afoot, by car and carriage, but weirdest of all were the endless lines of thousands of bicyclists lighting their way with, of all things, Japanese paper lanterns bobbing and dancing in the moonlight. At the roadside, stands had been set up where the excitable mob could buy everything from croissants to champagne, bicycle clips, and gas. Automobilists were hard put to force their way through the jam. They blew exhaust whistles, rang bells, and even used sirens, still legal on private cars in those

days. To add to this delightful French uproar, an outfit called the Vincennes Motor Corps showed up en masse to bellow out songs calculated to encourage one of their number who was starting in the race.

First off was Girardot, on a 60-hp C.G.V. After him went Fournier on a Mors; S. F. Edge, the publicity conscious Englishman who was later to promote Napiers and A.C.'s, on a Napier, and then the brown-bearded and flamboyant chevalier, René De Knyff, on a big Panhard.*

A special train was waiting to take those spectators who wanted to see the racers arrive at the Belfort control. And they were delighted to see Fournier, followed by a great cloud of dust, come alongside and then pass the fast express as if it were welded to the tracks. For Fournier was really moving on his 60-hp

---

*This first group of cars was not only running in the big race, but also for the annual Gordon-Bennett Trophy put up by the spectacular owner of the *New York Herald*. This magnificently ugly cup was first offered in 1900, not for competition among manufacturers, but for racing between nation and nation. Each country was allowed to enter three cars. Every bit of each machine had to be made on the soil of its own country — every nut, bolt, and cotter pin, the tires, the battery, even the spark plugs. The Mors, the Panhard, and the C.G.V. were, of course, the French team. A Wolseley was to have joined the Napier to represent England, but it never reached the starting line. The Gordon-Bennett part of the race ended at Innsbruck in Austria where Edge, surprisingly, was the winner.

Mors, *averaging* over 70 mph for the first fifty miles out of Paris. But, near Chaumont, some 125 miles from the start, the train passed Fournier. He was out with a broken gearbox. But he wasn't the only one. Before Belfort, near the Swiss border, was reached at the end of the first day's run (and where the cars would be put in a locked parking area overnight), the roadside was strewn with sick and smashed cars, including Girardot's C.G.V.

The real racing didn't begin again until the cars had passed out of the territory of the suspicious Swiss, who permitted the cars to pass—but not to race—through their country. The crossing of the 6,000-foot Arlberg Pass in Austria is typical of the special kind of hell those early racers endured.

To quote Gerald Rose's *Record of Motor Racing:*
"The pass was nearly 6,000 feet above sea-level, and shortly before the competitors were due the roads were almost impassable from snow. And such roads! Hardly more than tracks in some cases, winding along precipices with nothing but boundary stones between the road and the drop beyond, crossing torrents on improvised bridges made of a few planks, climbing hills of extraordinary steepness with descents on the other side of equally terrifying appearance, with the constant fear of the precipice before the eyes of the driver should he miss his corner at the bottom. Small wonder that the competitors imagined at times that they had mistaken the road, and were only reassured by the constantly recurring flagmen. Up the drivers went, climbing to the clouds through the snow-covered passes, with nerves strained to the utmost by the unknown peril behind every bend in the road. Max, whose escape is now historic, missed his corner and charged a boundary stone; the shock somehow broke the fastenings of the seats, and Max and his mechanic were over the edge to the bottom. Max climbed down a little way to see what had become of the car, and, reappearing just as Baras came up, gave the latter the impression that he had followed the car to its resting-place on a ledge a hundred feet down, and had climbed up unhurt; a story which Baras subsequently retailed in the controls, to the no small astonishment of his hearers."

Finally, the road behind them strewn all the way back to Paris with wrecked cars, forgotten tools, oil cans, and shreds of tires, the finishers, covered in white dust, their hands torn and bleeding from constant tire-changing, limped into Vienna. Amazingly, no fewer than seventy-four cars, including light cars and voiturettes, made it.

The winner of the heavy car class was Henry Farman, on a 70-hp Panhard, who finished in 16 hours and 25 minutes. But amazingly, it was one of the light cars, a Renault, driven by Marcel Renault, which made the fastest time and won the race: 15 hours, 46 minutes.

A year later Marcel Renault was to die in the disaster of Paris-Madrid, the last of the country-to-country races. The London newspapers of May 25, 1903, in their sensational fashion called it "The Race to Death." It was, certainly, a nasty mess, and unfortunately some drivers and not a few spectators came to a sticky end. Starting on the very day of the race and continuing into our time, overblown accounts (among them one I wrote in my youth) have exaggerated the carnage and importance of Paris-Madrid which, of course, never reached Madrid. But the fact remains that the French authorities, frightened by the accidents, stopped the race at Bordeaux.

There were two chief reasons for the debacle. First, the manufacturers, not having learned the lessons of the Paris-Vienna Race, stuffed even bigger, overpowered engines into even more anemic and rachitic chassis. Gerald Rose describes these murderous machines as follows:

"Never before or since has the factor of safety in the chassis been so small or the frames so light, and had the race gone through on the rough roads of Spain the number of failures by the way would in all probability have been far higher than in Paris-Vienna. The engines also were light in structural details, though the power was high. In some cases the attention paid to the driver's comfort was ludicrously small, and one man was expected to take his car to Madrid, over roads known to be very rough beyond the frontier, seated on a board covered with a skin rug. Some of the cars were radically altered in design, and others, like the huge Gobron-Brillies, were far bigger than anything hitherto built. Most were riddled with holes, every possible part being lightened to the utmost extent. Piston walls were drilled out, beadings were taken off seats, bolts were chipped and filed away, frames and levers were slotted until they became a mere network of metal."

No wonder the cars spread themselves and their drivers all over the highway during even a minor flap, especially when you consider the speed of their going. Louis Renault, for example, on his 30-hp car, was timed between Bonneval and Chartres at nearly 90! The other big reason for the horror of Paris-Madrid was the suicidal spectators. Some 3,000,000 of them, pumped up into a fever of excitement by the newspapers, swamped the efforts of the French army to keep them out of the road. The tremendous speed of the cars was something their horse-and-buggy-age

brains just could not conceive. They stood in the middle of the road, opening a narrow path as an 80-mph car roared straight at them and closing in behind it again. The ones that didn't move fast enough either forced the driver into the ditch or got themselves killed.

No one has ever found out how many people lost their lives that day, but the man who was considered the winner of the shambles was Gabriel, on a 70-hp Mors, who averaged 65.3 mph for the 342-mile run to Bordeaux.

The French Government wouldn't even allow the racing cars to leave Bordeaux under their own power. Horses dragged them to the railroad station and they went back to Paris in freight cars.

Of all the wild and glorious racing in these past sixty years none has such an aura of romance attached to it as the series of races for the Vanderbilt Cup on Long Island, New York.

William K. Vanderbilt, Jr., whose name you'll find not only in early, musty, social registers, but also in those heroic lists of entries for the great European road races, offered the Cup. To encourage the building of American racing machines, he said. But we suspect that at least part of his reason was to transplant some of the foreign excitement to the dirt roads near the Gold Coast of Long Island, where he and his millionaire friends had their country seats.

He succeeded only too well!

The 30,000 spectators who showed up at 6 a.m. on that dark Saturday morning of October 8, 1904, had but a vague idea of what high-speed motor racing was all about. They were stunned by the crash and roar of the flame-spitting engines as the drivers, many of them from Europe, came up to the starting line. But they weren't, it seems, stunned enough to keep off the road after the cars took off. Only the yells of "Car coming, car coming" sent them diving for the ditches as a car shot past, leaping and swaying. Not that they hadn't been warned.

Before the race an imperious proclamation had been issued by the AAA, which was running the proceedings for Vanderbilt, in phrases worthy of a Roman proconsul addressing a backward province:

"An automobile race over a distance of between 250 and 300 miles will be held for the William K. Vanderbilt, Jr. Cup on Saturday, October 8. The start will be at Westbury at daylight.

"All persons are warned against using the roads between the hours of 5 a.m. and 3 p.m.

"Officers will be stationed along the road to prevent accidents. The Board of Supervisors of Nassau County has set aside the following roads for use of the racers on October 8:

"Jericho Turnpike, from Queens to Plain Edge;

"Massapequa Road, Jericho to Plain Edge;

"Plain Edge Road (Bethpage Road), Plain Edge to Hempstead;

"Fulton Street, Hempstead to Jamaica.

"A reduced rate of speed will be maintained while passing through Hicksville. Three minutes will be allowed to pass through the village. Six minutes will

be allowed to pass through Hempstead.

"All persons are cautioned against allowing domestic animals or fowl to be at large. Children unattended should be kept off the roads. Chain your dog and lock up your fowl.

"To avoid danger don't crowd into the road."

"Who in hell," said the red-necked potato farmers, "does this guy Vanderbilt think he is?"

The newspapers screamed—including the *New York Times* which hinted darkly at embattled farmers bearing firearms. Injunctions, counter injunctions, court orders failed to stop the race. But when the canny inhabitants of Long Island realized that there was a buck in it, they suddenly loved auto racing. Especially when they found they could soak the swells from New York $20 for a few hours on the sagging bed in the spare room, $5 to stand on a front porch facing the course, or $1 for a sandwich.

The crowd had a ball, with just enough gore and bent machinery to please everybody. Five Mercedes had entered. One driven by George Arents, Jr., an American, blew out a tire near Elmont, caught the rim in trolley car tracks, slewed around and rolled over, killing Arent's riding mechanic. Another Mercedes *mechanicién* crawled under his car to fix something just as its impatient and bemused driver drove off—with effects deleterious to the mechanic.

A big, 75-hp Smith and Mabley Simplex, driven by Frank Croker, had its chassis so drilled and cut for lightness that it gradually buckled and twisted. Before long the onlookers were treated to the rare sight of a four-wheeled car leaving a triple track in the dust. Joe Tracy driving a stripped-down American touring car, a 35-hp Royal Tourist, broke a pin in his universal joint, but far from giving up, headed for a local machine shop where he made himself a new one. This did him no good; his engine disintegrated and he had to quit. Webb, on a Pope-Toledo, suddenly found himself without steering and entwined himself around a tree. After 6 hours and 56 minutes, a 90-hp Panhard driven by George Heath, an American, came in first over the 284.4-mile course. Albert Clement on an 80-hp Clement-Bayard was second. Before Herbert Lytle, who was lying third on a 24-hp Pope-Toledo, could cross the finish line, the uncontrollable mob swarmed out on the road and the race had to be stopped to avoid carnage.

The 1905 race was an even wilder brannigan. This time the top drivers of Europe showed up, including Szisz on a 90-hp Renault; Camille Jenatzy, the "Red Devil," on a 120-hp Mercedes, Felice Nazzaro on a Fiat, and the fabulous young Italian, Vincenzo Lancia, also on a Fiat. Facing them was a newly formidable group of American drivers, including Joe Tracy on a 90-hp Locomobile.

The crowds were quite as crazy and disorderly as in 1904. One bunch from Bridgeport, Connecticut, where Tracy's Locomobile was built, anxious to cheer their home-town product, chartered the paddle-wheel steamer, *Isabel*, to take them across the Sound to Oyster Bay. But never giving a thought to the problem of getting to the race course from Oyster Bay,

Preceding pages: During the French Grand Prix of 1914, on the eve of the Kaiser war, few spectators could doubt, from their militarily precise strategy, that the Germans were out to win. The 4½-liter Mercedes with its single-overhead-camshaft engine is similar to the big white car that Lautenschlager rode to victory that day (left). He and his teammates—Wagner and Salzer—came in one, two, three, and appear liberally festooned in laurel leaves. Evidently this picture was taken after they had returned to the factory. There seems no other reason for the cars to have suddenly sprouted mud guards.

Ernest Henry revolutionized racing-car design with his 1912 Peugeot. (At right, a 1913 model.) The world's first twin-overhead-camshaft engine (above) with which he powered them has been the model for most racing engines since then. George Boillot battled the German Mercedes team in the 1914 Grand Prix in such a car.

they finally arrived just about when the race was ended. At that they didn't do much worse than some of the people who tried to get there by car.

Vincenzo Lancia was the odd-ball of the race and, naturally, the mob's hero. Only twenty-five years old, big and bull-like, he was given to bellowing snatches of grand opera between swigs of champagne. He drove his 110-hp Fiat with maniacal dash, averaging 72 mph for the first 100 miles of the race.

He was leading the race, when he pulled in at his supply depot on Willis Avenue for fuel. Just as he was leaving, Walter Christie on the front-drive car he had designed came snaking down the road. Lancia, impatient, took a chance and shot out in front of Christie. The Christie didn't give way, rammed the Fiat, and went end over end, smashing itself into scrap iron and hurling Christie's mechanic's body through a wild parabola into a field. Christie himself was only slightly hurt and lived to develop the famous Christie tank for the army, about which there was so much talk in the Thirties.

Lancia was lucky not to be lynched by the same mob that had so recently been cheering him. It took him an hour to repair the smashed rear wheels of the Fiat. Where he had been in first place, he was now sixth. He finally finished a poor fourth.

There were plenty of other frightful incidents to delight the spectators, but one of the craziest concerned Lytle on a Pope-Toledo. On a rough piece of road through a wooded area, his mechanic was bounced out of his seat into the brush. Lytle didn't slow down, but picked up a replacement mechanic at his pit. However, Vanderbilt and a doctor did head

into the woods to find and repair the used-up mechanic.

Hemery, on a 80-hp French Darracq, won the 283-mile race at 61.5 mph. Heath on a Panhard was second, and Tracy was third on the Locomobile.

For the 1906 race, the course included some fancy new turns, on a somewhat different route, including the murderous hills at Roslyn and Manhasset on Northern Boulevard. The European cracks—Lancia, Nazzaro, Clement, Wagner—all entered again, and Joe Tracy had a brand new Locomobile.

The Vanderbilt Cup, at least around New York, had become more popular than the World Series. Before daylight on that misty, rainy October 8, some 350,000 people had lined up around the course. One newspaper said that $50,000,000 worth of automobiles were parked or trying to park near the course by starting time at 6:15 a.m. Some of them had taken half the night to get there, driving acetylene headlight to kerosene tail-light, by way of the Brooklyn Bridge and the East River ferries and through the streets of

Brooklyn. The Vanderbilt Cup had a certain aura of classiness. There was even a successful musical called "The Vanderbilt Cup" running on Broadway, and it was the thing to have a fancy party at the Waldorf or Rector's before setting out in a big touring car, well-laden with hampers of lobster and pheasant, plus cases of champagne. Some manufacturers set up parking areas for cars of their own make, but the Long Island yokelry still made a fast buck fantastically over-charging city slickers who wanted to park in their front yards. There were the usual alarms and excursions, but only one killing. Elliot Shepard, W. K. Vanderbilt's cousin, on a Hotchkiss, went into the crowd at Krug's Corner where 20,000 people had set themselves up as targets.

The French won again: Wagner was first on a Darracq, Lancia second on a Fiat, and Duray third on a De Dietrich. Joe Tracy came in tenth on the Locomobile, although he had made the fastest lap at a dazzling 67.6 mph.

There was no race in 1907; nobody could figure out a way to control the suicidal mobs.

Meanwhile, Vanderbilt and a syndicate of his well-heeled friends were busily building a private road, the Long Island Motor Parkway, which ran from the dismal outskirts of Queens County, New York, to Lake Ronkonkoma. For a dollar anybody could use it as his private, fenced-in speedway. By the time I was old enough to drive on it in the early Thirties, it already seemed a narrow, twisty, old-fashioned road.

But in 1908 it was considered a super-modern superhighway. The 1908 race included almost ten miles of this road in every lap of 23.46 miles. The crowd was as unruly as ever, and even came equipped with wire cutters for snipping holes in the new fencing.

This time the 120-hp Locomobile won the race, but George Robertson was driving, not Joe Tracy. This car—"Old 16"—now belongs to the famous motoring artist, Peter Helck, and in 1954, during a fifty-year celebration of the race, I had the luck to follow it in

Continental road races and rallies like the Herkomer and the Prinz Heinrich ran over
public roads not usually cleared of normal traffic. Road races of those days not only battled dust and farm
wagons on the highways, but they never knew when a slow freight might come athwart their path.

an antique car around what was left of the 1904
Course, now partly covered with a cancerous growth
of ranch houses, shopping centers, and pizzerias.

Robertson, an elderly man, drove the Locomobile
again and, to the discomfiture of the local cops, had
himself a time. They couldn't even catch him to
threaten him with a ticket, except when traffic held
him up as he roared into the main street of Hempstead. The rest of the procession of fancied-up antique cars wheezed along miles behind.

The Vanderbilt Cup ran again on Long Island in
1909 and 1910, won both times by an American-built
Alco driven by Harry Grant. The crowds were as huge
and as bent on self-destruction as ever. When you
speak to oldsters who saw the races they speak with
awe of the half-million spectators, the score of injured
(mostly trampled by the hysterical mob), and the four
dead (two killed in the race, two in traffic). But it is the
1908 race somehow that lives as a fond memory; 1910
was *too* bloody, too much of a wild mob scene.

The race left the Island after 1910 and took to
the hinterlands—Milwaukee, Santa Monica, Savan-
nah, San Francisco. It was never the same again. The
days of the monsters were almost over.

After the hue and cry raised in 1903 by the much-
publicized horrors of Paris-Madrid, the Gordon-Bennett Races, which until then had been the tail on the
dog, became the chief event in European racing. Run
on closed-road circuits, protected by police and sol-
diers, the organizers were able to promote the happy
fiction that they were, somehow, safer.

S. F. Edge, as we have seen, won on his Napier in
1902. Therefore, under the rules, the 1903 race was
to be on British soil. The race was run in Ireland,
road racing being prohibited in England. (Evidently
Irish spectators were considered more expendable
than Englishmen.)

The Germans won this one, Camille Jenatzy, on a
Mercedes coming in first. In 1904, it was won at Hom-
burg in Germany by Théry on a Richard-Brasier. The
next year Théry on the Richard-Brasier won again.

But in spite of their wins, the French were getting
fed up. "We're the leading automotive country," they
fumed, "and yet we can't enter more than the same
three cars that some little country, very backward in
automobilism, can. It's unfair."

After much hassling, the French prevailed. The
Gordon-Bennett faded away, and in 1906 the French
Grand Prix (*Le Grand Prix de l'Automobile Club de
France*) took its place. This first Grand Prix was run
at Le Mans, but not over the same circuit as the fa-
mous Le Mans Sports Car Races of our day.

It was won by Szisz on a mammoth-engined Renault
of no less than 12,970 cc, at 63 mph for the 770-mile
race. If you think this was a big engine, consider the
cubic capacity of the 130-hp, four-cylinder Panhard
in the same race: 18,146 cc. Each *cylinder* was bigger
than the entire V-8 engine of many family cars today.

Imagine what it must have been like to handle such
nose-heavy brutes at high speed. And they did reach
high speeds. The Renault was timed over a kilometer
at a staggering 92.2 mph!

But the drivers had other troubles those scorchingly hot days of June 26 and 27, 1906. The rules said that the drivers and their riding mechanics had to make their own repairs and tire changes. The heat and the speed caused their tires practically to melt and many a crew changed a full set of tires ten or twelve times—no fun in those days of non-detachable wheels. They sliced the used tire away from the wheel with knives, frantically tearing at the remaining shreds with their fingers, refitted the new tire, struggled with the security bolts, then in the broiling sun pumped it up and restarted the engine. (Think of the horror of restarting an 18-liter engine by hand.) A lap later they might have to do the same thing all over again, unless they stopped sooner because they'd left a tire lever between the tube and the casing. One of the reasons Renault won this race was due to their use of the newly invented demountable rims, which saved time and labor.

Dust had long been a terror during races. To pass, a driver plunged blindly into the dust cloud raised by the car ahead without knowing whether the road went straight on or not. At least one driver who set his course in an earlier race by cleverly following the tops of the telegraph poles came to grief when the road curved and the line of poles didn't. For this first Grand Prix, the organizers had thought to lay the dust by tarring the road, but the sun soon turned the tar to liquid, almost blinding the hapless drivers.

For a few more years these dinosaurs among motorcars pitted their huge and foolish engines against each other in the French Grand Prix. In 1907 the organizers, in an effort to stop the crazy trend toward even larger power plants, ruled that the cars had to get along on one gallon of gas for 9.4 miles, but to no avail. Racing at Dieppe this time, a 16-liter Fiat—Nazzaro driving—was the winner, averaging 70.5 mph for 477 miles. Hardly anybody ran out of gas.

The next year, bore size was limited to 155 mm for four-cylinder engines and 127 mm for six-cylinder engines. But the effort was vain. To get around this, most of the boys merely made their cylinders longer. Lautenschlager won with a Mercedes at 69 mph.

From all this you might get the idea that the French Grand Prix was the only race in the world. True, it was far and away the most important, but there were other great races too: the Targa-Florio in Italy, the Kaiserpreis in Germany, and, of course, innumerable races like the Coupe de l'Auto, sponsored by *l'Auto*, the French sporting paper, for smaller, lighter cars such as Delage, Hispano-Suiza, and Peugeot. And it was one of these lighter machines that would soon slay the giants.

The French Grand Prix didn't run in 1909, 1910, and 1911. The big-potted monsters had almost done themselves in. So expensive were they to build and prepare, and so out of touch with the realities of automobilism, that they caused the Grand Prix, which depended on them, to sicken and almost die for want of entries.

In 1912 the giant racers ran again at Dieppe, but this time there were among them three machines that were to end their reign. These were the Peugeots designed by the Swiss, Ernest Henry, abetted by two famous drivers, Georges Boillot and Paul Zucarelli—the latter a notable conductor of Hispano-Suizas in the Coupe de l'Auto Races.

The Peugeots, mere striplings among Goliaths like Bruce Brown's gigantic 15-liter Fiat and the 15-liter Lorraine-Dietrich, were a mere 7.6 liters, but they had engines whose design has been the basis of almost every successful high-performance machine built in the last fifty years. Here, for the first time were twin-overhead camshafts, operating four inclined valves per hemispherically headed cylinder.

George Boillot, on one of the Peugeots, won the race at 68.45 mph. The other two Peugeots retired with plugged gas lines.

The age of the giants was over.

In 1913 and 1914 the twin-overhead-camshaft Peugeots were almost unbeatable. They won the French Grand Prix again and, invading America, Jules Goux won the Indianapolis 500 in 1913 in spite of a reduction of engine size to 5.65 liters.

In 1914 Boillot took second place at the brickyard, at 80.89 mph, with a startlingly modern 3-liter version of the Peugeot, breaking the lap record at 99.5 mph. (René Thomas, on a Delage, won that year.)

For the Grand Prix at Lyon in July, 1914, the blue Peugeots of France, headed by George Boillot, a combination which stirred the hearts of French patriots, went out to do battle with the Mercedes team of 4½-liter cars which was already organized as though for war. The German cars were prepared in secrecy in a village at some distance from the course. A complex strategy was worked out, with one of the German machines being assigned the role of decoy to break up the French cars. Pit work was practiced and re-practiced. The Germans were out to win—and win they did. And they finished in line-ahead formation—first, second, and third; Lautenschlager, Wagner, and Salzer—to a deathly silence from the stands.

A few months later George Boillot was shot out of the sky by a German airplane powered by a single-overhead-camshaft engine not unlike the one Lautenschlager had used to vanquish him on the ground.

The first car to go a mile a minute was an electric; the first car to go *two* miles a minute was a steamer. In the early years of this century electrics and steamers far outsold the cantankerous gas-engined cars. The first taxis were electrics. Yet today only a few zealots still diddle with electric and steam-powered automobiles.

What were these machines like? Why did they go the way of the Pianola and the Morris chair? The electric car is, theoretically, a simple device. It consists merely of a carriage loaded with electric storage batteries connected to an electric motor that turns the wheels. My twelve-year-old boy made one recently out of a twelve-volt starter motor, a couple of six-volt batteries, and a soap box on wheels.

Actually, an electric was rather more complicated. It had a steering system, chassis, and springing very much like that of a gasoline car. And although it had no clutch or gearshift, it had a cat's cradle of complex wiring to enable its batteries to be hooked up in various combinations, depending on whether it was starting, climbing a hill, or rolling along at cruising speed.

The electric car was the natural development of that clanking wonder of the early Nineties, the electric-batteried trolley car. A crude electric road vehicle using un-rechargeable electric cells had been run

by a Scot named Robert Davidson in Aberdeen as early as 1839. But it was the invention of the storage battery by Gaston Planté in 1865, and its perfection by Camille Faure in 1881, that made the electric vehicle possible. By 1888 Fred M. Kimball of Boston had the first American electric auto on the road and within ten years the electric was a commercial proposition.

On April 29, 1899, near Acheres, outside Paris, Camille Jenatzy, on *La Jamais Contente*, a peculiar electrical contrivance that looked like an aerial bomb on a trailer, set the world's land speed record by covering the flying kilometer at 65.8 mph. This was faster than gasoline-engined cars of the time could go, but the record was achieved at some cost. It is doubtful whether M. Jenatzy had enough juice left in his batteries for even one more kilometer, or that the batteries could even be recharged again. It is also likely that the wiring in Jenatzy's machine was close to melting away. As the London *Autocar* of the following week said, "The car had to fly or burn."

That always was the trouble with electrics. You could, if you wanted to, go quite fast for a very short distance, or you could go very slowly for a slightly longer distance.

This didn't bother those elegant American ladies who slipped silently from Le Bon Ton department store to the hairdressers and then, mayhap, to tea in those little glassed-in drawing rooms on wheels that were in their heyday just before we entered World War I. They seldom drove faster than 20 mph and it didn't matter too much that they could drive no more than fifty miles before they had to get home and have the handyman hook up the battery charger. By morning the batteries were up to running the car again.

It was their batteries that made electric cars such sluggards, for they used much of their power in moving their own great weight. A set of batteries in a fair-

Camille Jenatzy sits proudly on the world's fastest automobile of 1899 (preceding pages). This car, yclept "La Jamais Contente," was an electrically powered vehicle that had rightfully earned its flowery garlands. Driving her, Jenatzy set the world's land speed record at 65.8 mph for a kilometer. Later electrics were perhaps more attractively designed than this speedster, as the 1912 Woods Electric (above, right) may prove. The electrics were quiet and reliable cars when gas-engined buggies were still noisy, cantankerous bone-shakers. The 1908 Baker (above) exhibits a major disadvantage of the electric: its battery required continual recharging. The Morris and Salom Electric (right) ran on New York City streets in 1896. It was the world's first horseless hansom cab.

Faintly ludicrous, but too mannerly to be laughed at, is this 1918 Detroit Electric coupe with curtained windows and tiller steering. It was powered by a nearly indestructible storage battery developed by Thomas A. Edison.

sized electric car weighed close to a thousand pounds. They didn't last for the life of the car, either. You had to buy a new set every three years or so.

Electrics were wonderfully easy to drive. Most of them had tiller steering with some form of controller, similar to that used by a street-car motorman, either incorporated in the tiller or right close by. A foot pedal applied the brakes and a button on the floor activated the electric bell that politely warned pedestrians of your coming. Brakes were sometimes magnetic. The plushy interiors of electrics were lovely to see. Overstuffed chairs in conversational groupings—it was possible for the driver to sit in the back seat in some machines by means of an extra set of controls—tasseled silk curtains on the windows, flower vases, and window shades made them more like cozy boudoirs than road vehicles.

The manufacturers of electrics were continually trying to show how far they could run on one charge. Sometimes they'd go a hundred miles or more, but only if they kept their speed down to about 12 mph. It was, however, possible to tour for long distances in an electric if you went from charging station to charging station, or if you carried a kit along to charge your

batteries from the 550-volt overhead wires of the trolley car lines which covered the country.

The first auto taxis in New York were Columbia electrics, hundreds of which appeared in 1900. The batteries for these cars (weighing nearly a ton) lived in a box which could be removed from underneath the car for charging and instantly replaced by a box of freshly charged cells. Of course, the taxi company needed a pit and a sort of hydraulic elevator to do this, but it kept the money-making machines from being tied up. These taxis were not too successful. The thug-like drivers of the day, who make modern cabbies seem almost angelic, just tore the heavy brutes to pieces. The faster, lighter, cheaper gasoline taxi soon drove them off the streets.

The self-starter did as much as anything to doom the electric, since the more practical gas-engined cars now required no hand cranking. And it was the fearsome starting handle as much as anything that had made the electric auto such a favorite with women.

By the mid-Twenties the electric had almost disappeared. The last survivor, the Detroit Electric, finally bowed to the inevitable and ceased manufacture in 1938.

STEAMERS

To the man of the late Nineteenth Century, steam was the one truly logical source of power. It ran his railroads; a steam engine powered the wonderful complex of shafting and belts, which ran the machines in the factory that gave him his living, and it even ran the dynamos (and still does, mostly) which produced that strange new force, electricity.

To the practical man, a steam engine was more sensible, somehow, than a gas engine. A gas engine was a temperamental mystery. It didn't even seem as if it ought to work. And if it ran badly most mechanics of those days couldn't tell quite why. But there was some sense to a steam engine. If it stopped you could *see* why, and mechanics even in remote country districts had been familiar with steam for fifty years.

Just mention the words "steam car" to almost any man over fifty and he'll start spouting about the Stanley steam car. Although there was a whole gaggle of steamer types built before World War I, the name Stanley is the one that sticks in people's minds. Only a few remember the magnificent and popular White Steamer and the toylike and fragile Locomobile.

"Oh, boy," the fifty-year-old enthuses. "That Stanley Steamer was the greatest car ever built. Y'know the Stanley people would give you a new car if you just held the throttle open for three minutes. Nobody ever did, though. Those cars went so fast they couldn't be held on the road. Easiest car in the world to drive, though. No clutch, no shift, no nothing. But even so, they made you have a locomotive engineer's license to drive one. My pop had one for years. I drove it lots of times when I was no more than ten years old. The gas-car 'interests' put 'em out of business."

Ridiculous! I often have heard perorations like this about the Stanley, and in my youth I saw Stanley Steamers in operation—an undertaker in our neighborhood used a fleet of them for funerals. But until a few years ago I had never ridden in one. Finally, at that time I got a steam-happy friend (all steam enthusiasts are a bit odd) to take me for a ride in one of the many steamers in his collection.

He proudly rolled out a 1913 Model, 20-hp Stanley Roadster to show me what steam was all about. At first glance a steam car looks about like any other automobile. It has four wheels, a hood, a dashboard, seats, a steering wheel. But lift the hood and you'll be surprised to see a big, dirty-white, drum-like affair sitting in a tangle of sloppy plumbing. That's the boiler. Under the boiler, located where the crankcase in any other car would be, is the burner. Two holes in the front of the burner (about where you'd ordinarily stick a crank) give you a fine view of a terrifying mass of roaring blue flame. The holes admit fuel nozzles.

If you want to see the engine, it lives in close proximity to the rear axle and is a two-cylinder affair that looks as if it had been stolen off the side of a locomotive. Since it is covered with a big tin fairing (full of oil in later models), it's pretty hard to see, however. In the back of the car is a big tank full of kerosene. You do, however, carry a little tank of gasoline to prime the burner and to keep the pilot light lit. The dashboard is a really fearsome thing, with innumerable little wheels on long stems stuck in among some very unfamiliar-looking dials.

Furthermore, there is no clutch pedal, no gearshift, no accelerator pedal. The pedals on the floor of this one are a reverse pedal, a "hook-up" pedal, and a foot brake. On the steering column is a long throttle lever in about the same position as a modern gearshift, which is the main speed control and the water-control valve. On the floor, slightly aft of where an old-fashioned floor shift would be, is the long handle of a pump. In the old days people were braver than they are now and left the pilot light under the boiler burning all the time, so that there was always some steam up. If your wife suddenly realized that Aunt Minnie's train was due at the station in six minutes, you had but to nip out to the garage, release the hand brake, and without even monkeying with anything so foul as our present day self-starters, you were off to the depot. Nowadays Aunt Minnie would walk or have a long, long wait if she had to depend on steam-car transportation, because modern steam enthusiasts usually start with a stone-cold boiler and "steaming up" takes about half an hour. (Some real steam nuts claim they can do it in fifteen minutes; anti-steam characters claim it takes all day, with luck.)

If you have ever struggled with a kerosene pressure stove or a blowtorch, you know that you have to build up fuel pressure by pumping air into the little fuel tank, and that it helps to first heat the fuel jets with a little alcohol fire, so that the fuel coming from the tank through the jets will be vaporized and yield the necessary hot blue flame. The Stanley burner is not unlike one of these camp stoves, but on a Gargantuan scale. It is necessary first to build up pressure in a little auxiliary kerosene tank (so that the main tank won't be under pressure) and in that little gasoline tank on the running board. The gasoline takes the place of the alcohol primer of your camp stove and also feeds the pilot light. On a Stanley, however, it is usual to carry a little tank of acetylene in the tool kit. This has attached to it a short length of rubber hose ending in a nozzle. You open a valve on the tank, light the end of the nozzle, and play this flame over the pilot jet to get it really hot. Then you open the pilot valve a little. Now your pilot light is lit. Next you open the firing-up valve and let some gasoline burn on the main burner for half a minute or so to warm *it* up. Now you can open the main fuel valve and kerosene will soon be heating the water in your boiler. If the water in the boiler isn't up to the right level, an automatic valve will shut off the fuel, preventing you from idiotically burning out the boiler. Conversely, if the steam pressure gets too high, another gizmo ("the steam automatic," the Stanleys called it) automatically shuts off the kerosene.

The drum-like boiler of a Stanley carries the terrifying pressure of 600 pounds per square inch, but none has ever been known to explode. For strength the Stanleys wound it with two layers of piano wire—the way Armstrong's in England wound naval guns. These are fire-tube boilers—as opposed to water-tube boilers in which the water runs in the pipes—and there are as many as 750 tubes in the larger ones. The Stanleys tried to blow up one of their own boilers one day, but even after jamming in 1,500 pounds of pressure nothing happened. At that pressure some of the tubes started to leak, so that it was impossible to get a higher reading. But explode, no! The only time they succeeded was when they left off some of the wire wrapping. Almost blew Boston across Cape Cod Bay!

Once you have made enough steam, you can get behind the wheel and drive. As we climbed up and in, my friend pointed to the steam gauge. "Five hundred pounds per square inch. We could run on two hundred if we had to, but we'd have no reserve power." So saying he released the hand brake and a little locking

The two-cylinder compound engine of this 1904 White Steam Car lived under the hood, while its flash steam boiler warmed the underside of the driver. One of the boiler flues can be seen jutting from the side, in front of the rear fender. What looked like a normal radiator up front was really a condenser to allow exhaust steam from the engine to be cooled back into water. This made it possible to drive a White some 75 miles without stopping for a drink. The boiler made steam faster than the Stanley's fire-tube boiler, but could not hold as much power in reserve.

arrangement which kept the hand-throttle lever from being accidentally displaced. Then he slightly moved this lever, which was a long, shiny, nickel-plated affair attached to the steering post, and we moved off up a slight grade. Just like that!

My friend had turned no ignition key, pushed no starter button, had listened to no grinding, no sudden roar of engine. He hadn't stepped on any clutch or shifted any gears.

But softly, with a slight, odd creaking from the engine behind us we were off. It was an eerie feeling, coasting up a hill like that with just the merest suggestion of a chuff-chuff. I mentioned the chuff-chuff. "Oh, we steam people like that, but you can't even hear that much in the latest models."

We were rolling along a fairly twisty, hilly piece of country road now, doing about fifty, slowing for the turns with the rather primitive two-wheel brakes. I was glad we did, too, because the high, fully elliptically-sprung body rolled and bounced like a buggy. No sports car, this.

I still couldn't get over the strange effortlessness of the car's running. So quiet was it that every little squeak of the old bodywork, every little creak of the leather upholstery as we shifted our weight was oddly magnified, like people coughing in a library.

To stop for a crossroad, my friend just closed the throttle and stepped on the brake. The engine didn't idle; it stopped dead.

"Your power isn't made in the engine, as in a gas car," he explained. "It's in the steam you've made and saved up in the boiler, and if you think you have enough, you can just turn off the main fire and go home on the steam you have in reserve, which I think

In the early 1900's the White Steamer was the great rival of the Stanley. A 1907 model
(left) was the property of President Theodore Roosevelt. White Steamers were made until 1911, when they
abandoned steam and commenced the production of gasoline-powered cars. The Whites
had a wooden chassis frame "armored" with reinforcing plates of nickel steel. The underseat,
semi-flash boiler of the White could be fired by kerosene, as could the water-tube boiler of the
1913 Stanley Roadster (below). In spite of the oft-expressed fear of the timorous, boiler
blow-ups were unknown. Steam automobiles were quite safe.

I'll do right now because we've been driving around without license plates."

He reversed into a driveway by merely stepping on a reverse pedal which instantly made the engine go backwards without gearshifting or the manipulation of a clutch.

I noticed another pedal and asked about it.

"That's called the hook-up. When you push it part way down it'll stay there until you push it again. It limits the valve opening on the engine and saves steam when you're cruising. At low speeds or in traffic, you can run more smoothly without it."

When we got back I took a closer look at the Stanley's innards. There was a lot more to it than just a burner, a boiler, and an engine.

First, there were the pumps: pumps for air pressure, pumps for water, fuel, cylinder oil. These little pumps are situated under the floor boards and are mechanically operated from the engine. Then there are gadgets like the superheater; this dries and heats the steam for greater power. And there is the condenser. The 1913 model I rode in had no condenser and it had to stop for water every fifty miles or so (it carried a strainer-ended hose for sucking the stuff up from brooks and horse troughs). But from 1915 on the Stanley had what looked like a normal radiator out in front which condensed the used steam back to water, greatly increasing the range (to 300 miles or more) you could travel before having to make a water stop. All these devices were interconnected by what seemed miles of piping, valves, and joints.

The engine—I examined one removed from a car—was a much simpler device than I had imagined: two cylinders, side by side; simple slide valves, crossheads,

107

eccentric link and crankshaft with a big gear to couple it to the axle, no flywheel, and only thirteen moving parts, which were all on ball bearings.

Later models than the one I sampled also had a rather simplified electrical system for lighting and, in later models still, an electric heating device for lighting the pilot from the dash.

The twin brothers, F. E. and F. O. Stanley, who invented the Stanley Steamer, were born in Kingfield, Maine, in 1849. Like many farm boys they were tinkerers. More especially they were whittlers—violin whittlers. Until they died they were passionate whittlers of violins, F. O. particularly. If he liked you, he'd take you into a little room he had fixed up in the factory and proudly show you the latest violin he was working on.

They never had much schooling. One of them went to college for a few weeks, but didn't like it and came home. Oddly enough, they became school teachers, but their real enthusiasm was inventing things. They invented and successfully marketed a home gas gen-erator and X-ray equipment. They manufactured violins. They experimented with photography and came up with the famous Stanley Dry Plate, which they sold to Eastman Kodak for a fabulous sum.

They saw their first car in 1896 at the Brockton Fair and decided that they could do better. Their first steamer appeared in Newton, Massachusetts, in 1897 and an early photograph (made on a Stanley Dry Plate, I'm sure) shows the prim-looking, bearded, bowler-hatted, lap-robed brothers sitting in this little machine which caused such a sensation in its day. By 1899 they were making two hundred cars a year and F. O. drove one of the spidery little steam carriages, complete with wife, up the rocky, unpaved carriage road to the top of Mount Washington in two hours and ten minutes.

Everybody wanted to buy a piece of them and, finally, to get rid of a particularly persistent pest, they set an astronomic sum as a selling price for the whole works. Unfortunately, the buyers didn't scare, and the Stanleys found they had sold their business

At left are the boiler and the engine of an 1899 Stanley
Steamer; the complete car is at right. The Locomobile Steamer
of the next few years was almost identical, since the
Stanley brothers sold their rights to this machine to the
Locomobile Company in 1899. Later the company split
into two groups: Mobile and Locomobile. These little cars,
although very pleasant to drive, acquired a reputation
for fragility due to the rough treatment their unknowledgeable
owners gave them on the sandy and rocky roads of their day.
Rudyard Kipling in his charming story, "Steam Tactics,"
which concerned the Locomobile Steamer he owned, has First-
Class Engine-Room Artificer Hinchcliffe complain that
the machine was as delicate as a "wicker-willow lunch basket"
and that the "boiler's only seated on four little
paper-clips." Yet, it was on an 1899 Stanley that F. O. Stanley
and his wife drove up the ten-mile road to the top of
Mount Washington, a feat no car had ever been able to perform.
Above is a 10 hp 1910 Stanley Roadster.

to what eventually became the Locomobile Company.

In two years, unable to keep away from the things, they were back making steam cars, having had to redesign the whole machine in order to circumvent the patents they had sold. The Stanleys were so much better that the Locomobile people gave up in disgust and sold the patents back for peanuts. No more steamers for them, only gas cars.

The Stanley brothers hated advertising and seldom in all their years did they run a paid ad. But publicity from racing success was something different. For their really serious speed tests, they employed the now almost legendary Fred Marriot. For him they built a special racer, something like an inverted canoe, called the Stanley Rocket. She weighed but 1,600 pounds and Marriot broke five world's records at Ormond

Beach, Florida, doing 127.6 mph in 1906!

In 1907 he tried again, pushing the steam pressure up to 1,300 pounds per square inch. The speedometer stood at 197 miles per hour when something went wrong. The car took to the air, bounced, broke up. The boiler shot down the beach for a mile. Marriot flew clear but was badly hurt. Luckily, he lived, but the Stanleys never tried for record speed again.

In the twenty-five years or so that Stanleys were in production, only some 18,000 of them were made. In view of the number of people who claim that their fathers or great-uncles always took them riding in Stanley Steamers on Sunday afternoons, each car must have had about one thousand owners.

Using mass-production methods, the Stanleys could have made—and sold—more cars. They were always behind on their orders, especially in the days before the self-starter. But they just didn't care to make cars

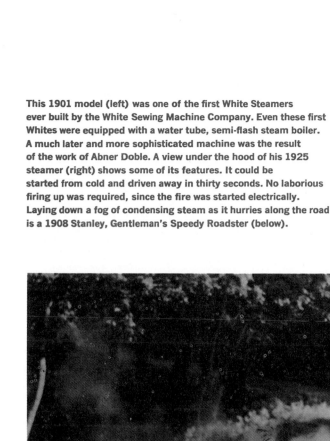

This 1901 model (left) was one of the first White Steamers ever built by the White Sewing Machine Company. Even these first Whites were equipped with a water tube, semi-flash steam boiler. A much later and more sophisticated machine was the result of the work of Abner Doble. A view under the hood of his 1925 steamer (right) shows some of its features. It could be started from cold and driven away in thirty seconds. No laborious firing up was required, since the fire was started electrically. Laying down a fog of condensing steam as it hurries along the road is a 1908 Stanley, Gentleman's Speedy Roadster (below).

except by meticulous handcraft methods. Nor would the Stanley brothers give you a new car if you held the throttle wide open for three minutes. You could hold it open for three hours for all they cared. They never gave anything away. They were Yankees, remember, and Maine men to boot. That business about needing an engineer's license is cut from the same cloth, too.

In 1918, F. E., making time in one of his steamers on the Newburyport Pike, ran it off the road rather than run into two farm wagons which were filling the whole road while their drivers conversed. F. E. died. His brother had no heart left for the steam-car business and pulled out. Others tried to reorganize the company and carry on, but in 1925 the last Stanley Steamer silently left the factory.

With the tremendous success of the early Stanleys, all kinds of steamers were built in competition. Per-

haps the most successful of these was the White Steamer, which used a water-tube boiler on the flash-steam principle. Although it could make steam faster, it did not have the reserve power of the Stanley. The beautiful and complex steam cars built by Abner Doble were perhaps the last and most modern of the steam cars. Starting cold, these could be driven away in half a minute, and everything worked from the dash-board by means of a beautiful electrical system, so that all of the drudgery of firing-up was eliminated. But the Doble cost too much—up to $20,000 or so. The Stanleys had never been priced at more than a tenth as much.

Steam types mutter darkly about the "interests" having done in the steam car. This sounds very dramatic, but just isn't true. Steam cars disappeared because nobody bothered to make them anymore.

OF THE LONG LINE OF AUTOMOBILES THAT HAS TAKEN TO THE ROAD THESE SEVENTY YEARS, A NOBLE FEW STAND FORTH ABOVE THEIR FELLOWS. THEY HAVE GIVEN US JOY. THEY HAVE CHANGED OUR WORLD. LET THE GREAT NAMES HERE SPEAK FOR THEMSELVES.

ROLLS-ROYCE

The engine's sealed up, isn't it?"

"They guarantee 'em for life, don't they?"

"Are the latest models still handmade?"

For twenty-four years now—as long as I've owned Rolls-Royces—I've happily listened to these same questions every time I've stopped the Rolls I was driving long enough to be engaged in even a few moments of conversation. The facts are: Rolls-Royces never had sealed engines, they are not guaranteed for life (but for three years), nor are they handmade (no car ever is or was).

Nonetheless, these are genuine questions. Whatever people may ask about other machines, in the case of the Rolls they are really telling me, letting me understand that they know as well as I do that the Rolls-Royce is "The Best Car in the World."

But why this awe, why this veneration for the "name"?

It is simply this: The Rolls-Royce is perhaps the finest mechanical artifact that has ever been made, that an individual can own, that he can get his hands on and operate.

A famous and perhaps slightly jealous engineer many years ago cracked that "The Rolls-Royce is the triumph of craftsmanship over design." He meant it as no compliment, but his quip penetrated into the very core of the reason for Rolls-Royce's success for almost sixty years. For every Rolls-Royce has been a triumph of craftsmanship and if its design has often seemed behind the times, it is because flashy mechanical tricks have always had to take second place to the homely virtues of silence, smoothness, and, above all, unbreakability; and the not-so-homely virtue of luxurious travel.

A Rolls at 50,000 miles is just nicely broken in. There are Rolls-Royces which have done 500,000 miles and still delight their owners. But don't imagine that such mileages can be attained if a Rolls is maintained in the offhand manner that is standard treatment for the appliances from Detroit. In its 1929 instruction book for the Phantom I, Rolls recommended, "as the safest and most economical course," that "the car should be sent to its makers for dismantling and report at least every 50,000 miles." And of course Rolls-Royce expected you or your paid

driver to follow the encyclopedic, two-hundred-page instruction book to the letter. If you liked, they'd send an inspector to your house to check up on your darling. You could—and still can—send your chauffeur to Rolls-Royce's school to teach him how to drive and maintain a Rolls by Rolls-Royce standards. Or, if you're too poor to maintain a Rolls *and* a chauffeur, they'll let you take the course yourself.

One of the things about older Rolls-Royces that has tickled me as much as anything else is the deliciously precise system of small hand controls for adjusting things like the spark, which has always been marked "Early" and "Late" rather than "Advance" and "Retard" as on lesser machines, and the throttle, which is marked "Open" and "Shut." At the driver's finger tips is a wondrous system of rods and levers that proceeds to such various parts of the car that may require his personal adjustment. On most cars such adjustments are vague and variable, but on a Rolls moving the throttle control just one tiny notch makes a predictable and tiny difference in the speed of the engine. Nor do the joints and bearings of these beautifully made rods and levers seem ever to wear—if you keep them lubricated according to the book. If one notch of the spark control retarded the magneto two-fifths of a degree on your Rolls new in 1934, it still retards it two-fifths of a degree today.

The car that more than any other made Rolls-Royce's reputation and is the basis upon which much of Rolls-Royce's present fame still rests was the Silver Ghost of 1907. In a day when automobiles were expected to be noisy and smoky and unreliable, the Silver Ghost burst (or, I should say, oozed) upon the scene like a revelation of automotive heaven. It was so silent that it was necessary to post in the yard at the works signs which said, "Look out for silent cars," to keep the help from being run over. Such silence could only be obtained by meticulous fitting and machining of parts, by myriad experiments with manifolds and mufflers, and, it must be admitted, at some loss in performance. Nor did the Ghost leave a trail of oily smoke. In a day when most cars used a primitive system of external oilers, which sometimes fed the engine too little oil and

Preceding pages: A 1912 Mercer Raceabout. Left: With an eight-cylinder V engine and an automatic transmission, the Rolls-Royce Silver Cloud II can do 100 mph. It is identical to the Bentley except for the radiator shell.

most times too much, the Ghost had a hollow crankshaft, fed by oil from a pump, like your smokeless car of today.

The Ghost was well-nigh indestructible, too. For example, the chassis of most other cars were riveted together. The Ghosts (and later Rolls', too) were bolted together by means of a special type of square-headed, tapered bolt which fitted a hole in the chassis reamed by hand to just take the bolt without shake, without forcing. Where other manufacturers were satisfied to fasten the torque tube, say, to the differential housing with a dozen big bolts, Rolls used a multiplicity of tiny bolts, almost touching each other, to "sew" (Henry Royce's word) the parts firmly together.

Once a chassis was finished, testers gleefully took it out on the worst roads they could find to see if they could expose some hidden fault. Woe betide the poor wight in the factory if some part he had designed gave way.

A year or so ago, I had a chance to drive a 1912 version of such a "Ghost" upon which a friend had just spent upward of two years in restoration after rescuing it from a tumbledown shed where it had lain, forlorn, since the late Twenties. As he swung open the door of his garage in which sat some half-dozen other ancient beauties, he said: "Let's push her out, I like to start these old timers outside."

As he released the glistening, nickeled hand brake, I resigned myself to a few heavy moments of puffing and sweat, braced my legs and started shoving. Miraculously, the long, heavy machine seemed almost to glide away from our hands of its own volition. Never have I known a car to roll so easily. (No, it wasn't on a downgrade!)

Once outside I could stand back and admire the easy grace of the Rolls' lines. Its rather squat, nickel-silver radiator was mounted well back, on a line with the front axle which, devoid of brakes, gave the front of the car a feeling of lightness and readiness for movement. My friend diddled with a switch on the steering wheel's hub, then lifted the starting crank effortlessly, with a slight flick of his wrist, and the engine was running. But so sweetly and smoothly that one was almost unaware of it.

As I slid behind the wheel, the Rolls' owner removed the stick holding down the clutch pedal. (You do this on old Rolls' when they're not in use to keep the leather faces of the clutch from adhering to each other.)

On the road the old Ghost was a joy. Noiseless, but for the swish of the tires, it was like gliding along in a sailing yacht. And no wonder. For these machines are high geared (2.9 to 1), and their big six-cylinder, 7½-liter, side-valve engines just laze along. Once in high you rarely shift gears. I found it possible to slow to five miles an hour in the top gear of its three-speed box and then, merely by opening the throttle, to bring it up smoothly to a top speed of almost 70. (Earlier Ghosts had an overdrive fourth speed; later Ghosts had normal four-speed boxes). It was a bit tricky to shift gears. Although as in every early Rolls the beautiful gear lever worked with oily smoothness, it was not only necessary to double-clutch between shifts, but imperative to gauge the engine and car speed just right if I was not to make shameful noises, which, unfortunately, I contrived to do.

When the owner took over, he showed me up by making beautifully silent gear changes, up and down.

"Sorry I made such a racket shifting," I apologized meekly.

"Oh, that isn't what worried me. What bothered me was your getting so close behind other cars on the thruway. You seemed to forget that these babies only have two-wheel brakes."

I had forgotten. The brakes seemed fine to me.

In 1907, when Rolls-Royce started building the Silver Ghost, they had been in the automobile business only three years. Frederick Henry Royce hadn't even owned a car until 1903 when he bought himself a French Decauville, considered a pretty good car in its day. Royce hated the thing. He thought it noisy, fussy, and put together by French plumbers. You could expect Royce to sneer at any mechanism put together by anyone but himself. He was not only a consummate mechanic, he was a self-made engineering genius. Only Ettore Bugatti, perhaps, had this same feeling for metal, this same unerring sense of what was exactly the right shape for a piece of steel which would do its job without being either too

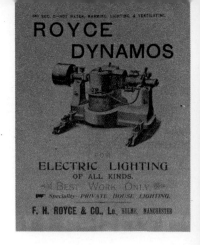

Preceding pages: A 1932 Phantom II, Continental Rolls-Royce. The original 1907 Silver Ghost (right) can still be viewed in Rolls-Royce's London showroom. Before he began building motor cars, Henry Royce built electrical equipment. The advertisement (far right) appeared in an architectural magazine in the 1890's.

heavy or too light and would, withal, have a sculptural grace to delight the eye. But unlike Bugatti, who dreamed his design on paper, Royce could actually shape what he wished with his own hands. He had been apprenticed as a child in the hard Victorian school of the Great Northern Railway shops, where a man was not considered a journeyman fitter until he could file, by hand, a square on the end of a brass rod and a square hole in a brass sheet so accurately that the rod would just fit the hole in any of the four positions without light showing through.

By 1903, Royce had a successful business building dynamos and electrical cranes, but his annoyance with the Decauville changed that. He knew he could build better cars himself. Within a short time, after driving his mechanics into a state of near desperation from overwork and his demands for perfection, he had several finished cars which satisfied him. These were by no means yet in the class of the Silver Ghost, but by the standards of the day his little two-, three-, and four-cylinder machines were marvels of mechanical excellence.

These cars were brought to the attention of an aristocratic young man named Charles Rolls. Rolls, the son of a Lord Llangattock (a good thing they didn't name the car after him), was like many of the bloods of his time—crazy about ballooning, aeroplanes (he was killed in one in 1910), and cars—mostly cars. He knew everything there was to know about them, wrote about them and raced them. He was the dealer for Panhard and Levassor cars in London when he saw and was entranced by Royce's cars, and almost immediately the firm of Rolls-Royce was born to market them.

Although these early cars were a success in sales and in racing—Rolls won the Tourist Trophy Race in 1905 with a 20 hp, four-cylinder machine—it was not until 1907 when the first Ghosts were delivered that the name started on its road to greatness.

The Silver Ghost was made from 1907 to 1926, from the Edwardian era through World War I, when it did yeoman service as the chassis for armored cars, to the Jazz Age and Calvin Coolidge. Certainly

there were slight changes in the car. Toward the end, some Ghosts even had front-wheel brakes, and a factory in Springfield, Massachusetts, started to manufacture an Americanized version. Basically it was still "The Best Car in the World," but never again would there be such a wide gulf between it and other, less regal machines.

In 1926, to meet the competition of great luxury cars like the Isotta-Fraschini, the 37.2 Hispano-Suiza, and the 6½-liter Bentley, which was already on the stocks, Rolls announced a successor to the Silver Ghost: the New Phantom, which we now call the Phantom I.

The chassis of this new machine was basically the same as the Ghost's, with torque-tube drive and long cantilever rear springs. But the new car had front-wheel brakes as standard plus a servo-mechanism (borrowed from Hispano?) to apply the new braking system.

The engine was entirely new. Still a six, with the cylinders cast in pairs of three, it now had overhead valves and was slightly larger (7,668 cc). It had slightly more power than the old engine. (Rolls never divulges the horsepowers of its engines, but the Phantom I developed about 100 hp, not high for some of the weighty arks it was expected to drag around.) But unhappily it did not have nearly its sweetness and charm.

In general, the Phantom I was rather a lump to drive, especially the Springfield lefthand-drive version, which had a three-speed gearbox. (The Derby cars had four speeds.) The Springfield Rolls also dispensed with the magneto of the English version. Although the three Phantom I's I have owned were capable of about 80 mph, they were not too pleasant at high speed owing to their less than perfect handling qualities. I must admit, however, that the Brewster coachwork on the cars I owned was not only beautiful (especially the Ascot Tourer and the Riviera Town Car), but was perhaps the most honestly built and sturdiest I have ever seen built anywhere. And I include in this judgment the fanciest *carrossiers* of England and France.

Within four years Rolls-Royce discontinued the unloved Phantom I. In 1929 the Phantom II was announced, as fine a car as the firm has ever built. The engine of the Phantom II was basically the same as that of the earlier car, but minor modifications somewhat increased its power to perhaps 125 hp. Its chassis, however, was entirely new. The heavy torque-tube drive was eliminated and long, supple, half-elliptics replaced the cantilever rear springs which had been a Rolls habit for so long. The frame itself was also considerably stiffened. The car now had superb road holding and steering, and even with the heavy, formal bodies that some of the stuffier customers demanded, it would do over 85 mph.

In 1930, to satisfy its less stodgy clients, Rolls introduced what is perhaps the finest sporting luxury car ever built by anybody (except Hispano-Suiza?). This was the "Continental Touring" model built on the "short" 144-inch chassis. (The "long" chassis had a 150-inch wheelbase.) It had flatter springs, a higher compression engine (5.25 to 1), and a slightly higher rear-axle ratio. Late models had four-speed, synchromesh, close-ratio gearboxes and adjustable shock absorbers.

I now own a 1935 Phantom II Continental upon which is mounted a convertible body by Binder of Paris. It is truly a joy to drive. Its high-geared and accurate steering and excellent road holding make it possible to drive almost as if one were in a much smaller sports car. It is fast, too. I've seen a 100 mph on the clock, but Rolls never claimed more than 93, albeit a few cars had high-lift camshafts (later eliminated because they were faintly audible) with which it was possible to exceed 100. Its gearbox is a pleasure to use, but the tremendous torque and power (160 hp?) of the huge engine makes shifting almost redundant except for starting from rest. It is possible to crawl along at four miles an hour in high when you want to show off, and then tramp on the loud pedal to get right up to top speed without any sounds of displeasure from the engine room.

In 1934, Sir Henry Royce died and in 1936 there appeared the first Rolls-Royce designed without his

Isle of Man Tourist Trophy Race of 1906 was won by the four-cylinder, 20 hp Rolls-Royce (upper left) at an average speed of 39 mph. Edwardian exaggeration: Joseph Cockshoot of Manchester built the body for this 1908 Silver Ghost (upper right). This regal equipage was the first Rolls-Royce in India. Known as the "Pearl of the East," it had a removable top and could be used in open form. The "Silent Sports Car" (above), a 1938, 4¼-liter Bentley, was more of a sports car then.

involvement. This was the fabulous Phantom III, powered with a marvelous and somewhat complicated V-12 engine of about the same cubic capacity as the earlier engines. And now for the first time there was a Rolls-Royce with independent front suspension. The P-III was probably the very last truly great luxury car the world will ever see. Usually fitted with huge palaces among bodies, lined in rare woods, fitted out with bars and vanity sets, these 100-mile-an-hour giants could be steered over rough, potholed roads and through dense traffic with greater precision and comfort than an ordinary small car. It would be nearly impossible to build such a machine today. One of these cars with a good bespoke body cost nearly $20,000 in 1939, delivered in the United States. Today $60,000 would hardly give its makers a profit.

Parallel with these "battle-cruiser" Rolls-Royces, there appeared in 1923 a line of smaller machines from which descend the Rolls-Royces and Bentleys of today. The old line of giant, long wheelbase ma-

Functional elegance marks the dashboard of a 1912 Silver Ghost (above). At left, the Dudley family diligently polishes its 25/30 hp, 1937 Barker Landaulet for a Concours d'Elegance. The author's 1935 Phantom II Continental Rolls-Royce appears below. Its convertible body was built by Henry Binder of Paris. A 1914 Rolls-Royce Alpine Silver Ghost (right) was especially designed to take milord on the Grand Tour. The Bentley Continental (lower right) is a lightweight version of the standard V-8 engined automobile. Fitted with custom bodies of small frontal area, like this Milliner four-door "Flying Spur," these delectable high-geared cars are capable of more than 120 mph. They can cost over $25,000 in this country.

chines really died out with the Phantom III at the start of Hitler's war in 1939.

The first of the "baby" Rolls-Royces was the 20 hp model. Its big brother was rated at 40 to 50 hp, but these figures have no real relation to actual horsepower, since they are a peculiar British measurement for an odd taxation system in force in England until recently. Over the years these Twenties grew into 20/25's, 25/30's and just before the war, the Wraith. All of them were in every respect as meticulously made as the larger cars, although the earlier smaller machines, especially the Twenty, were painfully underpowered. Nevertheless, the Twenty was dearly loved by the British, who found that in spite of its slowness (60 mph maximum), it was just the thing for "going up" to London from the family demesne. It was wonderful in town traffic. Further, on the twisting, two-lane roads of England, it could put up very nearly as good an average as its haughtier sisters. It was from these smaller Rolls-Royces that the Rolls-built Bentley was developed.

In 1931, Rolls bought out the assets of Bentley Motors (just edging out Napier), and in 1933 the first of a new breed of Bentleys appeared. Based on the 20/25 Rolls, but with a lower and considerably more sporting type of chassis and a higher compression engine fitted with S.U. carburetors, this new 3½-liter machine — the Silent Sports Car — drew groans of disappointment from devoted partisans of the rugged old he-man Bentleys of Le Mans. I felt that way myself. But we were wrong. The new Bentley with its butter-smooth engine, its silent, silky, close-ratio gearbox, and its near-noiseless exhaust fooled us into thinking that it was a pussycat of the highways. In fact, in its day it was a lion, even if it didn't roar.

In 1936, after its engine had been slightly increased in size to 4¼ liters, the Bentley was capable of over 95 mph. With sensibly light coachwork (some Bentleys had ridiculously heavy sedan bodies), it could go from 0 to 60 in under fifteen seconds.

For five years, I owned one of these charming machines, a 4¼, 1938 model with a Thrupp-and-Maberly convertible body. I still can't imagine why I sold it, unless it was that upon hard cornering it sometimes evidenced a certain instability in its hind quarters that, for a Bentley, was disconcerting.

In the summer of 1939, Captain G. E. T. Eyston on a 4¼ specially streamlined Bentley did 114.63 mph for an hour on Brooklands track. This machine was most likely the prototype of the stillborn 110 mph Corniche model with independent front suspension, which during the "phony war" period in 1940,

was on test in France. Standing at the dock at Dieppe awaiting shipment home, it was destroyed by German bombers.

Since the war, Rolls has been making cars which are still "The Best Cars in the World." Certainly it is almost impossible to expect that in these shoddy and expensive times, Rolls-Royce can still go to the fantastic lengths to insure perfection that it went to in 1939. In those days Rolls brought metal in at one end of the plant and drove the finished chassis out at the other. They made their own castings, their own honeycomb radiators, their own electrical equipment, and their wonderful self-locking hubs for the wire wheels.

Now Rolls buys many things from outside suppliers, including steel bodywork which would have been anathema in the old days when the company made chassis exclusively. Still, every bit of metal is to Rolls-Royce specification, every component bought from the outside is examined by an army of fussy inspectors using electronic devices. Each engine is run for eight hours on a testing rig fueled by cooking gas, thirty minutes idling, thirty minutes at medium revolutions, and seven hours at full power. Then every twentieth engine is taken down to its smallest bolt and every single part carefully examined, some under a microscope. And then, if there is some suspicion about any part, every one of the previous twenty engines is ripped apart for examination. Every fiftieth engine goes through an even more stringent trial, running for twenty-four hours. If, upon being stripped down, it doesn't please the sourpuss inspectors, the previous fifty engines are torn down. Not only the engine, but every single part of a new Rolls or Bentley is treated with equally cruel suspicion by the testers. It's a wonder any finished cars ever leave the plant.

I was at the Rolls-Royce factory recently watching them build the new V-8 Silver Cloud II and the Bentley. I asked a Rolls engineer how many cars a day were produced.

"Well," he said, "we finished five yesterday, but the blasted testers brought every bloody one back."

Yet all the electronic measuring gadgets and microscopes and listening devices didn't impress me as much as a group of quiet men in a corner of the plant who were doing something with shining sheets of stainless steel. They were making Rolls-Royce radiator shells and they were soldering them together by hand. I wouldn't have been a bit surprised if one of their big, coke-heated, soldering irons had been the selfsame one used to solder together the very first radiator shell of the very first Royce car.

300 SL Mercedes-Benz

f Rolls-Royce, during the great years of the Grand Marques, typified the British ideal in a road machine —silence, superlative craftsmanship, together with a certain lean and quiet understatement of quality— then Mercedes-Benz was typically German. While also of superb construction, the Mercedes-Benz of those days was an altogether different sort of animal, especially in its sporting versions which are the ones most worth considering. They were flamboyant in look, Teutonically harsh in character.

The firms of Mercedes and Benz were married in 1926. We are not here concerned with the Benz, which was an undistinguished machine except for some flashes of brilliance in the early pre-Kaiser war Prinz Heinrich Trials. As a racing machine, it had some success, notably the Blitzen Benz's raced by Barney Oldfield and by Bob Burman, who broke the world's land speed record in a special 200 hp model in 1911.

Mercedes, before joining Benz, was in its own right one of the great marques of all time. It had been so ever since Wilhelm Maybach (who, you may remember, was associated with old Herr Daimler) designed in 1900 the machine which instantly made every other car in the world impossibly old-fashioned.

This new car had a honeycomb radiator, gate-change gearshift, and accurate control of engine speed by means of a throttle, made possible by mechanically opened inlet valves. (Until then the inlet valves in all cars opened by suction.) Although made by Daimler in Cannstatt, this new *wunder-wagen* bore for the first time the name Mercedes, after the daughter of one Emile Jellinek.

Jellinek, Daimler's agent and Austro-Hungarian consul in Nice, was a sharp little insider of the fast-moving, gilded set on the Riviera in those free-spending Edwardian Days. He contracted to dispose of the entire factory production if Daimler would name the car after the apple of his eye. He had no trouble selling the new Mercedes to his rich friends who were enchanted by its silence and reliability as a touring machine and its near invulnerability as a racing car. For in 1901 a fast tourer was a sports car *and* a racing car (once you undid the back seats).

In 1903, there appeared the legendary "Sixty" Mercedes. No matter how many millions of pounds your father, the belted Earl, had, no matter if you were first cousin to the Czar of all the Russias, or if your name was Vanderbilt, you were just a square in the eyes of your moneyed cronies of the international social register if you didn't own a "Sixty." A "Sixty" cost some $12,000 in 1903. But, consumed with heart-burning eagerness, many a gold-laden young buck paid several times this much to get one ahead of his friends. Herr Jellinek became much richer, and so proud of his cars, that he changed his name to Jellinek-Mercedes.

The "Sixty" had a giant four-cylinder engine of 9,236 cc, and low-tension, make-and-break ignition. To make it easier to start, a ratchet-and-pinion device was fitted to raise the exhaust valves from their seats. Lubrication was by a drip-feed device which clung to the windshieldless dashboard, good enough for an engine which developed its full power at 1,000 rpm. A coil spring that could be tightened around the drive shaft served as a clutch, which transmitted

Lusty-looking giants such as the SSK Mercedes-Benz of 1929 (preceding pages) were the beau-ideal of the wealthy young blades of the late Twenties. Their prodigious, 7-liter, supercharged engines delivered 225 hp, with the "kompressor" engaged (it only engaged when the throttle was shoved to the floor). An 18/22 hp Mercedes-Simplex of 1903 stands above left. At full bore the engines of these charming small Mercedes revolved at no more than 1,000 rpm. They are remembered for the silence of their running and the delightful ease of their gearshift. Camille Jenatzy won the 1903 Gordon-Bennett race on a stripped version of the famous "Sixty" chain-drive Mercedes' of 1903 (left). Although these were dangerous cars, they were favorites among the haut monde. In 1903 they cost a princely $12,000. Above: The engine of a 1901 Mercedes.

the drive to a four-speed gearbox which then drove the rear wheels via side chains. A little tankful of water was carried on the car and every time you pressed the brake pedal some water sprayed the brake drums.

The "Sixty" was fast. In 1903, when three 90-hp cars ready for the Gordon-Bennett Race were destroyed in a fire that levelled the Cannstatt works, the factory borrowed three "Sixties" from private owners and, with one of the cars driven by Jenatzy, the red-bearded Stirling Moss of his day, won the race. He averaged 49.25 mph for 325 miles and at times reached 85 mph. Perhaps the "Sixty" was *too* fast for its steering and road holding, for a fair number of the young gentlemen who owned them never lived to collect any of papa's millions.

Between 1903 and the end of World War I, Mercedes built a spate of fine cars for both touring and racing, but not until the Twenties did they build machines that delighted autophiles as much as the memorable "Sixty."

If in the early Thirties you had hung about the purlieus of an establishment known as the Zumbach Motor Repair Company in New York, as I did, you would have panted over as breath-taking a parade of Mercedes-Benz's as ever rolled through a garage

door. Long, lean machines whose hoods seemed to take up two-thirds of their length, these were the cars of Mercedes' great vintage years. And though they were in a repair shop, it was only rarely, I remember, that they were hospitalized for any serious malaise. I saw few cases of blocks being resleeved, sick crankshafts, or gear dentistry. Mostly they were in because their loving owners, even during the Depression, were anxious to spend money babying their darlings. Looking back it seemed to me that Werner Maeder, the chief mechanic, concerned himself largely with purging constipated carburetors with blasts of air and strong chemical cathartics. Or else they did such things as I remember the scion of a department store owner doing. He had the already stiff springs of his machine bound in white cord and ordered the huge brake drums to be copper plated. It was also *de rigeur* to bind the steering wheel in cord.

The first sporting Mercedes-Benz was the 33/180, or K, and it was certainly the least desirable. It appeared in 1926, the year the firm became Mercedes-Benz. Designed by Ferdinand Porsche, who had come to Mercedes from Austro-Daimler in 1923 and who was later to design the Auto-Union Grand Prix cars, the Volkswagen, and the Tiger Tank, it was claimed to be the first "off-the-floor" car anybody could buy (if he had $10,000 to spare) that would do 100 mph.

A friend of mine owned one and I was terrified every time I rode in it. It had the usual long loco-motive-boiler hood from which huge external exhaust pipes curled like nickel-plated pythons. Filling the cavernous space under the hood was a 6.2-liter, sin-gle overhead-camshaft engine complete "mit kom-pressor" which cut in when you were daft enough to press the gas pedal well down.

I don't recollect ever seeing anything like 100 mph on the speedometer of this high and unwieldy con-veyance, but I do remember that at 40 or so it took the best part of a city block for its hopeless brakes to bring it to a halt.

It would seem unlikely that so cumbersome and dangerous a car as the K could be redesigned and made usable, but Porsche not only made it usable, he made it one of the great cars of all time. He low-ered the chassis, bored out the engine slightly (to 6,789 cc), and installed power brakes (which still didn't stop too well).

This new model was called the 36/220, or S, and its 6.8-liter engine developed 120 hp at 3,000 rpm without the supercharger and 180 hp when the super-charger was cut in.

This supercharger or "kompressor" was the unique feature of these cars. Gear driven from the front of the crankshaft and running at three times engine speed, the standard-size blower (there were two larger sizes) blew air at eight-and-a-half pounds per square inch *into* the carburetors instead of sucking a gas-air mixture *from* the carburetor and *then* pumping it into the cylinders, as is usually the case. A clutch cut the blower in only when the gas pedal was mashed down, so that most running was done with the "kom-pressor" out of action. Cut in, the blower howled mightily and made you think you were motoring rather faster than you actually were, meanwhile im-pressing the peasantry. The factory frowned on owners using the blower more than twenty seconds at a time and never in bottom gear for fear of over-stressing the engine. A delightful canard is the claim that continual use of the blower will cause the engine to distintegrate and then discharge the bits through its own exhaust pipe.

This six-cylinder engine also had a single overhead camshaft driven from a vertical shaft at the rear. Two valves per cylinder were operated by rockers while the cylinders, of cast iron, were of the wet liner type and sat in a bath of cooling water in the light alloy block. The crankcase and head were of alu-minum, the only gasket being between the block and the head. Elsewhere, precisely ground and lapped surfaces were of such high accuracy as to preclude gaskets. The crankshaft rode on four main bearings and a pump delivered heated oil to the crankcase from an auxiliary tank.

In 1929 this engine was enlarged to 7 liters and put into a new model known as the 38/250, or SS. With a 7-to-1 compression ratio, it now delivered 170 hp unblown and 225 hp with the "kompressor" cut in.

In spite of their "Kriegshiff" construction these Mercedes' were surprisingly agile when moving rap-idly, and though their steering was heavy at park-ing speeds they weren't meant to be used for taxiing around town.

The SSK was a variation of the SS, but with a shortened chassis (K for *kurz*). These cars were lighter, had a higher blower pressure, and more horses (250).

The SSKL was a similar machine, but with a chas-sis drilled as full of holes as a Swiss cheese to lighten it (L for *leicht*). This type was used for racing and with the so-called "elephant" blower developed some 300 hp. Private owners could buy an SSKL, but somehow (and this is still true of Mercedes-Benz to-day) they could never approach the results the fac-tory got out of its cars. For example, in 1931 Rudolf Carraciola in an SSKL won the German Grand Prix against two Bugatti Type 51's driven by Varzi and Chiron.

It would be twenty years before you could again buy such superb sporting machines from Mercedes-Benz. For with the coming of the Nazis, the marque degenerated. True, this was the period of Mercedes' greatest racing successes, but the production sports cars of the mid-Thirties were the obese, Goering-esque 500K and 540K (this time K stood for "kom-pressor"). Softly sprung, and woolly engined, albeit well-made and beautifully finished, these machines had lost the purposeful character and performance of their predecessors. They sold quite well in this country (delivered in New York with dummy wooden tires because the Germans were conserving rubber) and are even today much in demand by collectors of "classic cars."

Nowadays, Mercedes-Benz, in addition to a line of excellent lesser cars, also manufactures the 300 series. The de luxe 300 Touring machine and the superb 300 SL sports car certainly qualify as Grand Marques. If you own one, cherish it and treat it with kindness, for, doubtless, thirty years hence, it will be sought after as eagerly and prized as highly as its ancestors are today.

BUGATTI

At best, I've never been more than a *demi-Bugattiste*, a heretic, unfaithful to the cult of *Bugattisme*. Although I have owned and driven and even suitably revered the name of Bugatti, I have committed the unpardonable sin of flirting with other gods, of allowing myself to think that other cars sometimes, under special conditions, and for particular purposes may be almost equal to the Bugatti.

Your true-blue *Bugattiste*, under pain of having his Bugatti Owner's Club badge torn from his car, would admit no such heresy. He's almost right, for the Bugatti was as unique as its maker, Ettore Bugatti.

Bugatti sprang in 1881 from a family of artistic Italians in Milan who hoped that young Ettore would follow the family traditions and go in for sculpture. Luckily for the world, he didn't. Instead of producing mediocre art to embellish Italian palazzi, he became a master sculptor in metal for motor car chassis. Each part of every car Bugatti ever designed bears the stamp of his genius. It is crisp, functional, and beautiful for its own sake.

As I write this I am looking at some of those brilliantly clear photographs people used to make, early in this century. They are close-ups of the mechanism of a De Dietrich of about 1904, one of the great cars of its time. The clean, flat surfaces, the sharp edges are as pleasurable to look at and as efficient as those in the very last Bugattis. And Bugatti was a mere boy, not yet twenty-one, a minor whose father had to sign the contract when Ettore joined De Dietrich in 1902 as their designer.

Nor were the De Dietrich people fools, for Bugatti had already made a name for himself as an automotive genius who had designed and built race-winning machines since he was eighteen — and this without any formal engineering-school training.

The De Dietrich works were in Alsace, then a German province. In time, Bugatti left to work for other car builders — Mathis, Peugeot, Duetz — but when he set up his own factory in 1909 it was in Alsace, at Molsheim.

Factory is the wrong word. It was a kingdom and Ettore Bugatti was its absolute monarch. No one, whether he were draughtsman, fitter, foreman, or sweeper, bore a title. To Bugatti, they were but extensions of his brain and will. Bugatti loved horses and there were great stables. He loved fine wines and his barony contained vineyards. There was a hotel for customers come to receive their cars, and if their manner pleased "Le Patron" there was no bill (although they paid for their cars in cash — no checks). The factory itself was of surgical cleanliness. Much of the machinery was designed by "Le Patron" himself and even the vises bore the same red oval name plate as the cars. Scratching one with a file was *lèse majesté* not to be tolerated.

I saw the master but once, at a race at Deauville in 1936. He had arrived at the course in a sort of electric bath chair which he designed himself. (He was dissatisfied with the design of many common objects and designed his own variable-focus spectacles and a new, fabulously expensive bicycle, among other things.) Bugatti was a dandy. That day he wore a tan pongee suit and a brown bowler and leaned on a thin whangee cane.

He stood a little away from the pits, and as a

Preceding pages: The Type 55 Bugatti. La Royale, the Type 41 Bugatti (right), often called the Golden Bug, was designed as a "voiture de grande luxe" for the use of kings and princes. Its chassis alone cost $30,000 in 1927, the year it first appeared. It had a fourteen-foot, two-inch wheel base and a Gargantuan 13-liter engine, which developed no less than 300 bhp. It was capable of 125 mph and could be throttled back to 3 mph without shifting. At 72 mph the engine only turned over at 1,000 rpm. The Royale was guaranteed and maintained free of charge for the life of its owner, each of whom Ettore Bugatti presented with a special white elephant radiator-cap ornament. On the running board sits the late Jean Bugatti, son of "Le Patron."

B.253

Type 59 which lay first came in for refueling, he watched impassively as one of the pit crew struggled with the crank (which stuck out of the car's flank) and failed to start the engine. The mechanic was shoved aside by his superior and *he* cranked to no avail. Then the "chef" of the Bugatti pit, grand in pristine white coveralls, grabbed the crank, spun it mightily, and as the engine started, fell over in a faint, his nice white suit speckled with blood, presumably from a ruptured blood vessel overstrained in the service of "Le Patron." As two bearded medical types lifted the casualty onto a stretcher, M. Bugatti turned his back and strolled away.

From 1909 until 1939, Bugatti turned out fewer than 10,000 cars, but they were of thirty-six different models. Of these many were racing machines, the most successful ones ever built. In 1925 and 1926 alone, Bugattis won over 1,000 races!

Bugatti never built an uninteresting or unexciting car, unless it was the relatively quiet Type 44, which is sometimes known as "the Molsheim Buick." But my favorites, perhaps because I knew them best, were the Types 43 and 55.

The Type 43 was the sporting version of the Grand Prix 35B, the car that had done most of the race winning I just mentioned. The 43 had a straight-eight, 2.3-liter engine and was supercharged by means of a Roots blower at eight pounds per square inch. It developed some 120 hp and a good 43 could exceed 110 mph, a remarkable speed in 1927 when it first appeared. The three valves per cylinder were operated from fingers actuated by a single overhead camshaft. Expensive maintenance never bothered Bugatti. He assumed you were rich. Roller bearing con-rods and crankshafts — which meant disassembling the crankshaft in case of trouble — and non-detachable cylinder heads were normal in his designs. The Type 43 was typical. The chassis, too, is typically Bugatti, with deep side rails just below the dash area, but tapering to unbelievable delicacy at the front end. The springs were reversed quarter-elliptics in the rear and half-elliptic in front, but of such stiffness that one almost feels M. Bugatti might as well have left them off. (He once did build a race car without rear springs.) The front axle, common to almost all Bugattis, was nothing less than jewelry. Of polished steel and hollow, it had square apertures through which the springs were thrust. The flat-spoked wheels were of cast aluminum, with the brake drums an integral part of them.

Ettore Bugatti designed this Type 59, 3.3-liter car as a full Grand Prix
racing machine. The model seen on these pages was converted for road use and is
now the property of Mr. F. R. Ludington of New York. In racing trim, its
supercharged, twin-overhead-camshaft engine developed 250 bhp and propelled
the car at 175 mph. First produced in 1933 as a 2.8-liter,
it was unable to compete with the Alfa Romeos backed by the Mussolini government.
In 1934, the Type 59's had their engines increased to 3.3 liters, but
by then the Nazi-sponsored Auto-Unions and Mercedes-Benz's were too much for them.
Individualist Ettore Bugatti fitted the Type 59 with his famous piano-wire
wheels and continued to use his cart-sprung polished front axle at a time when
other makers were already using independent front suspension. Although it does not
show, the axle was split centrally to allow slight movement. The Type 59
retained the elegant shape of earlier Bugs, including their wedge-shaped tails.

This four-cylinder, 1½-liter Brescia Bugatti
of 1923 (top) was the Type 30 and was made in
two forms: the Brescia and the Brescia Modifé
(the Modifé was the detuned form for sports use).
A Type 35 2-liter appears below it, running
in a prewar road race at Alexandria Bay, New York. Dick
Wharton is driving. In this the usual aluminum-
spoked wheels have been replaced. Touring
the course at Le Mans (above) is one of the few
3.3-liter Type 101 Bugattis made for a short
time after the war. Two of these Type 101's are in
the U.S. John Straus' Atalante coupe-bodied, 3.3-liter
Type 57C (right) is the supercharged version of the
Type 57. Both have higher chassis than the
ultra-low, ultra-sporting Types 57S
and 57SC, which are the ultimate Bugattis.

But what is it like to own and drive one of these high-strung animals—say, a Type 43?

In the first place you must be a very special kind of man, imbued with the fervor of *Bugattisme* to stand the machine's foibles. On a cold day, for example, it is nearly impossible to start. (Bugatti told complainers to keep their cars in heated garages.) So you drain the oil and water, heat to taste, and re-feed to your engine. If it is going to start it will now burst into life at the first turn of the starter. But if you are a true believer, you'll hand crank first with the switch off to ease the pistons in their cold cylinders. You then idle at, say, 1,000 rpm for ten minutes to warm things up. Idle much slower and you'll be taking out the spark plugs for cleaning.

But a Bugatti is worth the trouble. Once on the road, nothing except perhaps an Alfa Romeo of the Thirties can give such joy. The front wheels point exactly where your hands on the steering wheel tell them to. You corner like a god. The clutch feels light at first, but as you gain speed it needs a swift kick to allow you to flick the gear lever from notch to notch. (At low speeds, however, the multi-plate clutch —a tricky device on a "Bug"—doesn't quite release and you make embarrassing noises unless you just slam the lever through.)

When a Bugatti needs work you'd best be an enthusiastic and knowing mechanic yourself, for there are not half-a-dozen men in this country who can be trusted to operate on it. To do a carbon and valve job means removing the cylinders—the head doesn't come off—and before you can do this on some models you have to remove the rear axle. On the Type 43 and some others, the roller bearings of the crankshaft are lubricated from jets set in the side of the crankcase which receive their oil through small-diameter copper pipes. A little lint in a pipe can mean trouble, of course. But *Bugattistes* never go near a dismantled engine with a rag. Camel's hair brushes only, *mon vieux!*

The Type 55 which came out in 1932 was one of the great sports cars of all time. It had a Type 51 Grand Prix engine (slightly de-tuned) in a Type 54 Grand Prix chassis, which had proved lethally dangerous as a race car. This 2.3-liter engine had twin-overhead camshafts, eight cylinders, and a slightly larger supercharger than the Type 43. It blew at ten pounds.

The 55 was very much like the 43 on the road but rather faster and with much greater acceleration. It was capable of going from 0 to 60 in just over nine seconds and had a top speed of 120. It could do 100 mph in third!

In 1935, a new kind of Bugatti appeared, designed for use by people impatient with the charming idiosyncrasies of the near-racing type of Bug. This new series was the Type 57, with a 3.3-liter, eight-cylinder, twin-overhead-camshaft engine. Although built in the usual Bugatti style, this "Normale" model somehow caused the cognoscenti to weep into their Pernod. "Bugatti is 'going Cadillac' like everyone else," they moaned.

But soon Bugatti brought out additional versions of his new machine, first a supercharged 57, the 57C, and then a much lower chassis-ed, higher-compression type, the 57S (for sport), which in supercharged form was known as the 57SC. The weepers could dry their tears now, for these 57's proved themselves to be the greatest cars for road and sport that Bugatti had ever built. They compared in power and speed thus: The 57—130 hp, 95 mph; the 57C—160 hp, 105 mph; the 57S—190 hp, 125 mph, and the incomparable 57SC—220 hp, 135 mph.

Ettore Bugatti still had not been convinced of the benefits of independent front suspension. He compromised by splitting the ever-beautiful, polished-steel front axle in its middle and joining the halves with a knurled collar. This allowed an almost imperceptible amount of independent movement for each front wheel. (You can't blame him for not wanting to give up that wonderfully handsome axle.) Further, he fitted De Ram shock absorbers, marvels of complexity which theoretically adjusted themselves to the exigencies of the road.

In 1936, a stock 57S driven by Robert Benoist crammed 135.4 miles into an hour on the Montlhéry autodrome in France, and in 1937 and 1939 57S Bugattis won first place at Le Mans.

The war ended the Type 57's. The Germans, the Canadians, the Americans all had their way with the Bugatti factory. Bugatti even had trouble getting it back, since he was still an Italian citizen and, therefore, technically an enemy alien.

Ettore Bugatti died in 1947. He had during the war designed a 350 cc, overhead-camshaft engine and a 1½-liter engine for a new small sports car, and it is said that he had redesigned the 57, but, sadly, nothing has come of these.

At the Paris Auto Show in 1951 a new Bugatti was exhibited, the Type 101, and although a few of these exist (two in the U.S.), no real production ever got started. In 1955 the people who now run Bugatti's factory brought forth a 2½-liter, Grand Prix car with a transverse rear engine. It bore the red oval name plate, but is it a Bugatti? Is any car that Ettore himself didn't design a Bugatti?

JAGUAR

Preceding pages: Monocoque, stressed
shell, steel bodywork eliminated the conventional
chassis in the XK-E Jaguar introduced in 1961.
This car uses the well-tried thirteen-year-old,
twin-overhead-camshaft XK engine. With a capacity
of 3.8 liters and three carburetors, it is
said to develop 265 bhp. The factory claims it is
capable of 150 mph. Dunlop bridge-type
disc brakes are fitted to the wheel hubs forward,
but are inboard at the rear. The XK-E is
commendably light, weighing but 2,600 pounds in
coupe form. It has a wheel base of only eight
feet and is but 48 inches high. The prewar
SS-100 (above) was the bargain-priced sports car
of its day. It cost only $2,175 in 3½-liter,
push-rod-engined form and provided exhilarating
performance, reaching 60 mph from a standing
start in under 11 seconds. It was said to
be able to approach 100 mph. In 1934, the SS-I
(right) captivated sporty interests with its
low and rakish bodywork. Its six-cylinder, L-head
engine gave it a top speed of 75 mph, a
great improvement over the first SS-I's and
SS-II's which, although equally sporting
in build, had a rather mediocre performance.

top at a traffic light in a posh $20,000 Continental Bentley and the taxi driver next to you is likely to lean out of his window and rasp, "Hey, Mac, 'at's a Jaguar, ain't it?" Tell him it's a Bentley and he's disappointed. To him, as to most people, the Jaguar is *the* fancy foreign car.

Today's Jaguars are very fine motor cars, but for the price of a Continental Bentley you can, happily, buy four of them.

Before the war it was the other way around. Jaguars tried to look like Bentleys. Rude types called Jaguars "Wardour Street Bentleys"—Wardour Street in London being the haunt of the flamboyant impresari who made movies on a shoestring.

The Jaguar started out as a sidecar for motorcycles. In 1923, a twenty-one-year-old youth named William Lyons (now Sir William), noting the burgeoning sales of sidecars, went into the business of building, at a low price, a sleeker, racier looking "bathtub" than anyone else in England. He gave this tiny enterprise, which consisted of himself, a partner, and five workmen, the resounding and comprehensive name of "The Swallow Side Car and Coach Building Company."

Business boomed. Before long, "Swallow" was building special de-luxe bodies for many of the popular small cars: the Standard-Swallow, the Austin-Swallow, the Hornet-Swallow. Lyons was doing fine, but he wasn't satisfied. He wanted to turn out a car that would be uniquely his own. To that end, Lyons made a deal with the Standard Motor Company whereby it would supply him with specially designed, underslung chassis upon which he could build his dream cars.

The cars (the SS-I and the SS-II) Lyons unveiled at the London Show in 1931 were certainly dream cars, the kind of machines imaginative schoolboys might doodle in their notebooks. They were excruciatingly rakish: Much of their length was taken up by a many-louvered hood; they had low, low passenger compartments whose inmates peered out at the world through slit-like windows; they had wire wheels, cycle-type fenders, and looked as if they might do 150 miles an hour.

Unfortunately, their performance was miserable. The larger of the pair, the SS-I, which was available with either a 2-liter or 2½-liter L-head engine, could barely exceed 70 mph, even with the bigger engine.

Both the Jaguar XK-150 convertible and the "Three-Point-Eight" five-passenger sedan of 1960 (right) were powered by the familiar 3.8-liter, twin-overhead-camshaft, six-cylinder XK engine. When it was first introduced in 1948, the XK engine displaced 3½ liters and developed 160 bhp at 5,400 rpm. By 1960, with its size increased, the engine was producing 265 bhp at 5,500 rpm (with three S. U. carburetors and a 9:1 compression ratio). This engine permitted the phenomenal performance of the XK-150S. From rest to 60 mph, it took but 8.9 seconds; to 100 mph 22.4 seconds. Top speed (in overdrive) was 135 mph. Both the lushly appointed 3.8 sedan and the most decidedly un-Spartan convertible, using the standard 3.8-liter engine, were able to better 120 mph. Each of these machines was fitted with disc brakes on all four wheels. Sir William Lyons has always amazed the automotive world with his uncanny ability to offer a combination of tremendous performance and superb finish at prices far lower than comparable cars.

The smaller SS-II had a 1-liter engine and was, if possible, even less sparkling.

But this didn't prevent the SS's from selling like mad. For despite their exciting looking and quite well-finished coachwork, they were amazingly cheap. The SS-I cost a mere $1,500.

Rapidly, the SS got better. A new, well-designed, six-cylinder, 2½-liter, push-rod, overhead-valve engine with a sturdy, seven-bearing crankshaft was developed and two versions of a potent sports car, in quick succession, were added to the line of much-improved sedans and sporty looking open tourers.

The sports cars were the SS-90 and the SS-100. (The numbers referred to their top speed.) The SS-90 appeared before the overhead-valve engine was in production and, surprisingly, was capable of reaching its advertised speed with a much-tuned, two-carburetor version of the old L-head engine. The SS-100 had the new 2½-liter ohv engine, and later a 3½-liter version which put out 120 bhp.

The SS-100 looked exactly like the popular ideal of a sports car in the mid-Thirties, with extravagantly sweeping fenders, a long hood, giant, staring headlights, a squarely chopped-off stern, and cutaway doors. Its 104-inch-wheelbase chassis was quite ordinary, with half-elliptic springs at its four corners. But it was light and thereby gave wonderful performance for its price ($1,925 for the 2½-liter, $2,175 for the 3½-liter). Vintage sports car collectors will pay more than that for an SS-100 today.

Driving an SS-100 at near its top speed could be a shattering experience for one not used to its foibles. For although it went from 0 to 60 in about eleven seconds, an exhilarating performance in its day, I recollect being quite frightened by its peculiar tendency to hop sideways at anything over 80 or so.

Perhaps the one I drove had a maladjusted front end. But I think not, for there have been murmurs about similar peccadillos in other SS-100's.

By the mid-Thirties the SS was much more Lyons than Standard. The whole line—sedans, tourers, and sports cars—had a new name added to its initials: Jaguar. The cars were known as SS Jaguars until World War II.

The first car produced by Lyons after the war was the Mark IV Jaguar. The initials SS, with their slight connotation of sleaziness, disappeared. The company had a new name, too, Jaguar Cars Ltd.

The Mark IV of 1946 was almost identical to the 3½-liter SS Jaguar of 1939. But where the prewar car had sold hardly at all in this country, the Mark IV Jaguar was an instant success despite its high price of nearly $5,000 (before the pound was devalued). Many Americans were pleased with its comparatively accurate steering, its four-speed gearbox, its classic Bentley-ish look, and its leather upholstery. There was a murmur of complaint, however, about its hard ride, which was due in part to its lack of independent front suspension such as American cars had used for years. In 1948, the Mark V remedied this by appearing with torsion-bar front springing. The 3½-liter engine remained basically the same (a 2½-liter version was available in England), but the bodywork was made smoother and roomier, the headlights were faired into the fenders, and the expensive, knock-on wire wheels gave way to bolt-on discs.

The Marks IV and V were still developments of prewar machines. In 1948, however, Sir William took the wraps off a new car and engine which broke entirely with the past and which were destined to make the Jaguar one of the world's great cars.

It's hard to realize that the XK-120 goes back as far as 1948. We take its descendants, which are still basically similar, almost for granted, but when the XK-120 appeared it seemed fantastic, almost unbelievable, that a nicely made sports car, with a 3½-liter, twin-overhead-camshaft engine of 160 bhp (at 5,400 rpm) could be bought for less than $4,000.

Twin-overhead-camshaft engines with hemispherical combustion chambers were nothing new in racing cars, Alfa Romeos, Bugattis, or even in the 3-liter Sunbeam, among others. But it was a startling innovation—even with chain-driven camshafts instead of gears—in what was, after all, a low-priced, mass-produced car.

The new XK engine was not dissimilar in its dimensions from the earlier push-rod types, but it was by no means a development of those engines. True, its stroke was within a hundredth of an inch of that in the old Mark V's 3½-liter engine (4.17 in.), its bore was identical (3.27 in.), and its carefully balanced crankshaft, revolving in seven main bearings, was very similar. The designers, W. M. Heynes and the famed Harry Weslake, had started with a clean sheet of drafting paper to build what was considered impossible: a tough, almost indestructible, high-speed racing type of engine at a low price. Weslake, the great expert on the respiratory problems of engines, was mainly responsible for the light aluminum cylinder head with its nickel/cast-iron valve-seat inserts and its patented port shapes.

The XK-120 had a 102-inch chassis with independent front suspension through torsion bars. Surprisingly, it was quite heavy—about 3,200 pounds. In spite of this, it had excellent acceleration. Going from 0-60 took slightly less than twelve seconds, 0 to 100 twenty-eight seconds.

Although the few people in this country who were used to "real" sports cars carped about the Jag's "softness," mushy brakes and steering, and the poor positioning of its foot pedals, Americans newly exposed to sports cars thought it was wonderful. Most of them had never driven anything more ambitious than the M.G., which was immediately abandoned by those who had Jaguar-size pocketbooks. Starting in 1950, when the first XK-120's became available, no less than 10,000 were sold in two years. The rush to the Jag was hurt not at all by a run of 132.6 mph that a stock XK (sans windshield, plus undershield) made at Jabbeke in Belgium around this time. Sourpusses like me were not overwhelmed, however. We were quick to point out that the 3.3-liter, 57S Bugatti had put 135.4 miles into an hour at Montlhéry track some ten years earlier.

Although the XK-120 had not been designed for racing (its engine had, indeed, been designed originally for use in a high-performance sedan), it was immediately, gleefully, brought to the starting line of races—many of which it proceeded to win handily. Not only did it score well in amateur competition, but factory teams started cleaning up races and rallies which until then had been the private preserve of great continental marques.

Since the first XK-120 appeared in 1948, it has steadily been developed and improved. Its basic engine has been modified for use in hot racing machines, in luxurious sedans, in new generations of sports cars. Its chassis has gone through continual metamorphoses, through tubular frames, space frames, no frames. Disc brakes, automatic transmissions, manual transmissions have come and gone, but the XK engine evidently will go on and on, powering new incarnations of great Jaguars forever.

141

FERRARI

Preceding pages: A ferocious, frontal aspect of the 250-GT Ferrari. The V-12, 3-liter, three-carburetor engine (right), as fitted to the 250-GT Berlinetta, develops 270 bhp at 7,000 rpm. Unusual carrosserie for a GT Ferrari is the four-seater by Farina (center). This V-12 engined "family car" has a top speed of about 130 mph and is luxuriously equipped all around. It weighs only 2,800 pounds. The Ferrari 4.1-liter Super America (far right) was also bodied by Farina and is the most potent of all of Commendatore Ferrari's machines.

A sports car, ideally, should be a de-tuned racing machine rather than a warmed-over touring automobile whose engine is either a puny mechanism tuned to within an inch of its life or a gross and trucklike oaf of a "motor" out of an American passenger car.

A sports car should have a built-in feeling of excitement. It should be as taut and nervous as a racehorse. It must certainly be quick off the mark and very fast. Further, its mechanism should be good to look at, its bodywork decently finished and functionally sober in design. (No Detroit gold-flecked, G-string-material upholstery, please.)

The one maker in the world who builds cars that most closely approach this exciting ideal is the Commendatore Enzo Ferrari—the modern version of Ettore Bugatti—who builds his cars in a tiny factory in Maranello, in the north of Italy.

Ferrari's three hundred or so workmen build a multiplicity of machines: Grand Prix cars, sports racing cars, Gran Turismo cars and even a "cooking" model (by Ferrari standards), called "the California" (with a modicum of disdain, perhaps?).

Currently, the 250-GT Berlinetta is the hottest practical machine you can drive on the public highway and then, by merely slapping a number on its flank, take racing—with a fine chance of winning. (The 250 stands not for horsepower, but for the cubic capacity in centimeters of each of its twelve cylinders; the GT, for Gran Turismo; Berlinetta, for its coupe body style).

"Is it true?" you ask. "Is this car so very different from other cars I've driven?"

Yes, it is!

Turn the key to start the engine and in an instant it is making scalp-prickling music. Its valves, its chains, its rocker arms—all the beautifully finished parts of its engine rub and click and revolve to make their own wonderful noises. A touch on the accelerator and these lighter sounds are drowned by a screaming roar which makes you tighten your abdominal muscles.

Once on the road you can drive this car as one drove the Alfas and Bugattis of the Thirties, before the family sedans got too fast for them. In those days an Alfa, for example, was so much faster and more maneuverable than other cars that it was possible to treat domestic machinery like stationary obstacles which you ignored as you blasted up the road, moving from lane to lane as necessary. At speed you got no impression that you were pursuing anything but a straight course. It seemed merely that Plymouths and Fords at anchor appeared now to port, now to starboard.

Aboard this quick-steering Ferrari, with such amazing accelerative power underfoot (0 to 60 in 6.4 seconds) and so much top speed (145 mph), plus superlative disc braking, you can again play such games, except, of course, if another damn fool in another Ferrari is playing the same game on the same road at the same time.

This 250-GT, although it certainly cannot be driven as absent-mindedly as your wife's station wagon, does not have to be driven with quite the concentration and worrisome care that were a nerve-wracking necessity when conducting a Ferrari just a few years ago. No longer are the clutch and crash gearbox something only maestri dared handle without breaking something. The plate clutch and four-speed, all-synchromesh transmission are now rugged and nearly foolproof and, if you're as un-Ferrari-ish a driver as to want to lug along at 40 mph in high gear, you can do so without wetting the spark plugs.

But make no mistake in thinking that this tough machine, with all its brutal power, is somehow crude and rough riding. Its cockpit has all of the quiet luxury anyone would want. Its chassis, independently sprung forward, but with a solid rear axle and leaf springs aft, of necessity has a certain firmness, but is far from uncomfortable.

The 3-liter engine of the 250-GT Berlinetta, as in almost every non-Grand Prix Ferrari ever made, is a V-12 with a single chain-driven overhead camshaft over each bank operating the two valves per cylinder via rockers. The "over-square" cylinders are wet liners in the aluminum block. Three Weber carburetors lie in the valley between the heads. At 7,000 rpm it develops 280 hp.

Ferrari (b. 1898) is no engineer, in the formal

sense. When he was a boy his father owned a small garage in Modena, and like many young Italians he was obsessed with cars and racing drivers. Even in those days motor racing was Italy's national sport (after grand opera). Ferrari was torn between opera and cars for a while, but instead of *Il Trovatore* he chose Alfa Romeo, where he got a job as a mechanic. By 1923 he was a racing driver. Those were the spectacular days of the P 2 Alfas and the 3-liter RLSS 22/90's and of drivers like Campari, Sivocci, and the elder Ascari. Ferrari, not quite of the racing caliber of these giants, didn't drive the P 2's much, but did very well in hill climbs and sports-car races and minor Grands Prix. It was during one of these races that the prancing horse shield which is the Ferrari trademark came into his life.

Ferrari had just won a race at Ravenna when a man and his wife rushed forward to present him with a charred and blackened shield which had been the emblem of their fighter pilot son, Francesco Baracca, the Italian ace shot down in flames in 1918. Years later, like Guynemer's stork on the Hispano-Suiza, an airman's blazon was to herald another great car.

However, as Ferrari became involved with the organizational and construction problems of the Alfa Romeo racing team, he raced less often. When Alfa decided to give up its racing department, the famous "Scuderia Ferrari" was formed to handle Alfa Romeo's racing cars.

During the Thirties, the giant vans of the Scuderia Ferrari, with the prancing horse shield on their flanks and potent racing cars within, ranged from Monza in Italy to Mineola, Long Island; from the Nürburg ring to Tripoli.

At first the Alfas, driven by such legendary greats as Nuvolari, Farina, and Varzi, had things all their own way and all but swept into limbo the Bugattis that had been the kings of the Grand Prix circuits. But by the mid-Thirties, the Mercedes-Benz's and Auto-Unions of the Third Reich were giving the Alfas a hard time, and in the last years before the war, Ferrari's Alfa Romeos, to Mussolini's discomfiture, were completely overshadowed by the Germans.

In 1938, a new management at Alfa Romeo, in a hopeless effort to make a comeback, formed a company-run Scuderia called "Alfa Corse" and Enzo Ferrari was free to go his way.

Thus, in 1940, Ferrari entered two cars with 1½-liter, eight-cylinder engines in that odd, shortened, wartime Mille Miglia (the Italian 1,000-mile race) which was won by a German BMW. These machines built in Ferrari's shop in Modena, where he had prepared the racing Alfas of the Scuderia Ferrari, were not destined to be the progenitors of what we now know as Ferraris. The first real Ferrari took to the road in 1947. This was the 1½-liter Type 125, designed by Gioacchino Columbo, who had been chief designer for Alfa Romeo. It had the first of the V-type, twelve-cylinder engines which were to become a Ferrari feature and which are now the only V-12's produced anywhere. With its extreme "over-square" cylinder dimensions, its light reciprocating masses, and very short con-rods, it was hoped that 10,000 rpm would be possible. Columbo was disappointed when only 7,500 could be reached.

However, variations of this highly successful twelve have been made in sizes up to 5 liters and developing as much as 450 hp. There is no doubt that these engines have been among the most successful ever built, not only for racing but also in the eminently desirable cars which for so many years now have dominated sports-car racing.

The first Ferrari to reach this country, a Type 125, was brought in by Briggs Cunningham in 1949. By the early Fifties, famous American drivers like Bill Spear and James Kimberly were cleaning up every sports-car event they entered.

A Ferrari at around $14,000 is still the fanciest and fastest sports car you can buy, and wealthy sporting gentlemen from Hollywood to the Riviera, from Buenos Aires to Biarritz, feel positively naked without one.

But what does the Commendatore, Enzo Ferrari himself, drive from the factory at Marenello to his offices at Modena?

He drives a 1200 cc Fiat. Ferraris are just too rich for his blood.

ALFA ROMEO

In 1934, this 2.3-liter, supercharged Alfa Romeo (preceding pages) with its exquisitely built engine (right) developed 140 hp. Note the beautifully-finned intake manifold. Next is a 1925 RLSS 22/90 which had a 3-liter, push-rod engine. A Bat-9 Bertone bodied Alfa and Giulietta Spider follow.

At the risk of having a band of fanatical *Bugattisti* show up at my house some dark night to make me eat old Chevrolet catalogues until I recant, I hereby make this daring statement:

The Alfa Romeo of the Thirties was as great a car as the Bugatti—and vice versa.

These are the only two sports cars ever made about which there can be any argument as to which was better. No others were even in the same league.

True, Bugatti types can boast about the devilish service problems they have with their cars and they can amuse each other with the stories they invent about the romantic eccentric who built them. Alfa owners must sadly admit that their machines are easy to service, even though they do have twin-overhead camshafts and superchargers, and that the only odd character even remotely connected with them was one Benito Mussolini, a dreadful bore.

A.L.F.A. (Amonima Lombarda Fabrica Automobili) built French Darracqs as far back as 1909. Business was just so-so until a young engineer named Nicola Romeo took over at about the time of World War I, added his own name, and called the outfit Alfa Romeo.

Almost immediately after World War I, Alfa Romeo began to make its name known on the road circuits and race tracks of Europe with the famous P 2 racing two-seaters. These had 2-liter, twin-overhead camshaft, eight-cylinder, supercharged engines and dry-sump lubrication. Driven by such crack drivers as Ascari, Sivocci, and Mazetti, they cleaned up in enough races to win the world's championship in 1925.

But Alfa Romeo had not yet learned the lesson that a great sports car should be a de-tuned racer rather than a hopped-up tourer. The sporting machine they offered in 1925 was the 3-liter RLSS developed from their 15-55 four-cylinder and 21-70 and 22-90 RL six-cylinder touring machines.

The very first sports car I ever owned was one of these 22-90 RLSS Alfas, which I bought in 1932 for $400. It had a six-cylinder engine with push-rod operated, overhead valves, and twin Zenith carburetors. Its 129-inch chassis sat on semi-elliptic springs and it had a four-speed gearbox which I remember as a brute to handle. For that matter, the whole car was rather a noisy brute, but I loved it, for compared to the American cars of the period, it was a revelation. Its steering particularly amazed me. I hadn't realized that any car could be steered so quickly and with such precision. The car was fast for its day too, bettering 85 mph.

But the 22-90 did have its little faults. Its four-wheel brakes had no linings. Cast-iron shoes rubbed directly against the steel of the drums making the most blood-curdling howl imaginable. This might have been forgivable if they had done much toward stopping the car. But due to an ingenious brake linkage system, utilizing little bits of chain and cable in addition to the long steel tapes which formed the brake rods, response was discouragingly slow. By the time the pressure of your foot had been transmitted to the brake drums, you were likely to have hit what you were trying not to hit.

I remember, too, that I couldn't wear rubber-soled shoes while driving the 22-90 because its aluminum footboard got so hot the soles began to melt and got as sticky as chewing gum.

This Alfa had dry-sump lubrication and no oil was supposed to be poured into its crankcase. The oil was kept in a tank under the dash and then automatically pumped into the engine. The first day I got the Alfa I ignorantly filled both the dash tank and the crankcase. When the overtaxed dash tank of warm oil burst its seams right over the lap of a young woman who was getting her first ride in my new car, nothing I could do with handkerchiefs and oily rags from the tool box helped. From then on she'd have nothing to do with me or my Alfa.

In 1927, however, Alfa Romeo started building cars which owed much to the designs of the successful P 2 racing machines. The first of these had a 1½-

liter, single-overhead camshaft, six-cylinder engine. This freely revolving engine (about 4,500 rpm) in a car weighing about a ton, developed 60 hp and prodded the little thing along at about 75 mph.

By 1929 these machines had developed into the most delightful of sporting conveyances: the six-cylinder Gran Sport 1750 cc. supercharged twin-camshaft 17/95 model. I have owned several of these charming and exciting machines and I still think that they and their later and larger brothers, the eight-cylinder 2.3's (like the one in the picture), are the most exhilarating sports cars I have ever driven—and I include everything up to the latest Ferraris.

The engine of the 1750 Alfa is one of the most exquisitely finished mechanisms ever to be installed in a motor car. Even the Bugattis must take second place to it. Its twin-overhead camshafts are driven by a vertical shaft at the rear of the engine. The Roots supercharger (blowing eight pounds) is driven from the nose of the crankshaft. On the left of the blower is affixed a dual Memini carburetor, and from its right springs an amazing tour de force in light-alloy casting technique — the intake manifold. The wafer-thin cooling fins following its every convolution must be seen to be believed.

The clutch is a small, dry, multi-disc affair. The satisfying and tough transmission has four, non-synchronized speeds.

The 109-inch chassis is quite conventional, though made of the finest materials. The bodies were usually by Zagato; simple, graceful two-seaters with lean sweeping fenders and typically Italian, high-off-the-ground running boards. Within the tucked-in uncallipygian tail there is room for a top, a pair of batteries, a 30-gallon gas tank and, surprisingly, some luggage.

When you climb behind the wheel, after having first tickled the carburetor to flood it, you wonder how anyone with a normal behind can sit next to you, for the cockpit is only half as wide as the front seat of a 1961 Pontiac. The instruments are cunningly hidden under the cowl. To see them you must bob your head, thus blowing the horn on the steering-wheel center with your chin.

Turn the key and press the starter button and the engine literally explodes into action. Select first gear and let in the clutch (which has an undeserved reputation for fierceness) and you're off with the oddly Alfa-ish whew-p, whew-p from the exhaust. The gears, the camshaft drive, the blower add to the music. As you go up through the gears you realize that this little baby can *go!* (0 to 60 in under ten seconds — 105 mph in high — in the latest types of 1750 which put out 105 hp.)

The steering is characteristically Alfa. You learn not to grip the wheel, but to let it oscillate through your fingers slightly as the front wheels hit irregularities in the road. Otherwise the car snakes.

You take corners at impossible speeds—I firmly believe a 1750 will outcorner any car ever built—by just wishing the car around, helped by an almost imperceptible movement of your wrist.

The eight-cylinder, 2.3-liter Alfa which came out in 1931 (though the 1750 was made until 1934) was more of the same, but more powerful (140 hp). Its blower, however, lay alongside the engine and was driven by a train of gears. Racing versions of the 2.3 and the later 2.9 ended Bugatti's mastery of road racing.

The 2.9 Alfa Romeos had basically the same eight-cylinder, twin-cam engines as the 2.3's, but by 1938 the 8C-2900-B, as it was known, had become a little decadent, with enveloping bodywork and independent front suspension. Although its 180-hp engine could propel it at 125 mph, it wasn't nearly as much fun to drive as the Alfas of a decade earlier.

Right after the war Alfa Romeo brought out a 2½-liter machine at a fabulous price, but I think they'd just as soon forget about that one.

The nicest machines Alfa Romeo makes today are the Giulietta's, but I do miss that wonderful intake manifold of the 1750.

HISPANO-SUIZA

Had you been a gay young Continental in the feverish Twenties, a dashing blade who found it absolutely necessary to transport himself and his blonde of the moment from Maxim's in Paris to the gaming tables of Monte Carlo, there would have been only one eminently correct machine for the journey — a Hispano-Suiza.

True, a Bugatti or two on a similar errand might have leaped past you with a sound of tearing calico issuing from its exhaust, but the young man in its cockpit would have had at least part of his mind occupied with things mechanical: for instance, was that No. 1 plug oiling up again? You in the Hispano could keep more of your mind on the delicious creature at your left. As for the English milord in his Silver Ghost Rolls-Royce — a rattle of gravel against the varnish of his elegant Hooper coachwork and you were by him.

The words "Grand Marque" might well have been coined to describe the great Hispanos of the Twenties: the 37.2 hp model and the 45 hp Boulogne which developed from it.

Mark Birkigt, their designer and, with Royce and Bugatti, one of that great triumvirate of original automotive minds, first showed an awed motoring world his new car in 1919. Not unexpectedly its engine was based on the highly successful Hispano-Suiza aircraft engines which he had designed and of which some 50,000 had been built to power the French

Preceding pages: Leslie Saalburg's water color of a 1926, wood-bodied, 37.2 hp Hispano-Suiza. A Boulogne 45 hp model appears above, its cleanly designed overhead-camshaft engine below.

Spads, the English SE-5's and American JN4H's of the First World War. Such famous aviators as René Fonck, Eddie Rickenbacker, and Georges Guynemer had flown behind them to many victories. It was from Capitaine Guynemer's personal blazon that the stork, which graced the radiator caps of post-war Hispanos, was evolved. (The Hispano instruction book, worried lest careless owners harm this stork, warned: "The stork placed on the radiator plug is silver plated. Never brighten it up with copper-cleaning substances.")

The aero-engine had been a V-8 with a single camshaft over each bank, but the new car engine was a 6½-liter six, like one of the banks with two cylinders added. It too had an overhead camshaft. The method of valve adjustment — almost identical to that of the Alfa Romeos of the late Twenties and Thirties — employed gear-toothed steel mushrooms upon which the cams pressed to open the valves. The aluminum cylinder block was merely a cooling chamber into which the outwardly threaded, nitrided steel cylinders were screwed. This "cooling jacket," to quote the instruction book again, "is made corrosion-proof by a special process of enameling under pressure." The seven-bearing crankshaft which had completely circular webs was made from a single billet of steel weighing some 700 pounds before machining and only about 90 pounds after. I remember a mechanic striking one lightly with a steel rod to let me hear the sweet, bell-like sound it made.

The engine had dual ignition by specially designed coils and distributors, a twin carburetor whose innards could be instantly detached with a lever, and a huge oil filler into which a whole can of oil could be dumped at one swoop. The entire engine was of such wonderfully clean design — all shining black lacquer and bright aluminum — as to make one swoon with covetousness.

The first 37.2's engines turned over quite slowly (aircraft practice again) to deliver their power. At 3,500 rpm the engine generated 135 hp, but at a mere 2,000 rpm, 120 hp was produced. This from a compression ratio of but 4½ to 1. So enormous was the torque that in spite of a high rear-axle ratio of 3.37 to 1, it was possible to crawl along at four mph in high gear! Who needed Hydramatic?

Power was transmitted through a single-plate clutch (a cone clutch in earlier models) and a short, stiff torque tube to a handsome rear axle (a pity it wasn't visible). The chassis was of conventional design, but quite stiff and light, with half-elliptic springs. The whole car was light for its size. The chassis weighed a mere 2,500 pounds in road trim.

The four-wheel brakes were operated by a servo-mechanism through a clutch at the side of the gearbox—à la Rolls-Royce—but Birkigt didn't copy it from Royce. Royce was the copy-cat. The finned brake drums were of aluminum with shrunk-in cast-iron liners (such as Buick recently invented). The stopping power was phenomenal. The steering—two-and-a-quarter turns from lock to lock—was light and positive, making Hispano another of those rare big cars which feel small in traffic.

I discovered this (in 1932, I think) when Ray Gilhooley, who tried to sell us used sporting cars in those days, let me drive a Boulogne he was demonstrating for me. With its 133-inch wheelbase, the car was no baby and as I was driving it down Broadway in New York I gave the taxis swarming around me a wide berth, not engaging in any cut-and-thrust duels with them. My gingerly driving annoyed Gilhooley, who growled, "Pull over to the curb, I'll show you how to drive this bastard." And he did. With mere flicks of the steering wheel while his foot stayed well down on the gas pedal, he carved up those taxis as they'd seldom been carved before. The big car seemed to bend in its middle and sailed as effortlessly in and out of the heavy traffic as a Western Union boy (they're gone, too) on a bicycle.

I didn't buy the Hispano, though. He wanted too much for it—$150!

This Boulogne had a bigger engine than the 37.2. It had a capacity of 8 liters and was known as the 45 hp. (Both the 37.2 and the 45 were known by their British horsepower ratings.) It would do well over 100 mph. The 37.2 would approach 90 mph or so.

These glorious vehicles were in production for some twelve years, during which time they made some record runs. André Dubonnet, the aperitif manufacturer, drove the 580 miles from Paris to Nice, carrying three passengers and their luggage, in 12 hours 35 minutes. In 1921, he won the Boillot Cup at Boulogne at an average of 64 mph for 237 miles. Woolf Barnato, who later controlled Bentley Motors, took several records at Brooklands, doing 300 miles at a brilliant 92.2 mph.

Over the years, too, the Hispano became a symbol of all that was chic. It showed up in the literature of the period in books like Michael Arlen's *The Green Hat*, a bit of which I quote: "Open as a yacht, it wore a shining bonnet; and flying over the crest of the great bonnet, as though in proud flight over the scores of phantom horses, was that silver stork by which the gentle may be pleased to know that they have just escaped death beneath the wheels of a Hispano-Suiza car, as supplied to His Most Catholic Maj-

esty." There was even one opus of the gilded life called *L'homme à l'Hispano* by Pierre Frondaie.

People wonder about the name Hispano-Suiza: "What's this Spanish-Swiss stuff got to do with a French automobile?" Mark Birkigt was a young Swiss who got some rich Spaniards to back him in 1904 and formed the *Société de Construction d'Automobiles Hispano-Suiza* in Barcelona. Even the very early cars to come from Birkigt's drawing board were full of new ideas that became commonplace years later. The T-head, the cylinders cast as a unit (*en bloc*), the shaft drive with torque taken up by the rear springs (Hotchkiss drive), and, on a racing Hispano of 1912, a piston-type pump supercharger, which not only pumped mixture into the cylinders, but also pulled the burnt gases out through an extra exhaust valve.

But it was the so-called Alfonso XIII model, developed from the successful racing cars of 1910, that first made the Hispano famous. This was officially known as the 15T, and if the term "sports car" had been known in 1912, that's what it would have been called. It was a delightful little machine with a T-head, four-cylinder engine of 3,622 cc, and an incredible bore-stroke ratio of 80 x 180 mm. It would do better than 70 mph—fast for 1912—and better than 90 when souped up and stripped down for racing. Furthermore, it made a distinctive and musical exhaust noise which captivated the motor sportsmen of the day, including the Bourbon on the throne of Spain whose name it acquired.

Most of these Alfonso models were, by the beginning of World War I, being made in the recently opened factory near Paris, but the Barcelona factory continued them in production until 1920, although with a new four-cylinder, overhead-camshaft engine not unlike the aero-engine in concept.

In 1931, Hispano-Suiza took over the Ballot Company and brought out some very nice but unexciting six-cylinder, push-rod engined machines, hardly to be mentioned in the same breath with the fiery aristocrats of the Twenties.

However, there was to be one more fabulous Hispano, the V-12, which was launched in 1931, just in time for the Depression. This lordly *voiture de Grande Luxe* had a 9½-liter engine and developed 220 hp. It was capable of about 105 mph and would go from 0 to 60 in 11½ seconds, not bad for a 5,000-pound carriage.

But somehow this king of cars never generated the excitement of the 37.2. The Hispano had been a car for the great wild days of the Twenties. The Thirties were a time for lesser machines.

BENTLEY

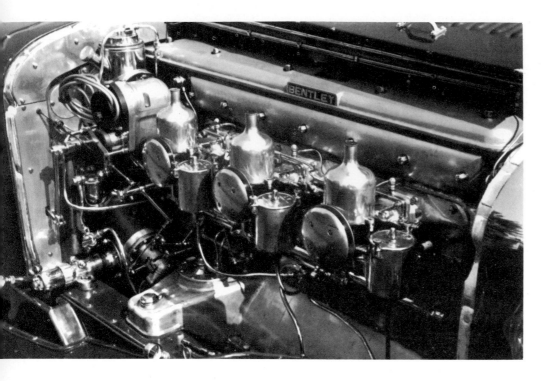

Mention the words "Bentley" and "Le Mans" to a Briton. A bugle shrills in his head, he straightens up a little, he stands with Nelson at Trafalgar, in a British Square at Omdurman.

For it was the thin green line of Bentleys at Le Mans that, in the Twenties, successfully upheld the motoring prestige of England against the onslaughts of the savage machines from the European continent and even from America (in the form of Stutzes and Chryslers).

During the Twenties, those years of the locust for other English racing machines, the Bentleys won again and again at Le Mans as no cars did before and none have since. And they won most years, as the English love to win, by nearly losing.

Their win in 1927 is a good example, albeit, perhaps, a too-oft-told tale. In the twenty-four-hour race (*Le Grand Prix d'endurance de vingt-quatre heures*) at Le Mans, south-west of Paris, three Bentleys were entered: two 3-liter cars, one 4½-liter machine. The race started at 4 p.m. Just after sundown, Leslie Callingham on the 4½, braking for White House Corner, was horrified to find a French Schneider across the road in front of him. Callingham, doing better than 80, desperately tried to skid clear of the Schneider, but his Bentley smashed itself to pieces in the right-hand ditch and Callingham went flying into the road, fortunately unhurt. George Duller, on one of the 3-liter Bentleys, came skidding and screeching into the corner and added *his* car to the shambles. S. C. H. Davis, later a famous British motoring writer, was dead-astern on the other 3-liter. He re-

members that dirt and stones on the road warned him of wildly skidding machinery. He stood on his brakes hard as he entered the wreckage-choked corner, swinging the car to confine the damage to its rear, but without complete success. The Bentley was sorely wounded. But Davis got it back to its pit—under the rules drivers did their own repairs at Le Mans—and with spit and string and wire he put things roughly to rights. Dr. Benjafield, his relief driver, took the car over and roared off at 90 in the darkness and pouring rain. A damaged headlight went out; Benjafield taped a flashlight to the windshield and rushed on, his brakes done for.

Twenty-three hours and twenty minutes after the start, this glorious wreck came into the lead and held it. It won the race at an average of 62 mph.

This was no fluke. Bentleys won again in 1928, in 1929, in 1930. In 1929, four Bentleys out of four entered crossed the finish in line-ahead formation—1, 2, 3, 4—like Admiral Beatty's Fifth Battle Squadron at Jutland.

The Bentleys of those years can rightly be compared to battle cruisers. From the 3-liter car that left the drawing board of W. O. Bentley in 1919, right up to the 8-liter of 1930, all were massive, honestly built machines. Other sports cars depended on lightness and low silhouettes to outwit the wind. The brass-bound, deep-chested, bellowing Bentleys with their in-built headwinds forced their bluff, honest radiators forward by sheer brute strength—and no nonsense about weight saving and such-like sneaky continental practices.

Walter Owen Bentley, like many other great British engineers, first learned to revere fine mechanism and honest workmanship as a premium apprentice in the shops of the Great Northern Railway. But a few years before World War I he deserted locomotives and became a partner with his brother in a small company which had the British concession for the sale of a French car, the D.F.P. (Doriet, Flandrin et Parent). For a few years the Bentley brothers had a moderate success selling, and even racing, D.F.P.'s. The war put an end to D.F.P. sales, but not before Bentley had made a notable innovation in engine construction—the aluminum piston.

Intrigued by an aluminum souvenir paperweight in the form of a piston that a French foundry had sent out to its customers, Bentley got the idea of having aluminum pistons made up for his racing D.F.P., with exciting results. Until then pistons were made of cast iron or light steel and broke at high revolutions. The light aluminum pistons not only permitted higher engine speeds but higher compressions, due to better heat dispersal. And, of course, greater engine power resulted.

During the war, W. O. Bentley sweated over the design of rotary aero engines and, in fact, succeeded in coming up with what were considered to be the most successful rotaries used in British aeroplanes, the B.R. 1 and B.R. 2 (B.R. for Bentley Rotary).

But even while he was immersed in the hectic business of aero-engine design under wartime pressures, Bentley must have been thinking of the kind of car he'd love to build and sell after the war.

By November, 1919, he had a chassis to show at the Motor Show at Olympia in London. It wasn't, however, until September, 1921, that the first 3-liter Bentley was delivered to a customer.

The 3-liter was just the car wealthy young Britons of those feverish postwar years were waiting for. It had, for its day, the speed and ferocity of a racing machine, but yet was docile enough to drive to a tea-dance in Mayfair. Almost instantly the name Bentley became synonymous with all that was smart and sporting in motor cars, and long before production ceased only ten years later, 1931, it was easily as prestigious as that of Rolls-Royce.

This 3-liter model had a four-cylinder engine of 80mm bore and a long stroke of 149mm (whatever the disadvantages of a long stroke, it certainly gives high torque at low revs). This beautifully constructed power plant had a non-detachable head with a single overhead camshaft which operated four valves per cylinder. The camshaft was driven by a vertical shaft at the front of the engine, while two magnetos supplied the sparks to two plugs per cylinder and a Smith five-jet carburetor the sustenance. These early engines had a compression ratio of only 4.3 to 1. But still had enough power (65 at 2,500 rpm) to push the car along at 80 mph. The high and fairly whippy chassis had half-elliptic springs, and a leather cone clutch transmitted the power to a robust rear axle.

But nowadays, when we talk of the 3-liter Bentley we mean the famous "Red Label" model (for the color of its radiator badge which was changed in the various types).

It was a friend's "Red Label" model which had twin S.U. carburetors and four-wheel brakes which gave me so much pleasure in the early Thirties. With its light, accurate steering—through which bumps in the road could be felt—its big, powerful, sixteen-inch brakes and a lovely burble from the exhaust, it was indeed difficult for a young fellow (which I must have been in those days) to restrain his exuberance on the road. Although its acceleration was not, by modern standards, breathtaking, it was capable of almost 90 mph.

Before the 3-liters went out of production in 1927, they were developing 88 bhp at 3,500 rpm; the specially tuned versions for Le Mans nearly 95 bhp.

During the six years or so that the 3-liter cars were made, various other models were included in the 1,600 or so machines that left the factory. (Some 500 still exist.) Among these were the "Green Label," short-chassis, 100-mph model and the standard, stodgier, "Blue Label" types.

In 1926, a 6½-liter Bentley appeared—the "Big Six"—with an engine whose six cylinders had exactly the same dimensions as the 37.2 Hispano-Suiza (100x 140mm). In this engine the camshaft, unlike that in the 3-liter, was driven by a fascinating system of connecting rods and eccentrics from the crankshaft.

A hotter version of this "Big Six" appeared in 1929, called the "Speed Six." It had twin S.U.'s (a compression ratio of 5.3 to 1 in standard form and 5.8 to 1 in Le Mans trim) and could do 100 mph.

Between these two variations of 6½-liter car, an enlarged version of the 3-liter appeared in 1927: the beloved 4½-liter Bentley. Since its four-cylinder engine had cylinders of the same dimensions as the six, many parts were interchangeable with it. These 4½'s are today considered most desirable by the connoisseurs who are the members of the Bentley Drivers Club in England. And who can blame them? For snugged down in the leather seats of an open Van den Plas four-seater, with its cutaway door for the driver's right arm, its outside brake lever, and its satisfyingly-purposeful, if not easy, gear change, a lover of vintage cars is as close to heaven as he'll ever get.

Some fifty 4½'s were supercharged; the wonder-

fully complex Roots blower complete with carburetors sat out in front of the radiator with only a coarse chicken-wire screen for protection. The supercharged cars developed 182 bhp from a ten-pound boost and were capable of 105 mph, compared to the 92 mph of the unsupercharged machines whose engines developed some 110 bhp.

In 1930, that formidable, almost unbelievable motor car, the 8-liter Bentley, arrived to stun motorphiles. This noble carriage was not designed as a sporting vehicle, but to transport nabobs in the height of luxury at speed. Most of them were limousines, but a few of them carried open coachwork. A friend of mine owns one, a short-chassis model, with a wheelbase of 144 inches. (The standard chassis was 156 inches long!) Huge as it is, it steers with the ease and precision of a racing bicycle once it is rolling, although at low speeds the steering does take a bit of muscle. The gears illustrate that old cliché, "like a hot knife through butter."

The owner tells me that he has done over 110 in his near antique, but highly tuned and lightened 8-liters

have been timed at far greater speeds. The late Forrest Lycett, for example, who devoted years to tuning his 8-liter model was timed in 1956 on the Herentals-Antwerp Express Highway in Belgium at 141.7 mph for the flying kilometer.

Bentley Motors during its short lifetime had always been in parlous financial circumstances. The company had almost faded away as early as 1926, but Woolf Barnato, a famous Bentley driver and son of Barney Barnato, the South African diamond king, put up some money, for which he got stock at bargain prices, which kept things going for a while.

In spite of their racing successes in the next five years, Bentley Motors went under in 1931. At first it was thought that Napier's would acquire the name. Indeed, W. O. Bentley even started designing what could have been one of the great cars of all time: a 6¼-liter, overhead-cam Napier-Bentley.

But it was not to be. At the last moment, in court, at the receiver's sale, Rolls-Royce snatched the prize.

In 1933 a new car, a warmed-up and lowered small Rolls appeared. It too was called a Bentley.

A battled-scarred war horse, the 3-liter Bentley of the early Twenties (far left), competes in a vintage sports-car race a few years back. The unblown 4½-liter Bentley of 1928 (left) was one of the entrants in the 1955 Anglo-American Vintage Car Rally. Its engine develops about 110 bhp and can propel the car at over 90 mph. Note the fabric-covered coachwork aft of the chrome-plated curve on the cowl and the freight-car-like bracing under the chassis frame. A lovingly cared-for, 3-liter Bentley engine (above) powered the 1926 "Red Label" model. The vertical shaft which drives the single-overhead camshaft is visible at the front of the engine. These developed 88 bhp and were able to achieve a speed not far from 90 mph. The Le Mans versions put out some 95 bhp when especially tuned. About 500 of these 3-liter machines still exist.

MERCER

We used to build great sports cars in this country—before World War I, before the term "sports car" was even heard of. The Stutz "Bearcat," the Simplex "Speed Car," the Marion "Bobcat," the Apperson "Jackrabbit," and the Mercer "Raceabout." Of all this great company, it is the little Mercer Raceabout that is today, after nearly fifty years, the most beloved. And with good reason. It wasn't the fastest or the most expensive, but it was one of those rare cars that look so exactly right and feel so exactly right to drive as to make a young man expire with yearning.

Consider the look of the Mercer Raceabout. What was there about it that made it the heart's desire of four generations?

First, it wasn't "styled" (Detroit argot for "designed"). Its appearance is but the happy result of its parts being so disposed for efficiency that their very placement makes the whole good to look upon. The chassis sat low for its day. Upon the chassis, under a simple "doghouse" hood, behind a classically-shaped, brass-bound radiator is nothing but an engine. The rear of the hood is enclosed by a slanting mahogany board carrying a few simple, brass-cased instruments. From this same board springs the long brass tube that carries the steering wheel. Aside from this, there is nothing but a pair of bucket seats. A cylindrical gas tank, a little rounded tool compartment, plus a pair of spare tires, are slung on behind. The big wheels stand unashamedly at the four corners of the machine, their nakedness but skimpily covered by austerely shaped mudguards. There was no useless decoration, except for a touch of striping on the paintwork and the honest gleam of brass for the owner to lovingly polish.

How does a Raceabout feel on the road? What's it like to drive?

Ralph Buckley, the famous car restorer and Mercer exponent, once let me drive his. This Raceabout had been literally resurrected from junk: three-fourths of a chassis frame, part of an engine; Buckley even had to make a new radiator and its brass surround. But when Buckley showed it to the man who had originally designed the Raceabout, Finlay Robertson Porter, even he could not distinguish it from a new one.

Once I got into the driver's seat, I could easily see why the young sports of Wilson's first Administration were so crazy about Mercers. You sit low, but still have perfect visibility. If you turn the steering wheel you can actually watch the right front wheel follow your action. Your right foot rests on a brass stirrup outboard of the narrow chassis. The accelerator is, of course, outside the chassis frame, too. A glass monocle, perhaps eighteen inches in diameter, mounted on the steering column keeps but part of the wind out of your eyes. Your passenger has no protection at all.

The four-cylinder, T-head engine makes a light poom-poom sound. The clutch action and gear shifting are surprisingly light and easy for a car of that period. The gears particularly are a surprise. It is possible to shift up and down noiselessly, without recourse to double clutching and with but a modicum of thought about synchronizing gear speeds with that of the engine.

I once asked Mr. Porter about his amazingly easy gearbox. "Oh, I had nothing to do with that," he said. "We just ordered the transmissions from the Brown and Lipe Gear Company and those are what they sent us."

On most cars of that period, gearshifting was just used for starting from rest or for hill climbing. But on the Raceabout the gears are meant to be used as on a modern sports car. It is possible to loaf along in high with the engine "making one explosion per telephone pole." For even at, say, 75 mph, this Mercer's engine is turning over at only 2,000 rpm. But drop down into second or third at 2,000 rpm and the Raceabout turns into the wildcat it was designed to be.

The Raceabout steers like a modern sports car, too. No, I take that back. It steers *better* than a modern sports car—more like an Alfa Romeo or Bugatti of the Thirties.

If there is anything wrong with the Raceabout, it is its miserable braking. The foot brake works on the drive shaft and its retardation is almost imperceptible. If you really have to stop, you haul back on the brake lever at the same time and wish, *hard*.

Another problem the Raceabout had was an unfortunate habit of cracking its chassis frame. Almost every one we see nowadays has been welded and reinforced. This was due to the wild abandon with which the Raceabout was driven on the appalling roads of its day—plus the fact that its shock absorbers were either seized solid, or adjusted into immobility.

The Mercer got its name from Mercer County, New Jersey. It was built in the town of Trenton, in that county, by the Roeblings, the same family that built the Brooklyn Bridge. From 1909 on, they built all types of machines, including touring cars and limousines, with L-head Beaver or Continental engines. For 1911 they announced the Type 35 Mercer "Raceabout" with a T-head, 5-liter engine, at first with a three-speed gearbox and, after 1912, with the more desirable four-speed.

The Mercer Raceabout (preceding pages)
was the supreme example of the true American sports
car of pre-Kaiser war days. Its 5-liter,
T-head engine at 75 mph was only turning over
at 2,000 rpm, giving the driver
the feeling that he was just loafing along.
This could be disconcerting when an obstacle appeared
ahead and it became necessary to apply
the rather ineffective brakes. The Raceabout
steered and handled as well as the very best European
sports cars of the Thirties. Carrying open-air
motoring to its extreme, the Mercer was never quite
the machine in which to take a girl on a date.
Affording somewhat more weather protection was the
L-head Mercer (above) which appeared in 1915.
Right: The T-head engine of a 1912 Mercer.

The factory guaranteed a mile in 51 seconds, but many Raceabouts were faster. Like the Bugattis of a later day, it was the kind of car a man could take from the showroom, drive to a race, enter, and win.

Specially prepared Mercers came in fourth and third, in 1912 and 1913 at Indianapolis, and in 1914 Eddie Pullen averaged no less than 87.8 mph in the Corona Road Race.

Mercer Raceabouts cost about $2,200 when they were new. All told, some 500 were made before they went out of production in 1915, but only some two dozen of them now survive. Ralph Buckley told me recently that at least one oil-rich Texan has been offering $10,000 for a nice Raceabout, with no takers.

In 1915 an entirely different machine was introduced, what we now call the L-head Mercer. The T-head was dropped, the car now had left-hand instead of right-hand drive, and Mr. Porter was no longer the designer. The new Raceabout, as it was still called, was designed by Erik H. Delling. The Type 22-70 engine of this new car developed more power— some 70 hp against the 50 hp of the old T-head—and was notable for having the unusual bore-stroke ratio of 3¾ inches to 6¾ inches, which required connecting rods as long as your forearm—fifteen inches!

Furthermore, it had an electric starter, windshield (in 1919), and even *sides* to the bodywork. Even though the new L-head cars were heavier (3,500 pounds) than the T-heads (2,850 pounds) they were guaranteed to do a mile in 48 seconds.

By 1918, the Roeblings, who had made the Mercer such a success, were dead and from then on the company, in the hands of hard-headed businessmen, went downhill until it ceased production in 1925.

163

A 1911 model still lacked front doors.

By 1912, the tourer had grown front doors.

"Flivver" still had gaslights in 1914.

"Lizzie" entered high society: a 1915 town car.

This early sedan boasted center doors, carriage lamps.

An electrically lighted, vertically styled, 1917 model

Bedizened with brass in 1909

Brass radiators lasted until 1915.

A classy Ford "Tudor" of 1923

Of all the automobiles ever built, none did more to change the world than Henry Ford's Tin Lizzie.

Its life span almost exactly paralleled that of Henry Royce's Silver Ghost—from 1908 to 1927—but while only a few thousand Rolls-Royces were made in those nineteen years, 15,456,868 Model T Fords rattled their way off the assembly lines. On one busy day, October 31, 1925, an amazing 9,109 flivvers were built. Between 1917 and 1927 Ford made half the cars produced in the United States.

Like a million other farm boys of the Eighties, Henry Ford was crazy about mechanisms. At first he tinkered with clocks and watches, but by the early Nineties, when he had a job with the Detroit Edison Company, he was desperately involved with an automobile. In 1896 he finally got it running.

This brakeless, reverseless, two-cylinder buckboard wasn't much of a machine compared to the fairly sophisticated automobiles already running in Europe, but it was good enough to get some friends of Ford's to advance him a little money to go on experimenting. By 1899 he had built a much better machine, quit his job with the electric light company and become superintendent of the Detroit Automobile Company, one of the myriad little outfits rushing into the car business.

Ford already had his mind on a cheap car almost anyone could afford, but he wasn't the boss, and the Detroit Automobile Company went under while trying to sell the few dull and expensive machines it succeeded in building.

Now, to make his name known, Ford began to build racing cars. With spectacular success he beat the great Alexander Winton's 70 hp machine and almost immediately new money became available to start the Ford Motor Company, first as a partnership with

An expensive machine, this six-cylinder Model K Ford (top)
cost $2,800 and was not a success. By the time the Model T went
out of production in 1927, over 15,000,000 of them had been
built. About to be displaced by the Model A, the T,
like the 1926 model roadster (above), had begun to look pretty
snappy. Although it still had the pedal-controlled
planetary transmission, it had straight-line bodywork, domed
fenders, wire wheels, and even bumpers.
It was a wonderful value. In 1926 it cost only $380.

Alexander Malcolmson, a Detroit coal dealer, in
1902, and then as a corporation in 1903. In the five
years or so until he hit the jackpot with the Model
T, Ford brought out a series of fairly successful light
cars and at the insistence of his partners, one fancy
lemon, the Model K. This was not at all the sort of
machine Henry wanted to manufacture. It was big,
it had a fuel-hungry six-cylinder engine, and it was
expensive. Even at the high price of $2,800, the com-
pany lost money on it. Further, it had a too-flimsy
planetary transmission, which was most likely Ford's
fault (he just loved planetaries and later put one in
the Model T).

By 1906, Ford was building the Model N and was
approaching his ideal of "The Universal Car," as he

called it. This Model N was the direct ancestor of the
T—it even looked like a T in the shape of its radiator
and its transverse front spring.

But although thousands of N's and its de luxe versions, the Models R and S, were sold at quite low
prices (the N cost a mere $600), they had not acquired
that stamp of pure genius which was to make "Ford"
the best known car name in the world.

On October 1, 1908, the most maligned and the
most praised, the most reliable and the most cantankerous, the ugliest and the most functional of all
cars was born—the Model T.

It was about as beautiful as a kitchen coal stove
precariously balanced on a cat's cradle of springs
and rods above four impossibly skinny wheels. Its
huge top, which ballooned aloft over the passengers,
may have offered protection from the elements, but
it looked monstrous.

Contrary to that oft-quoted remark of Henry
Ford's: "They can have any color they like as long
as it's black" (which he very likely never said), the
early Ford T touring cars were dark Brewster green
with red striping. There were even very early T's with
red bodies!

But looks meant little to tough old Henry. When
someone asked him how far behind the front seats
the back seats were to be placed, he said, "Far
enough for a farmer to get his milk cans on the floor."
And with the farmer in mind again, the T was hardly
more complicated than a plow. Baling wire, pliers, a
screw driver could keep one going, and in later years
you could buy parts for Ford T's in the dime store.

With all its simplicity, the Model T was full of
innovations:

Its 2.9-liter, 22-hp, four-cylinder engine was cast
in one piece, but it had a detachable cylinder head in
a day when such a convenience was unheard of. Although the very earliest European machines' heads
had been made separately because of casting problems, most manufacturers fought shy of having to
make a water-tight, gas-tight joint at such a crucial
point in their engines.

The narrow chassis sat on transverse springs fore
and aft which made for steering of phenomenal lock
—a T could turn on an Indian-head penny.

The driver sat on the left where he belonged in a
right-side-of-the-road country. The early Autocar
was first with the notion, but Ford made it stick. In
a few years most U.S. car builders had followed suit.

The Model T made its own electricity from a magneto built into the flywheel. (I can remember very
well playing with the greasy horseshoe magnets we
pried out of the derelict Fords with which the junk-

yards of my youth abounded). The English Lanchester had a similar magneto and might well have given Ford the idea.

The engine, clutch, transmission, flywheel, and universal joint all shared a common oil chamber; when you poured oil into the crankcase every part was certain to get some.

Although the last days of the T slightly antedated my debut as a driver, I can well remember the oddities of control necessary when managing one. The T, of course, had no hand gearshift. Its two speeds and reverse were controlled by means of three foot pedals, which tightened the brake bands of the planetary transmission and that of the foot brake inside the gearbox. A hand lever operated the tiny brakes on the rear wheels. There was no gas pedal. To vary engine speed you diddled with a lever on the steering column, where also lived the spark-control lever. Once the engine was started—until 1919, by hand cranking —you pressed the left-hand pedal halfway down, which put the gears in neutral. Then you released the handbrake, which had kept the gears in neutral while you cranked. To get moving, you tramped all the way down on the same left-hand pedal, meanwhile opening the hand throttle. You were now in low. At about eight miles an hour you eased the throttle a bit and took your foot right off the pedal. With a neck-snapping bound and a mournful howl from the transmission the flivver catapulted ahead. You were now in high, in which speed you could do 40 mph if all was well with the engine.

If you wanted to back up, you pushed the left pedal down again halfway, into neutral, and trod on the middle pedal. You could if you liked use this middle pedal as a brake. (The instruction book recommended this to equalize band wear.) Being able to bound back and forth like a rubber ball on an elastic was one of youth's joys in a T.

To stop you tramped on everything. It didn't matter which two pedals your feet hit.

T drivers became expert at driving rearward, for even in low, due to chronically worn bands, smallish hills were sometimes unclimbable. Undaunted, drivers went up backwards. But there was another reason for being a virtuoso in reverse. The gas tank was under the front seat and fed the carburetor by gravity. With a near-empty tank on a hill the gas was unable to climb up to the carburetor. Going up backward raised the tank above the carburetor.

With all its little foibles, the T was nearly unbreakable, mostly because it was made of superlative materials, better than many of the more expensive machines of its day. In 1905, Henry Ford was at a

speed trial on a Florida beach when a French car wrecked itself. Impressed by its stamina before the debacle he quietly put a bit of metal from its engine in his pocket. Back in Detroit, Ford had a metallurgist analyze the fragment and discovered that its was chrome-vanadium steel. From then on every Ford car had some of this steel in its construction, made in a small steel mill built by Ford.

As the farmers realized that here, at last, was a cheap, reliable machine to lift them out of the mud, to set them free from the horse, and to end their isolation, production zoomed and prices went down.

In 1909, when the first T's reached their owners, the price was $850. By 1912, it was $600; by 1918, $450. In 1924 it reached its all time low of $290. Just before it went out of production in 1926 it cost $380. But by now it had electric starting and lighting and detachable wire wheels with balloon tires.

Of course, it was mass production that made these incredibly low prices possible. And although Ford had certainly not invented mass production, he was the first to use it on such a colossal scale. In August, 1913, it took twelve-and-a-half man-hours to build a chassis. But as the technique of the assembly line was perfected the time dropped. By December, 1913, it was two hours and thirty-eight minutes, by January, 1914, one hour and thirty-three minutes. After that the factory remained silent on how few man-hours it took to whip out a Tin Lizzie.

Although the Model T gave way to the Model A in 1927, it still lives on. For it is the most popular (especially the brass-radiatored, wooden-dashboard examples of pre-1915) of all the machines treasured by antique-car collectors. I didn't say the most desired. That is still the Mercer Raceabout.

Tin Lizzie's mother: the Model N of 1906 was directly related to the Model T of two years later. It had a four-cylinder, 15 hp engine, and was sold for $600.

ASTON MARTIN

Should some fairy godfather offer me my pick of the world's cars as a lordly, damn-the-cost present, I would certainly look long and hard at the DB4-GT Aston Martin before making up my greedy little mind. For this noble vehicle stands beside the 250-GT Ferrari as one of the great sports cars of our time.

Although the origins of the Aston Martin go back through several changes in management and ownership to 1913, the basic concept of what kind of car an Aston should be has changed but little down the years. In fact, Lionel Martin said one time that his ideal in a car was the combination of the qualities of a Bugatti and a Rolls-Royce.

Martin had an agency with a man named Robert Bamford for the sale of Singer cars in those automotively mixed-up, halcyon days before World War I, when car dealers so often were racing drivers and car designers as well as business men.

At first, Martin and Bamford raced specially tuned Singers and even offered these reworked machines for sale. But Martin was dissatisfied and decided that Bamford and Martin ought to turn out a high-quality sports car under their own marque.

The new machine was to be assembled from components built to their design by outside suppliers. Only the engine was already in existence: a 1389 cc, four-cylinder, L-head, 1400 Coventry-Simplex of excellent design and workmanship. Martin couldn't wait to try it out and dropped it into a small 1908, Bugatti-designed, Isotta-Fraschini racing chassis.

This strange, albeit high-quality, hybrid was called an Aston Martin (combining the name of Martin, who was much more involved with it than Bamford, and part of the name of Aston-Clinton Hill where the special Singers had done well in competition).

It wasn't until 1921, after the War, that an actual prototype of the new Aston Martin appeared, and even then changes were made before any cars got into private owners' hands.

The first L-head Aston Martins, true to the Bugatti-ish ideals of Lionel Martin, had first-class road holding, excellent two-wheel brakes (although slightly later models were among the first to have four-wheel brakes) and precise, quick steering by Marles. Marles, by the way, have long built superb steering gear for sports cars, but Martin had the steering boxes disassembled and even more accurately refitted to his standards. The chassis was underslung at the rear, with semi-elliptic springs all around (although a few earlier examples had three-quarter elliptics aft).

By now the four-cylinder engine was of 1487 cc to allow it to race in the 1500 cc class. It had a non-detachable head, a single carburetor, and a hefty three-bearing crankshaft. A feature to delight people who love interesting mechanical gadgetry was a trick oil filter sunk into one of the engine bearer arms. On the opposite front bearer arm was an oil filler whose lid, when raised, automatically opened an overflow tap in the engine to prevent overfilling. A multi-plate Hele-Shaw clutch (whose metal plates were pressed into concentric V's, something like the diaphragm of an aneroid barometer), a four-speed gearbox, much like a Bugatti, in appearance and finish (but with constant-mesh gears incorporating a device for locking them into the gear selected), and a torque tube transmitted the power back to a fully floating rear axle. Although capable of only some 75 mph in standard form, racing versions were surprisingly fast for their day, one of them pushing the 1500 cc hour record up to 86.21 mph with Kensington Moir at the wheel.

About the only thing one can hold against the Aston Martin people of that period was the ineffably cute names they gave their racing cars—"Bunny," "Sweet Pea," "Razor Blade"—some of which, by the way, had experimental twin-overhead-camshaft engines.

In spite of a comparatively low chassis price of $3,000 and the financial support of that famous and wealthy sporting motorist, Count Louis Zborowski, Bamford and Martin had rough sledding. By 1926, a mere fifty cars had been sold. But before the name Aston Martin disappeared altogether a new company was formed.

During the early Twenties a young, Italian-born engineer named Augustus Cesare Bertelli, in company with a man named W. S. Renwick, was experimenting with a new type of engine and built a car in which to run it on the road. They called this prototype machine an R & B.

When Bamford and Martin folded up in 1926, Ber-

Among the great sports cars of our day, standing as an equal of the Mercedes-Benz 300 SL and the 250-GT Ferrari, is the superb British Aston Martin DB4 and its more potent twin, the DB4-GT. The DB4-GT's engine develops 302 hp, the less powerful DB4, 240. Yet, it was this "street" Aston which performed the incredible feat of accelerating from a standstill to 100 mph and then braking to a stop—all within 27 seconds. With a normal rear-axle ratio of 3.54:1, the DB4-GT is capable of 138 mph. If you want "real" speed you can order it with a 2.93:1 axle and, according to the factory, reach 170 mph.

Aston Martin from its earliest days has engaged in racing. Clive Gallop (left) appears at the wheel of the 16-valve racing Aston which ran in the French Grand Prix at Strasbourg in 1922. Although it retired, it lapped the circuit at 75 mph. During the Thirties, Aston Martin produced a series of "he-man" 1,500 cc sports cars. The "Ulster" (below) was one of the more potent of these and could reach the magic 100 mph. This example left the factory in 1934 and is said to have been in action at Le Mans in the 1935 race. Below are visible the wind wings which become wind screens.

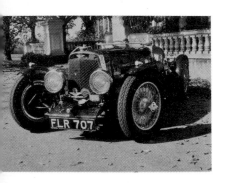

telli and Renwick, along with Martin, the Baron Charnwood, and a man named Benson, organized a new outfit called Aston-Martin Motors Ltd., in Feltham, a London suburb.

Bertelli's first Aston, which came out in 1927, was an almost entirely new machine, but he retained one important feature of the old cars—their superlative quality. In their heyday (and even now, if you can find one), the Bertelli Astons were among this world's more desirable sporting conveyances.

The unusual feature of Bertelli's new engine was its cylinder head, shaped like the inside of a pitched roof; the spark plug was at the peak, but the valves, instead of being placed one on each side of the plug, were both placed on the same side of the peak. A single, chain-driven overhead camshaft actuated the valves through rockers. It was possible to do a carbon job without disturbing the timing by unhooking the camshaft sprocket and hanging it in a little, specially made aperture in the head.

A distinguishing mark of Astons for the ten years or so of Bertelli's reign was an oil tank with a big, plated filler cap between the chassis members, forward of the radiator. This was part of the dry sump lubrication system that was such a nice feature of these cars. Sitting away out front it helped cool the oil a bit; it made for better ground clearance (the crankcase could be much shallower since it did not have to

serve as a deep oil reservoir—and, of course, it looked interesting). Engine oil from this tank was circulated through the engine and back to the tank.

Another unusual trick was the way the water pump circulated coolant only through the head by the natural movement of water of varying temperatures (thermo-syphon). The rest of the 1½-liter engine was fairly orthodox, with twin S.U. carburetors and a three-bearing crankshaft. The four-speed, close-ratio gearbox was not integral to the engine, but separated from it by a short driveshaft. Bringing the gearbox well back permitted the use of a short, stubby gear lever, perhaps the first of the type that is now a distinguishing characteristic of sports cars. A torque tube transmitted the drive to an underslung worm gear in the rear axle. This worm gear, stubbornly retained by Bertelli, was one of the few Aston parts that was not only unreliable, but wasteful of power.

Only a very few Astons actually reached private owners until 1930, when the "International" close-coupled four-seaters were introduced. Capable of barely 80 mph, these machines certainly looked much faster. In fact, their look alone was enough to make any sports-car lover dissolve with desire. I have always felt that they were the most beautiful sports cars ever built. Without any fraudulent "styling" or "streamlining," they looked just right for the job. Simple, rather angular hoods with lots of louvers;

helmeted, cycle-type fenders attached to the back plates of the brakes, so that they steered with the wheels; plated, outside exhaust pipes, and knock-off wire wheels all added to their delectable appearance.

But it wasn't all looks. These Aston bodies were wonderfully solid and well made by A. C. Bertelli's brother, Harry, who ran the body building department in a corner of the factory.

During those drear and depressed Thirties, other models of the Aston Martin were bravely brought forth. In 1932, after Bertelli and a co-driver named Driscoll won the Biennial Cup at Le Mans, it was inevitable that a "Le Mans" model should be introduced. In 1933, the Mark II appeared with a more highly tuned engine, supposedly capable of developing 75 bhp, quite high for a 1500 cc engine in those days. Now, too, the separate gearbox disappeared, as well as the torque-tube worm drive, which gave way to Hotchkiss drive.

One day in 1937 my brother Arthur and I were driving near Roosevelt Field, Long Island, in a 1750 cc, unblown Zagato Alfa Romeo when we fell in with a Mark II Aston being driven by George Rand, now an important official of the F.I.A., the august body which controls the world's racing. We were itching to drive each other's cars and we swapped. Immediately we started racing. George, in our Alfa, just left the Aston standing. But so comfortable, smooth, and rattle-free was the Aston and so refined in its manner of running, compared to the Spartan furnishing and seating of the Alfa, that I think I would have traded George even-up on the spot had he been willing.

This Aston, as I recall, had glass wind wings which could be detached and clipped into slots on the dash to serve as small racing wind screens when the main windshield was folded down. Very neat.

After the Le Mans model came the "Ulster," a much more potent machine capable of the magic 100 mph. Sadly, however, the Aston was beginning to lose something. There were now more stampings and fewer hand-finished castings in it. It was losing its precise, handbuilt charm.

In 1936, a 2-liter Aston came out, without cycle fenders and sump lubrication. This four-cylinder 15-98 was fitted with a synchromesh gearbox, a clue to the feeling that the old Aston was perhaps too "tough" a car for the new generation of drivers.

For the hardier, old-school driver, a new "speed model" was offered which *did* have a dry sump and a crash-type gearbox; 100 hp was available at 5,000 rpm in this machine.

Just prior to World War II, an experimental car called the "Atom" (really!) was built, using the 2-liter engine. This machine had an integral body-chassis and was the forerunner of the formidable Astons of today. During the war, Claude Hill, who designed this new car, continued developing the 2-liter, open sports machine. It was one of these cars which, in the hands of the late "Jock" Horsfall and Leslie Johnson, won the Belgian twenty-four-hour race at Spa in 1948.

In 1947, David Brown, head of the huge tractor and gear factories bearing his name, bought out Aston Martin and continued the development of the 2-liter. He also bought the ancient firm that produced the Lagonda. In 1950, the new company dropped the Aston 2-liter engine and decided to use the twin o.h.c. 2.6 liter engine that W. O. Bentley had designed for the Lagonda.

The new Aston which evolved was known as the DB2 (DB for David Brown). It had a six-cylinder (2580 cc) engine which developed 105 bhp at 5,000 rpm; a "Vantage" engine with a higher compression head developed 120 hp. The valves were operated by chain-driven camshafts in the cast-iron cylinder head, which had hemispherical combustion chambers. The crankshaft of this power plant (and, until recently, that of subsequent Astons) was supported on four large ring-type main bearings which were assembled on the shaft before being slid endwise into the rigid crankcase.

These earlier DB Astons also had an unusual body-cum-chassis whose entire coachwork forward of the windshield could be tilted upward to expose the engine, suspension, and other viscera to public view. There have been claims that this arrangement tended toward rattling, but I never found it so.

These DB2's were fast and would go from 0 to 60 in twelve seconds, but they were only a beginning. In the years since 1950, Aston Martins have been among the most successful sports-racing cars in the world.

The current Aston Martins—the DB4 and the DB4-GT (Grand Touring)—now have 3.6-liter engines with aluminum blocks and heads. They still have twin-overhead camshafts, but the trick crankshaft is gone. The new crankshaft has seven bearings and was proved in the racing Astons.

The DB4-GT puts out no less than 302 real horses at 6,000 rpm, the cooking DB4 a mere 240 bhp at 5,500. But it was one of these less puissant Astons that accelerated from zero to 100 mph and then braked to a standstill, with its four-wheel disc brakes, in a mere 27 seconds.

I could go on and on about their amazingly good road-holding, their precise steering, their beautiful coachwork—but I won't, for I'll just be writing myself into wanting to buy one. I'll just remind myself of one thing: they cost too damn much money!

DUESENBERG

In some of the ad pages of *Vanity Fair* in the early Thirties, you'll find full-page drawings of some excruciatingly wealthy people. One is of a gent in his den, which looks the way Grand Central Station would look if it had been paneled à la Tudor by Henry the Eighth. The gent, a leonine type, in a tuxedo, of course, is seated in front of a carved stone fireplace rather larger than the gate to Track 32.

Another drawing shows an imperious beldame talking to the third gardener. Behind them stretches a manicured landscape calculated to make the Hanging Gardens of Babylon look like the planting around a traffic circle. A yachtsman, oozing billions aboard one of his J-class yachts, fills another page.

On each of the ads there is but one line of chaste lettering: "He (or She) drives a Duesenberg."

Duesenberg's ad agency knew what it was doing, for it was peddling a car only for the very rich. Duesenbergs, even in those days when a buck was still a buck, cost upward of $14,000 and I know of one with ultra-posh coachwork that cost nearly $25,000.

The tycoons got their money's worth, too, for the Duesenberg (built in Indianapolis) gave them the comfort and size and prestige of a Rolls-Royce or Isotta-Fraschini, plus the tigerish power and speed of a Bugatti (although hardly a Bugatti's handling qualities). Furthermore, it was as beautifully constructed of the very finest materials as any car, any place, any time.

Imagine what a sensation the J Duesenberg must have caused when it was announced in 1928. Here was a car of 265 hp, with a top speed of 116 mph which would do 90 mph in *second* gear. This in a day when 100 hp and 90 mph in high was considered prodigious in this country.

The Duesenberg engine was a straight-eight of just under 7 liters. Its four valves per cylinder were operated by chain-driven, twin-overhead camshafts. It had aluminum pistons and connecting rods and a chrome-nickel-steel crankshaft with five main bearings no less than two and three-quarters inches in diameter. Although the crankshaft was carefully balanced at the factory, it had a unique vibration damper bolted on between No. 1 and No. 2 cylinders, consisting of two cartridges — one on each side of the crank cheek — 94 per cent full of mercury. The mercury churning about inside the cartridges effectively absorbed any torsional vibration. This huge engine developed its peak horsepower at 4,200 rpm, very high when you consider the weight and size of its reciprocating parts and its fairly long stroke of 4¾ inches. But Duesenberg engines were built to stay in one piece—as is proved by the number of them still running as sweetly as they did thirty years ago.

Three-speed gearboxes transmitted the drive from a two-plate clutch by way of a torque tube to the hypoid rear axle which had a duralumin housing. The semi-floating axles were an amazing 2³⁄₁₆ inches in diameter, but were bored out to save weight. You find this concern for weight-saving in greater use of light alloys than was common in those days — but not in places where weight-saving meant sacrificing strength. The alloy-steel chassis frame, for example, had a depth of 8½ inches and had six cross-members. Like Bugatti, Duesenberg knew that a rigid chassis meant good roadholding.

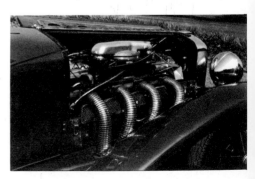

Preceding pages: "SJ" supercharged Duesenberg. This 1935 model was one of only two such short-chassised machines ever built. Its straight-eight, twin-overhead-cam, blown engine (above) was said to develop 320 bhp. The short wheel base (142½-inch) roadster accelerated from zero to 100 mph in 17 seconds and did 104 mph in second gear. Left: An unblown "J" Phaeton.

Springing was by semi-elliptics all around. Braking was hydraulic.

The Duesenberg had a fascinating dashboard. In addition to the expected instruments, it boasted an altimeter-barometer, a tachometer, a stop-watch chronometer, and a brake-pressure gauge. It also had four warning lights which were wired to a sort of mechanical brain. One of these lights went on every 750 miles to remind the driver to change the oil, another glowed at 1,500-mile intervals to tell him the battery needed water. The other two were connected to an engine-driven chassis lubricator. If this was sending the right doses of oil to various destinations, like the clutch throwout bearing or the spring shackles, a red light signaled that all was well. If its reservoir was empty a green light glowered at you.

In 1932 an even more potent Duesenberg was produced: the SJ (S for supercharger). This one had a vertical centrifugal blower which operated at six times engine speed. At 4,000 rpm it blew at five pounds, but revolved at 24,000 rpm. Centrifugal blowers, a peculiarly American type, don't do much at low revs, but even so the SJ engine was claimed to put out 320 hp; 104 mph in second gear, and over 130 mph in high. A 5,000-pound roadster on a short wheelbase (142½ inches) it could, they said, accelerate from 0 to 100 in seventeen seconds!

Nowadays some suspicious types (especially British motoring journalists) tend to pooh-pooh these claims, but Jim Hoe, who operates a repair establishment in Weston, Connecticut, that is the mecca of Duesenberg owners, tells of an *unsupercharged* J that, when properly breathed upon, puts out more horses than was claimed for the SJ.

He once took me for a ride in his lightened, almost bodyless Duesenberg, which he hurled about as if it were a tiny sports car. I took no acceleration times; if I had carried a stop watch I would most likely have crushed it in my clutching hand, for the acceleration of this saurian machine was, to state it conservatively, unsettling to the nerves.

Only once did I see a Duesenberg in action on the road in its heyday. I was driving a 1750 cc blown Alfa Romeo on Mr. Vanderbilt's Long Island Motor Parkway one day in 1933 and I was, I fondly imagined, acting quite the racing driver. I must have been doing about 75 (on one of the rare straight stretches) when, with a long trumpet blast, a black convertible sedan shot by me like the Twentieth Century Limited passing a hand car. I tried to catch it, and even though I gained a bit on the twisty parts of that narrow road, all I ever saw again was that huge light with the stenciled letter S-T-O-P which was standard

on Dusies, blinking on when the driver braked for the bends. I never even got close enough to find out if it was a J or an SJ.

Duesenberg built only chassis. Coachwork was built to the buyer's order by the great American bodybuilders who still existed in those early days of the Depression: Murphy, Le Baron, Judkins, La Grande (Duesenberg-owned). These, and others, constructed the loveliest sporting roadsters and double-cowl phaetons that have ever been seen in this country. And for gentry of more formal tastes they built, usually on the long, 153-inch chassis, stiff-necked, damn-the-chauffeur town cars to satisfy even the stuffiest nouveau-riche Midwesterner. Upholstered in the softest of leathers, the finest of broadcloths, and stuffed with goosedown; paneled in exotic woods and trimmed in gold and mother-of-pearl or ivory, with complete sets of instruments for the rear passengers, the ridiculous luxury of these bodies has never been surpassed by the fanciest *carrossiers* of Europe. Not that they didn't try, for some of them, too, built bodies for the relatively few Duesenbergs that were sold abroad.

The J and SJ Duesenbergs were by no means the first cars Fred Duesenberg and his brother, August, had built. Fred was the leader and, like Royce and Bugatti, he was a self-made engineer. Coming from Germany as a boy in 1885 he had, by 1903, already built a racing car. By the Twenties the Duesenberg was one of the more important racing machines in the world, winning the Indianapolis 500 in 1924, 1925, and 1927 after having been (in 1921 driven by Jimmy Murphy) the only American car to ever win the French Grand Prix.

In 1920 the Duesenberg Model A, based on the racing cars, with a 90-hp engine, liberal use of aluminum and four-wheel hydraulic brakes (pioneered by Duesenberg) created a stir. Although not expensive ($6,500) considering its quality, it was not a financial success and in 1926 Auburn-Cord, under the control of E. L. Cord, a shrewd stock-market operator, became Auburn-Cord-Duesenberg.

Now, for the time being, there was plenty of money and the Duesenberg J was the result.

Fred Duesenberg died in 1932 after an accident in one of his cars, but Dusies were produced until 1937 — amazing when you consider how few people would buy such a machine in the early Thirties. Of some 550 J's and SJ's manufactured, more than 200 still exist — a far greater proportion than that of any other great classic—Bentley, Bugatti, Alfa Romeo.

Perhaps they *were* built better than any other motor car ever made.

175

Grand Prix racing is the highest type of motor racing, the kind of racing that involves a very special breed of men driving very specialized cars. The Grand Prix driver is totally dedicated to winning. The Grand Prix engine is a brute of great power, yet so delicate and highly stressed as to be ever on the verge of mechanical disaster, and so fussy in its feeding habits as to gag on anything but exotic chemical mixtures.

Nonetheless, some people think Grand Prix racing is pointless. And this worries other people and prods them into making excuses for it. "The Grand Prix car of today is the touring car of tomorrow," they say. "Racing improves the breed." Or, "The racing circuit is the laboratory where new ideas are tried and proved." All of which is at least partly true.

For me, however, no excuses are needed. The excitements, the terrors, the noises, the colors of Grand Prix racing are wonderful in themselves, and the opportunity to appraise and appreciate fine driving and brilliant pit work is an added pleasure.

Until recently, only in Europe was there true Grand Prix racing—through the streets of towns. The "Race of a Thousand Corners," for instance, an insane chase through the center of Monte Carlo with thousands of spectators hanging from the balconies of the baroque buildings, a sidewalk's width from the cars. Or the Wagnerian Nürburgring, that up-in-the-clouds circuit hacked out of the Eifel Mountains in Germany, where each lap of 14.3 miles has one-hundred-and-seventy-four corners and a driver must make over fifty gear changes per lap. The "ring" has seen as many as half a million spectators, many of whom arrive days before the race and camp out in the mountains along the course.

But perhaps the typical Grand Prix race would be run on country roads outside some French town, where part of the course might be over a section of cement highway, part twisting over the tarred road through a forest.

For days before a race like this, the kiosks in Paris display posters advertising the race. The sporting newspapers like *L'Équipe* discuss it. The night before, thousands of cars head for the course, although true acolytes of the sport might have been there for

days, camping out or crowded four to a room in some bucolic fleabag. Long before dawn, special trains are already on their way, heavily laden with more spectators.

Once, in the Thirties, I took such a train to a Grand Prix in France. I found myself crowded into a compartment with five excited young Frenchmen vehemently discussing the race. Although I had little French and they had no English, I was almost instantly embroiled. We made our points by pointing at pictures of drivers and cars and scribbling figures in the margins of *l'Auto*, the prewar sporting daily.

Nothing in the world has ever stirred my blood so

Preceding pages: This Grand Prix Delage was a masterpiece of racing-car design in 1927. Its wonderfully complex, 1,500 cc, supercharged engine had eight small cylinders and ran on ball and roller bearings. Delages ran four times in G. P. races and won every time. Ray Harroun's Marmon (above) won the first Indianapolis 500 in 1911. Sunbeam-Talbot-Darracq ran similar straight-eights under all three names. Racing as an English Sunbeam (right) one of them won the Isle of Man I. T. in 1922.

much as the shriek and bellow of Grand Prix cars practicing on the course as I approached it on foot for the first time that day. As I got closer, the delicious castor smell of burnt racing-oil perfumed the air. And then when I saw the great vans which had brought the racing machines from across half a continent, vans bearing the prancing horse of Ferrari, the star of Mercedes-Benz, and the red oval of Ettore Bugatti, I almost expired with excitement.

Lounging with seeming unconcern around the vans and in the pits were the white-overalled drivers, absently watching the harried mechanics and fretful pit crews laboring over the cars. And all around were girls, gorgeous girls, hanging on the drivers, sitting on the pit counters, or frowning over still-blank lap charts and unstarted stop watches. You can see their daughters at today's races.

Then, almost suddenly, the platforms and the wattled fences were black with people. The cars stood in their places on the grid. The music from the loudspeakers stopped (you hadn't noticed it until then), and the crowd hushed. Only the photographers scuttled in and out, rapidly working the magazines of their Gaumont Spidos. As the loudspeakers gave the countdown (did they know this word then?), one and then another engine roared into life, some cranked by means of hand-held electric starters powered from storage batteries in little carts.

Ten seconds to go—and the air was vibrating with the shriek and clash of engines being blipped by their drivers. As the starter raised his flag, the engine noise rose to an unbearably shrill screaming and the cars on the grid shivered violently in a haze of oil smoke.

The flag whipped down. Like a single entity, twenty cars sprang forward in a horror of sound.

Pre-race atmosphere is still like that in Europe, and it's very much like that now at Sebring in Florida and Riverside in California.

Grand Prix racing is different at Indianapolis, Indiana. The track there is a two-and-half-mile oblong with rounded ends, upon which cars of nearly identical specifications tear around and around for five hundred miles every Memorial Day. And they buzz around fast, too. Indianapolis race cars are as rapid as any machines running anywhere.*

But they often have peculiar names, usually calculated to advertise the business of the man who is spon-

*Almost invariably they have four cylinder, 4.2-liter, twin-over-head-camshaft Meyer-Drake engines which develop over 300 bhp and are capable of urging the cars along at 180 mph. These engines are usually mounted on their sides, not only to reduce hood height, but, because Indianapolis has only left-hand turns, to throw more weight to the left for easier cornering. Since engines are virtually standardized, much ingenuity goes into chassis design,—although, oddly, rigid, non-independently-sprung front axles are almost universal. The cars have but two speeds (shifting is never done) and almost all now have disc brakes. In mechanical finish, few cars in the world approach them.

Straight-eight Ballot (left) came out in 1919 and was designed by Ernest Henry, who earlier had designed the twin-cam Peugeot. The Ballot engine was inspired by Bugatti's World War I aero engine. These 5-liter cars were capable of almost 120 mph. A team of them appeared for the Indianapolis 500-mile race in 1919, where it was expected that their chief rivals would be the new straight-eight Duesenbergs. Surprisingly, neither the Duesenbergs nor the Ballots won. The prewar, 1914 Peugeots took the race. In 1919, the Ballot did not have front-wheel brakes; they were added in 1921.

soring the car—like the McGlatchy Bagel Special, or the Spielvogel Nutcracker Special. Many of the spectators have a mid-continental aura about them. For days before the race they form long lines in front of the gates, temporarily sheltered in sedans whose windows have been covered for the sake of modesty. On the roofs of the vehicles tower home-built grandstands from which they intend to watch the race.

When the gates open, the mob engages in a mad Grand Prix of its own to be first at favored spots in the infield, usually near the corners they know from long experience will give them the best view of any sticky mishaps.

The start at Indianapolis has a flavor of its own, too. After a parade of massed brass bands in splendid uniforms, the race cars make a circuit of the track in formation, led by a pink or chartreuse convertible driven each year by some great nabob of the Detroit auto industry. As they approach racing speed, still in formation, the convertible dives off the track and the race is on.

Immediately, half the race-mad spectators lie down on the grass, cover their faces with copies of the *Indianapolis Times*, and go to sleep.

Obviously, Indianapolis has a style and tone that are individual and unique. Still, Indy is not too far out to have had European racers in its field from time to time. When Europe's spectators and drivers went off to World War I, the chief protagonists, Peugeot and Mercedes, continued to race against each other in the United States for two years. Ralph de Palma, driving his 4½-liter (ex-1914 Grand Prix) Mercedes; Dario Resta, a Peugeot. The results were inconclusive, the Mercedes winning at Indianapolis in 1915, the Peugeot in 1916. Indianapolis was not the only place where they tested each other. Among other contests was the famous one on the Chicago board track* in June, 1916, when the Peugeot and the Mercedes sped, wheel to wheel, for three hundred miles. Four miles from the finish, the Mercedes had to go into its pit with spark-plug trouble and Resta's Peugeot won at 98.6 mph.

In 1917 the United States entered the war and racing stopped. But from the aerial dogfights over the Western Front came new ideas in engine design, new techniques in construction, new ways in metallurgy. Most aircraft engines were sixes or V-12's, but Ettore Bugatti, the maverick, made an eight-in-line. Although little used in the air, it became the basis for successful racing-car engines for many years to come. Bugatti's plant in Alsace was occupied by the Germans, but it was not big enough to produce engines in volume, anyway. Other people undertook to build his straight-eight and a sixteen-cylinder version consisting of two eights geared together side by side. Among the factories building these engines were Bara, a French company whose chief engineer was Ernest Henry, late of Peugeot, and Duesenberg in the U.S.A. When the war ended, Henry went to work for the Ballot Company in Paris in order to design a racing car.

So, when Indianapolis had its first post-war Decoration Day race in 1919, what should appear but a Ballot straight-eight and a Duesenberg straight-eight. Neither of them won; a 1914 Peugeot driven by Howdy Wilcox was first.

In the next few years, however, the Ballot proved to be a quite successful racing car—and the Duesenberg was a sensation. Brash young Jimmy Murphy, in a road-racing modification of an Indianapolis Duesenberg, went over to Le Mans and won the French Grand Prix, something no American had done before and none has done since. Everything American was still exciting and admirable in those post-war days, and the French were captivated by the typically American Murphy and his *formidable* Duesenberg.

The slickly turned out Duesenberg team may have surprised the Europeans used to the rough bodywork of the usual Grand Prix machine of those days, but the superb finish and the sophisticated design of these 3-liter, single-overhead-camshaft engines and chassis astounded them, especially the beautifully executed four-wheel hydraulic brakes. The brake shoes were of spring steel, the hydraulic pistons at each wheel were machined out of blocks of marine bronze. The master cylinder was hinged to the chassis and moved as the brake pedal was depressed; the piston stood still. Oddly, the brake fluid was water with a little glycerine added to prevent freezing. It ran through a hollow front axle and kingpins to the front brakes.

*Wooden boards were once a favorite material for surfacing auto race tracks in this country. Although inexpensive to build and fast and smooth to run on, they were dangerous. They became slippery, and it was not unknown for a loose board to go through a car's radiator and impale the driver.

Although the eight-cylinder engine put out but 115 bhp, it was sufficient to push the 1,750-pound car along over the rough and rocky course at a winning average of 78.1 mph. Toward the end, it even ran with a pierced and empty radiator. Further, it set a lap record of 83.2 mph, which would not be beaten until 1929!

Now started a new era. The next eighteen years—until World War II—are considered by many to be the great period of Grand Prix racing. In the beginning, Fiat, Ballot, Sunbeam, Bugatti, Delage, Alfa Romeo, even the American Miller, all fought for supremacy. But after the mid-Twenties a pattern emerged that would last until the Second World War.

At first the Bugatti had its way. Then Alfa Romeo became the king of the racing circuits, to be displaced in turn by the unbeatable Germans, Mercedes-Benz and Auto-Union. True, these great cars won most of the races over the next fifteen years, but other contenders arose to challenge them and win important Grands Prix, too—Maserati, the English E.R.A., and Delage.

The Delage, in particular, was a fascinating, brilliantly conceived machine. Designed by M. Lory to run under the 1926-1927 international formula which limited Grand Prix engines to 1,500 cc, it was ostensibly a two-seater (although the riding mechanic was by then a thing of the past). It was very low for its time. The absence of a passenger made it possible to seat the driver with his behind almost scraping the road, and the short drive shaft beside his left elbow. The chassis was normal for its day, with half-elliptic springing and four-wheel brakes (servo-operated off the gearbox à la Hispano-Suiza). To keep the radiator low, it was placed forward of the front axle, with its bottom edge below the line of the axle.

But it is the Delage's incredibly complex, to-hell-with-costs engine that continues to astound us as it astounded people in its day. This supercharged engine had eight small cylinders, twin-overhead camshafts, and it ran on no less than sixty ball and roller bearings! The twin camshafts had nine roller bearings apiece; the magnificent, forged, one-piece crankshaft ran on nine main bearings—rollers, too. So were the bearings for the eight con-rods.

It was the incredibly complex train of gears at the front of the engine that really made it such a tour de force. Over twenty gears—all on roller bearings—drove the camshafts, the magneto, the water pump, and two oil pumps. This engine could put out 170 bhp at 8,000 rpm. The Delages ran four times in Grand Prix races and won every time. They also captured second and third place in two of the contests.

The Delage factory stopped racing in 1927, but ten years later Richard Seaman, the famous British driver, bought one of the old cars, and with the use of more modern fuel in a somewhat modified engine, was able to raise its horsepower to 195! He then went out and cleaned up in 1,500 cc class racing.

The Type 35 Bugatti, however, was the most successful racing car of all time. Ettore Bugatti certainly had been involved with racing cars for many years and with considerable success, but it was not until he evolved the Type 35 and its variations that he hit the jackpot. In 1925 and 1926, Bugattis were victorious 1,045 times. Obviously, these wins were not all in important races, for many amateurs owned Type 35's. They were not only factory racing cars, but catalogued models as well.

The chassis of the Type 35, which contributed so much to its unequalled controllability and road holding, was typically Bugatti. It had the extreme variations in depth of side members—tapering from six-and-three-quarters inches at the dash to a mere three-quarters of an inch at the front goosenecks, and tapering rearward to the reversed quarter-elliptic springs aft. In front, the Type 35's had, naturally, Bugatti's hollow, polished front axle.

The Type 35's of 1925, running under the 2-liter formula, had unblown, straight-eight engines. Bugatti inveighed against superchargers, claiming they unsportingly increased engine capacity. A vertical shaft at the front of the engine drove a single-overhead camshaft which operated three valves per cylinder. The crankshaft was the usual piece of built-up Bugatti jewelry, running in five bearings. The inner ones were roller bearings, the end ones ball bearings; the con-rods ran on roller bearings. The mechanical racket from these bearings has led many a *Bugattiste* to think his engine was about to give up the ghost. Lubrication employed the usual Bugatti system of jets squirting oil at the revolving machinery. The blocks were cast in two four-cylinder sections, but the head was in one piece. The crankcase had tubes running through it from front to rear that were sup-

INDIANAPOLIS MOTOR SPEEDWAY
15TH ANNUAL 500 MILE RACE 1927.
Frank Lockhart Miller Special.

posed to cool the oil. I doubt that this goal was ever realized.

These lovely, precisely built engines were easily a match for more puissant machinery due to their remarkable torque at low revs and their sturdy reliability. (Although they didn't develop much over 100 bhp at 5,200 rpm, they have been revved to 7,000 without disintegrating.) It was on these Type 35's that Bugatti's characteristic cast-aluminum spoked wheels, with their integrally cast-in brake drums, first appeared.

In 1926 the Grand Prix formula was reduced to 1½ liters, and Bugatti had no choice but to supercharge his new smaller engines by mounting a Roots blower, driven by gears from the nose of the crankshaft. He called this variation of the Type 35 the Type 39. At the same time he built for non-formula use *(formula libre)* his famed blown 2.3-liter Type 35B and in 1927 he added a 2-liter with supercharger—the 35C.

Although in the late Twenties the beautiful horseshoe radiator of a Bugatti was almost always first across the finish line, a new Grand Prix formula (with no engine-size restrictions) and a new contender were to bring Bugatti's supremacy to an end.

Alfa Romeo was to be the new king. Alfa had been successful in Grand Prix racing early in the Twenties with their P2's, but after a five-year lapse they returned in 1931 with new machines to glorify the name of Il Duce. Politics was getting into the act. Their first new car was the Type 8C—the "Monza"—with a 2.3-liter, straight-eight engine, supercharged from a blower mounted at its side and driven by gears situated between separately cast, four-cylinder blocks.

183

A René
la mia [...] amicizia -
Parigi - Giugno 1937   Gianfranco Comotti.

"Monoposto" P 3 Alfa Romeo (top). This late example, with Gianfranco Comotti in the
cockpit, has been converted from elliptic-spring suspension in the front to independent suspension on
the Dubonnet system. (Chevrolets once used this system promoted by the aperitif maker.)
Another P 3 (above), still with cart-springs, is compared with a 1924, 2 liter P 2 Alfa.

The same gears also operated the twin-overhead camshafts and the oil and water pumps. Unlike the Bugatti and the Delage, the Alfa used no roller bearings. The Monzas developed some 160 bhp at 5,200 rpm, and later Signor Vittorio Jano, their designer, raised it to about 190 bhp. It had a conventional chassis with huge brakes, and a two-seater body (required under the formula rules), even though a mechanic was not carried.

Meanwhile, Bugatti had fielded its new development, the Type 51, with twin-overhead camshafts. The 51's and the new Maseratis prevented the Monzas, even when driven by cracks like the great Nuvolari, from being decisively successful.

Alfa next experimented in some of their racers with two super-tuned, 1,750 cc six-cylinder, blown sports-car units side by side, with separate drive shafts, clutches, and gearboxes. The result was not too successful, but the next machine they produced —the Type B-2600, or the P3—was the most successful they ever raced. This was the "Monoposto." It had a single central seat, as two seats no longer were required under the rules. However, the twin-engined experiment had perhaps given Signor Jano the idea; the P3 had twin drive shafts in the form of a V, with the apex just behind the gearbox. The engine was similar to that in the Monza, except that the block was now of electron with steel liners, and two small superchargers were fitted on its left flank. It developed 180 bhp at 5,400 rpm. Between 1932 and 1935, the P3's, in the hands of such top drivers as Achille Varzi, Tazio Nuvolari, and Guy Moll, won over forty important races. In 1932 alone, P3's won the Italian, French, German, and Monza Grands Prix.

To counter the Alfa sweep, Bugatti built that greatest of racing classics, the 3.3-liter Type 59 which developed 240 bhp. Alfa Romeo increased its engine size to 2.9 liters and managed to maintain its superiority, but there was a pair of aerodynamically shaped storm clouds on the horizon—Mercedes-Benz and Auto-Union.

A new formula for the years 1934-1937 started the Germans building. The *Association International des Automobile Clubs Reconnus* (the A.I.A.C.R.), which controlled auto racing, decided that racing cars were getting too fast and proposed a new rule, hoping to slow things down. (They kept doing this and cars kept right on getting faster.) This new formula required chiefly that a racing car weigh no more than 750 kilograms (1,650 pounds) without fuel, oil, water, and tires.

In those days, rumors from Germany gave everyone gray hairs. The Germans were said to be building fantastic new machines—and the new government of Adolf Hitler was disposed to encourage the effort.

Hitler loved automobiles. Although too timid to drive a car himself, he wanted to show the world that the *Herrenvolk* could build better racing cars and drive them faster than anyone on earth—faster especially than those "*verdammte Italianer*"—and he of-

German Auto-Unions first appeared in 1934. By 1937, when the models above and left were seen, their 5.9-liter engines were developing over 600 bhp. Earlier models had fabric bodies, but these later ones were paneled in aluminum.

185

fered a prize of 500,000 Reichsmarks for the most successful German car. When the Mercedes-Benz's and the Auto-Unions appeared on the starting grids in 1934, the nightmares of Alfa Romeo, Bugatti, and Maserati became realities.

That first Mercedes-Benz of 1934—the M25—had a 3.3-liter, straight-eight, twin-overhead-camshaft, blown engine that developed 354 bhp, in a light chassis with independent suspension all around, and enveloped in a light, aerodynamic body. It instantly made every other racing car look ancient.

The Auto-Union (built by a combine that manu- factured the Horch, Audi, Wanderer, and D.K.W.

passenger cars) was designed by Dr. Ferdinand Porsche, and was known as the P-Wagen. It had a light tubular chassis—in early models the cooling water ran through the tubes—and independent sus- pension by means of torsion bars in front and a trans- verse leaf aft. Porsche put his engine in the rear. This fantastic, 4.9-liter V-16 had a single camshaft be- tween the cylinder banks which operated all thirty- two valves and produced 380 bhp at 6,000 rpm.

At first, the Mercedes and Auto-Union suffered teething troubles. Alfa Romeo, for example, took the first three places in the French Grand Prix of 1934. But after that the Germans were invincible. Until the

Tazio Nuvolari in a twelve-cylinder Alfa Romeo (upper left) at Roosevelt Raceway in 1937. The author (in beret) scowls in pit. Talbot Lago (left) had an unsupercharged 4½-liter, six-cylinder engine, which produced 250 bhp. These cars had fair success in the late Forties racing against 1½-liter, blown machines, because they made fewer pit stops for fuel. The Alfa Romeo "Alfette" (above) first appeared in 1938, then reappeared immediately after the war. These type 158-9's had 1½-liter, eight-cylinder engines and two-stage superchargers. Toward the end of their career, their engines developed no less than 310 bhp. Right: René Dreyfus, French Champion in 1939, poses with a blown four-cylinder, Type 37A Bugatti. Outwardly, the Type 37A resembled the Type 35 and its variations, but where the Type 35C's eight-cylinder, blown engine developed 130 bhp, the Type 37A developed 90 bhp, enough to propel it at over 110 mph. Note that the usual cast-aluminum Bugatti wheels have been replaced.

war, Grand Prix races were nothing more than contests between Auto-Union and Mercedes, between great drivers like Caracciola, von Brauchitsch, and Fagioli for Mercedes, and Rosemeyer and Stuck for Auto-Union.

But the manufacturers didn't let up. Mercedes enlarged the engine of the M25 to 3.7 liters. With 400 bhp it was clocked in speed trials at 197 mph for the flying kilometer! By 1937, with a further enlarged engine, it was developing 500 bhp. Under a revised 750 kg formula, a new model, the W125 using a 5.6-liter engine developed 646 bhp. It did 193 mph in road-racing trim! The W125 chassis was, however, a considerable improvement over the M25, which had been tricky to handle. It was tubular, with torsion bars and a de Dion axle astern, and a new, lower, smoother body.

The Auto-Union, too, became more powerful year by year. By 1936 its engine's size had increased to 5.9 liters and was developing over 600 bhp. Its chassis was no longer used as plumbing (leaks had shown themselves), and it now had torsion bars at the rear, too. But despite experiments with its suspension and weight distribution, the P-Wagen was decidedly tricky to drive—even compared to the Mercedes-Benz's, which the great British driver, Richard Seaman, likened to driving a family sedan at 100 mph on ice. **187**

Only one driver, Bernd Rosemeyer, ever succeeded in really mastering the peccadillos of the tail-heavy Auto-Union. Even Achille Varzi and Tazio Nuvolari disliked driving the P-Wagens.

Although Mussolini had not the millions to pour into racing that Hitler had, Alfa Romeo feverishly tried to improve their G.P. machines. In 1935 they increased their engine size to 3.2 liters and installed Dubonnet front suspension; in 1936 a 4-liter V-12 of 400 bhp was tried. It was hopeless. The Italians, with their outclassed machines (including some very potent V-8, 4.6-liter Maseratis), didn't stand a chance.

In 1936, at Roosevelt Raceway on Long Island, over a pretzel-shaped pseudo-road circuit, the Alfas and a 4.7-liter Bugatti showed what European racers could do against American cars. If I remember rightly, the best an American car could do was take thirteenth place. Nuvolari took first place, Wimille on the Bugatti, second. Even the primitive British 1,500 cc E.R.A.'s beat the pants off us. In 1937, the race was run again, but this time the Mercedes and Auto-Union teams arrived, too. The Alfas of the previous year had shocked us with their power; Nuvolari had disdainfully shown his low opinion of our drivers as he passed them on turns, seemingly going slower and

leisurely folding down his little racing windshield with one hand as he went by. But the Germans of 1937 overwhelmed us, turned our knees to jelly, and stunned our brains with the earthshaking crash and scream of their exhausts, their unbelievable speed.

Their organization and pit work were beyond our imagination. They took the temperature of the track and of their tires. They carried beautifully fitted cases containing hundreds of different-sized carburetor jets. Other fancy fitted boxes contained spark plugs of every conceivable heat range. They measured barometric pressure. One mechanic even tried to make me think that they had some mysterious new lubricant that they used instead of oil. He had a bottle-full of some blue stuff and pointed toward the oil filler of a Mercedes with it. I noticed later, however, that he poured good old American Quaker State into the Mercedes' crankcase. This display of technical proficiency apparently was intended to make us wonder how anyone could beat such Supermen in a war.

In spite of all this, when the German anthem was played and the swastika flags were displayed before the start, while the German pit staffs and drivers saluted in stiff-armed rigidity, one driver winked at me—ever-so-slightly. It was Bernd Rosemeyer. He

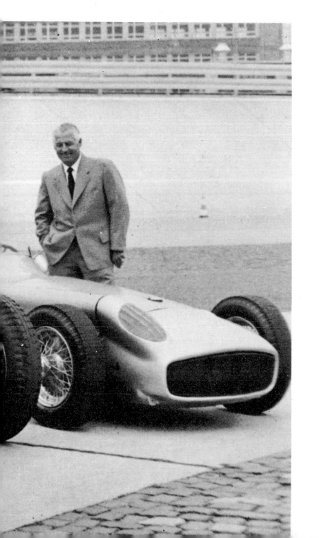

Nuvolari whips along in the 1939 Auto-Union (upper left). This twelve-cylinder model (earlier machines were equipped with sixteen) had its fuel tanks moved to the bulges on the sides of the car from their previous position behind the driver. A Teutonic reunion (left): Mercedes-Benz Grand Prix cars of 1937, 1939, and 1955 line up to be photographed. Note the removable steering wheel held over the head of the driver in center. Alberto Ascari —another great Italian driver—sits the D50 Grand Prix Lancia (above) at Monaco in 1955. This Lancia has a 2½-liter, V-8 engine with four overhead camshafts and a tubular space-frame chassis.

Above: Wolfgang Von Trips does a bit of grass cutting in a 1960 Formula I Ferrari. Upper left: The V-6 engine of the Ferrari "Dino" Formula I. At Spa, Tony Brooks drove this Vanwall (opposite page), winner of three Grands Prix in 1957, six in 1958. Its 2½-liter engine produced 270 bhp on Avgas in 1958. In 1957, when the use of racing dope was allowed, it gave 290 bhp. The British B.R.M. (upper right) has a four-cylinder, 2½-liter, twin-overhead-cam engine, capable of 275 bhp at 8,000 rpm, mounted in its tail. It is similar in name only to the sixteen-cylinder car of 1947 which developed 400 bhp, but was a failure. Right: Jim Rathman in a 1960 Indianapolis winner.

won that day on his Auto-Union, and Richard Seaman came in second. The Italians couldn't even place; Rex Mays, late of Indianapolis, driving like a demonic angel in an old Alfa Romeo discarded and sold to him by the *Scuderia Ferrari*, elbowed enough Auto-Unions and Mercedes's aside to take third place.

When a new formula was decreed in 1938, limiting engines to 3 liters, supercharged (4½ liters unsupercharged), Mercedes had ready a fabulous new creation with a V-12, twin-supercharged, 2.9-liter engine, producing 500 bhp at 8,000 rpm—at about two-and-a-half miles per gallon. This engine was set diagonally, permitting the drive shaft to pass next to the driver's central seat. These cars now had de Dion rear suspension, too. Amazingly, although they had

but half the engine capacity of the earlier machines, they were capable of 190 mph.

Auto-Union met the 3-liter rule by chopping its V-16 down to a V-12, now with three camshafts. They were having trouble with too much weight aft, so they removed the fuel tank that sat between the driver and the rear-mounted engine, slid the driver back, and put gas tanks on the sides. Alfa Romeo had no fewer than three new supercharged designs under the new 1938, 3-liter formula—a straight-eight, a V-12, and even a V-16. Maserati tried a blown straight-eight. But their situation remained almost hopeless.

With no chance of beating the Germans in formula Grand Prix racing, Alfa brought out the famous Type 158, 1½-liter car. Now they could at least beat the

English, who had been doing quite well with their 1,500 cc E.R.A.'s. This Type 158, which was to be so successful after the war, had a straight-eight, supercharged, twin-overhead-camshaft engine developing 205 bhp at 7,000 rpm. Maserati, too, built 1,500 cc machines, but it was no use. The Germans, ever eager to keep their Axis partners in their place, brought out a 1,500 cc job, too—a Mercedes V-8 that developed 260 bhp and surprised the Italians by beating them at Tripoli in 1939. Since the 1938 formula permitted the racing of 4½-liter unblown cars, two French machines appeared, the 4½-liter Delahaye and the Talbot. The advantage such cars had lay in their low fuel consumption, thereby saving pit stops. Taking advantage of this—and by dint of clever driving—the famed French crack, René Dreyfus, defeated Rudolf Caracciola and Herman Lang in their Mercedes-Benz's in the Pau G.P. in 1938.

In 1939, Grand Prix racing stopped. When it began again after the war, Bugatti was gone, and a new organization, the *Federation Internationale Automobile* (F.I.A.), was regulating Grand Prix racing. Only Italy had first-class racing machines ready to go: their 1½-liter, blown, Type 158 Alfa Romeos and the Maseratis. Also suited for modern racing, but to a lesser degree, were France's 4½-liter Talbots, and England's 1½-liter E.R.A.'s. The new F.I.A. formula for the period from 1947 to 1953 specified 1½-liter blown cars and 4½-liter unblown machines.

For the first few years nothing could touch the Alfa Romeo "Alfettes" which, through continued development and the use of two-stage supercharging (in which the compressed gas-air mixture of one blower is fed into another to be further compressed), now developed 310 bhp. Nor were the new 4 CLT/48 Maseratis, now made by a new firm to whom the Maserati brothers had sold their name, able to do much against the Alfas, although they, too, used two-stage blowers on their four-cylinder engines.

But a new star was rising which in years to come would completely dominate G.P. racing. This constellation was called Ferrari.

Before the war, Enzo Ferrari had operated the *Scuderia Ferrari* which, until 1938, had been entirely concerned with running Alfa Romeo's racing department. But now he decided to build his own machines. Over the years, Ferrari, with his knack for quickly designing and building new machinery to meet every changing quirk of Grand Prix racing, produced over thirty-seven types of Grand Prix machines. I have not the space here to deal with them all, so the highlights will have to suffice.

The first G. P. Ferraris were the Type 125's, which appeared in the Italian Grand Prix in 1948. These tiny, tubular-chassised, 1½-liter machines designed by Gioacchino Columbo already had the over-square V-12 engines which have since been so characteristic of Ferraris. Supercharged, these engines developed 230 bhp at 7,500 rpm, but were no match for the Alfas that year. In 1949, Alfa Romeo did no racing and Ferrari's 1½-liter machines had things their own way. However, in 1950, Alfa fielded a new version of

the Type 158. This was the 159, which developed 350 bhp at 8,500 rpm.

But Ferrari dropped his 1½-liter blown machines. Having noted the advantage the 4½-liter French Talbots had in not having to stop for refueling during a race, he made a quick turnabout and decided to build unblown 4½-liter machines to counter the nearly invincible Alfas. These 4½-liter, 330 bhp V-12's (later increased to 380 bhp) were the work of a new designer, Aurelio Lampredi, who also designed a new tubular-framed chassis with de Dion rear suspension for his new engine. This big new Ferrari was still unable in 1950 to vanquish the 1½-liter Alfas and their formidable combination of drivers, Fangio and Farina. But the next year it did better, winning the British and German Grands Prix, although Alfa was now squeezing 385 bhp from the 1½-liter engine—at a gas consumption rate of one-and-a-half miles a gallon!

After 1951, Ferrari reigned supreme for several years. For at the very height of their success, Alfa Romeo gave up Grand Prix racing.

In addition to the Grand Prix formula, the F.I.A. had for some years sanctioned another racing category known as Formula II, for 500 cc supercharged cars or 2-liter unblown machines. With Ferrari practically unopposed in Formula I, Formula II, by decision of the F.I.A., became the Grand Prix formula for 1952 and 1953. Ferrari had somehow known this was coming and had ready a Formula II four-cylinder, 2-liter unblown engine, plus a 2½-liter version for the new 1954 formula. In 1952 and 1953, the Formula II 2-liters cleaned up and Alberto Ascari took the world's championship both years.

Things changed in 1954 as real Grand Prix racing came back, although hardly with the wondrous sound and fury of pre-1939. All of the machines which appeared on the grids of the *Grandes Epreuves* that year were 2½-liter, unblown cars. No one took advantage of the other approved engine size—750 cc

blown. Maserati developed its old Formula II, six-cylinder machine into the potent 250 F, now with a space frame using a grid of small-diameter tubing.

Mercedes-Benz came back. Although the Germans had been personae non grata in Grands Prix for a few years after the war, they could have entered G.P. racing for several years prior to 1954. But Mercedes-Benz never races unless it has an almost certain chance of winning. Therefore, with racing at low ebb, Mercedes entered the lists with the new Type W196, 2½-liter racing machines. As usual, the Germans were ahead of the game in design. Their straight-eight, 275 bhp engines (a far cry from their 600 bhp engines of the Thirties) had twin-overhead camshafts driven by a train of gears from the center of the crankshaft; the cylinders were separated into two blocks of four (à la Monza Alfa Romeo of twenty years earlier). Further, they used fuel injection and desmodromic valve gear, in which the valves are positively closed as well as opened by the camshaft. This engine was mounted at an angle in a beautifully made space frame, which had independent suspension fore and aft. All four brakes were inboard to reduce unsprung weight.

Surprisingly, Lancia, which had never raced in *Grandes Épreuves*, announced that it was going racing, too. Their engines were V-8's with four overhead camshafts developing some 275 bhp. They used the fashionable space frame, too; their gearboxes were incorporated in the differential, and they used inboard brakes. To keep weight distribution constant, the Lancias carried their fuel in pontoons—long tanks mounted outboard of the flanks of the cars.

Ferrari had his work cut out for him. His car that year was the four-cylinder-engined, 260 bhp "Squalo," or Shark (later versions were called "Super Squalo"), which got its name from the bulbous body that enclosed its side-mounted gas tanks. This car, too, had a space frame. It was hated by its drivers because its

strong understeer made it want to go straight ahead on corners and also because of its poor road holding, a characteristic of G.P. Ferraris ever since.

In 1954 and 1955, the Mercedes-Benz's, the Maseratis, and the Lancias gave Ferrari a miserable time. But Enzo Ferrari's luck held. Mercedes withdrew from Grand Prix racing again in 1955 (they hadn't won *all* the races), and Lancia—in parlous financial condition—quit the game, too, presenting Ferrari with their V-8's. With this acquisition, Ferrari was back in business again in 1956. Ferrari improved the Lancias and Juan Fangio brought home the bacon, winning the drivers' championship. Fangio won the championship again in 1957, but not for Enzo Ferrari; that year he brought it home to Maserati.

But Ferrari had a new car now: the "Dino" 246 (named after his dead son), developed from a light 1½-liter Formula II machine whose V-6 engine ran on gasoline instead of the racing dope normally imbibed by racing cars. It had its engine enlarged to 2.4 liters for Grands Prix under the new 1958 formula which prohibited racing dope. With the Dino 246, Mike Hawthorn became world's champion in 1958, although he took only two first places. The English in their Vanwalls and Coopers unexpectedly were beginning to get difficult.

The British hadn't taken a Grand Prix since Segrave won at San Sebastian on a Sunbeam in 1924. It wasn't until 1955 that they did it again, when Tony Brooks on a Connaught won a second-rate *Grand Épreuve* at Syracuse in Sicily. This was only the beginning, for the British were suddenly going crazy over racing. But while the great continental racing cars were the products of famous factories that also built cars for sale, most of the multitude of English racing machines were the products of tiny workshops that, with the sole exception of Lotus, made only racing cars.

The Vanwall, which won no less than three Grands

Prix in 1957, first appeared in 1954 with a 2-liter, twin-overhead-camshaft engine, later increased to 2½ liters. This 2½-liter engine produced 270 bhp on Avgas in 1958—enough to win six Grands Prix that year. The Vanwall had a space frame designed by that busy bee of current English racing-car design, Colin Chapman, who builds the successful Lotus cars. The Vanwall also had disc brakes and a de Dion rear end. In one important respect, the Vanwall of 1958 was different from the current English machines. It had its engine in front.

The tiny new British cars, driven by a generation of British drivers second to none, have reorganized the entire concept of the Grand Prix machine. B.R.M., Cooper-Climax, and Lotus-Climax all have rear engines mounted in light, tubular-framed chassis. None of them weighs much over 1,200 pounds. The Cooper-Climax and the Lotus-Climax have 240 bhp, 2½-liter, four-cylinder, twin-overhead-camshaft, Coventry-Climax engines. The B.R.M. has a four-cylinder, twin-overhead-camshaft engine of its own make, delivering 275 bhp. In 1960, the Cooper, for example, won four big races in a row. Driven by Jack Brabham, it knocked off the Dutch, Belgian, French, and British Grands Prix.

No wonder Signor Enzo Ferrari has been given furiously to think. No wonder his new Grand Prix machines designed for the 1961, 1,500 cc formula look so veddy British.

193

SPORTS CARS

Just what *is* a sports car? This question has become as much a cliché as the answer given to it by a minor pundit we know:

"A sports car," he solemnly intoned, "is a machine which is driven for the sheer pleasure of driving. It must be fast, it must have impeccable handling qualities, precision steering, train-like road adhesion, powerful brakes. It must have perfect visibility, good lights. It should please the eye—not necessarily of the mob, whose tastes have been perverted by the Detroit stylists—but the eye of a connoisseur, who knows what to like. In other words, it should be a delight to wheel it, shining and growling, out of its garage just to drive it for the fun of driving it fast."*

In its day, some years ago, this pronunciamento was not too far off target. Today the sports car is a somewhat different animal. No longer is it considered a peculiar and exotic machine owned by that even more peculiar and exotic nut down the street. Today half the housewives on the block seem to be driving Jaguars and Porsches. I can remember suburban mothers protectively hanging on to their progeny while balefully glaring at me and my Alfa Romeo as I slowly "wheeled it, shining and growling, out of its garage." Today you can hear these same good ladies expertly blipping the throttle as they double-clutch and downshift for the corner before the supermarket.

It is sometimes claimed that a true sports car should be a Jekyll-Hyde machine, suitable for going to work in five days a week and then, on week ends, becoming a raging tiger on the track or road circuit. Fifteen years ago this was almost possible. A man could drive an M.G.-TC to work and race it week ends. In today's production sports cars this could not be done, except in smaller races organized by local sports-car clubs.

Most machines used in the bigger "sports-car" races around the country aren't sports cars at all in the sense that they can be used for normal driving on the public highway. Fitted, under the rules, with roll-bars, having no weather protection (unless they have closed bodywork) except a vestigial strip of plexiglas serving as a windshield, their headlights permanently covered with layers of tape, except when they are entered in a night-time race, they are hardly the sort of machine to take down the Freeway to the office.

In my narrow view, a true sports car is *not* a machine you can use both for commuting and racing. It really should be designed with *neither* purpose in mind. Ideally, it should be close kin to a racing car, with a responsive, nervous, eager-to-rev engine and a quick close-ratio gearbox, in a stiff chassis with steering and brakes of racing-car caliber. However, unlike the cars used in sports-car racing, it should have a practical top and windshield and, although I hate to say

Preceding pages: A Maserati in the twelve-hour sports-car race at Sebring, Florida. What we now would consider sports cars first made their appearances during the Prince Henry trials, prior to World War I. Among these was the Prince Henry type Vauxhall (above). This 1914 model had a 4-liter, L-head engine which developed 75 bhp. It was unique in its day because of its high-speed engine, which revolved at 2,500 rpm (fast in 1914), although the car speed was not much over 70 mph. The "Prince Henry" was the direct ancestor of the famed "E" type 30-98 Vauxhall (above, right) of the early Twenties. This example has the "Velox" body and a 90 bhp, four-cylinder engine which propelled it at 80 mph. Later models of this marque had overhead-valve engines and were known as the "OE" type. The OE 30-98's were capable of over 85 mph. In the Gallic idiom was this "Surbaisse" Amilcar built in 1928 (below right). These inexpensive and popular 1,100 cc sports cars had four-cylinder, 40 bhp engines, but were light and agile enough to win many races and hill climbs.

Sports Cars of the World, Scribner's, New York, 1952.

so, maybe even sedan bodywork. Moreover, it should have decent accommodation for luggage. Its amenities may limit its use as a sports-racing apparatus, but an enthusiastic sporting driver can enjoy its fierceness, its need for constant gear-changing, even its tendency to be almost on the boil in traffic. And every time he succeeds in reaching his office in his restive charger he'll have a sense of victory.

Such a machine is best used, of course, for driving that is an end in itself, for an exuberant sally upon empty, twisting country roads early on a week end morning, when you can play tunes on the gearbox, when you can use the full power of your brakes before each corner, which you take to the very limit of your car's adhesion while enjoying the precision steering which allows you to put the right-hand wheels so close to the road's edge as to cut the tops off weeds with their hubcaps.

It must have been as late as 1930 that I first saw the words "sports car" in print—in the English weekly, *The Autocar*. I had certainly seen what we would now call sports cars long before that—in particular a certain red Stutz Bearcat, circa 1919. This fascinating machine was owned by a horse-playing type who often visited a moldering Victorian mansion of a kind which still held out against the new apartment houses engulfing the Bronx. There must have been something odd about that house for I was never allowed to approach its *porte cochère*, in which the Stutz was often parked, so that I might examine it and perhaps engage its owner in conversation. There was also a pair of frowsty-looking Mercer two-seaters run by the same kind of youths who nowadays operate chopped-down Fords. The unlucky Mercers didn't run very often, however, for much of the time they stood disemboweled at curbside as their owners, black with grease,

worked on the entrails spread out on copies of the *New York World*.

A few years later, however, I discovered a real sports car. Again and again I took the subway 'way downtown to Sixth Avenue and 59th Street where this heavenly machine, an Amilcar, sat in a showroom otherwise devoted to Hispano-Suizas. When I described this wonderful little car to my friends I always referred to it as a Hamilcar. I thought that somehow its French makers had erred in spelling the classical general's name.

If I was ignorant about sports cars before 1930, the great mass of Americans was, too, and it would take some fifteen years before the words "sports car" became coinage in this country.

It had not always been so. In the early days of automobilism, one of the surest ways of advertising the virtues of a make of car was to have it win races. At first, manufacturers raced their normal production models against each other, but as competition became keener, the cars they brought to the starting line be-

Tubular-chassised Chevrolet Corvette SS (left) appeared briefly at Sebring in 1957,
before American manufacturers shied away from racing. Its chassis frame was not unlike that of the
300 SL Mercedes-Benz. It had a de Dion rear suspension and inboard rear brakes, plus
a Halibrand quick-change differential. Its aluminum-headed, fuel-injected engine developed 310 bhp
from a 9:1 compression ratio. At Sebring it was troubled by overheating due to difficulties
with its remote-mounted radiator header tank, which turned out to have been
improperly constructed. Above: A sleek, Italianate 250 GT Ferrari. Below: The E-type, 265 bhp
XK-engined Jaguar, available with roadster body shown here or with Grand Touring coupe body.
Because of an immensely strong integral body-chassis construction, the open model, capable
of over 150 mph, is no weaker structurally than its coupe-bodied sister.

came less and less like the machines they were offering to the public. These specialized versions were lighter. Through careful tuning and higher compression their engines were more powerful. Above all, their bodywork was leaner, starker, and rakishly charming.

Before long these machines, which helped sell the stodgier, seven-passenger tourers and landaulets of a manufacturer's line, became out-and-out racing cars. However, there were sporty types, impressed by their wins on the track and road circuits, who would have none of the landaulets. They wanted the race cars to drive on the road. Often they were able to buy last year's racing car, attach mud guards and acetylene lamps, paint the whole thing red, install a muffler—although with a cutout that was never shut—and out-roar, out-speed, and out-do with the girls every other young blade in the township.

Some manufacturers made and sold such "racers" as part of their regular production. They called them "Raceabouts," "Speed Cars," "Runabouts." Mercer, Stutz, Apperson, Stearns, Chadwick, and others all made sporting versions of their production cars. They were sports cars, all right—people just hadn't learned the words yet.

After World War I, American cars were made by the million in factories bent on supplying cheap transportation for the newly prosperous masses. They were

no longer a means of sport, but a prosaic appliance about as romantic as a gas range. The few factories which still persisted in building high-quality sporting machines at high prices fought a losing struggle against the rising flood from Detroit.

Another factor worked against sports cars in the U.S.A. The American woman had not only become emancipated—she had become the boss. And she didn't like stark, windblown, hard-riding two-seaters. Despite F. Scott Fitzgerald and John O'Hara, the flapper of the Twenties did not do her drinking and petting in a Stutz Bearcat. The day of the Bearcat was just about over by then.

There were to be no sports cars in America for many years; only rumble-seat roadsters. The situation in Europe, happily, was somewhat different. At first, as in this country, sports cars were merely road-equipped racing machines or, as was common, especially with big Mercedes, they were family limousines with their monumental bodywork stripped off in summer and replaced by a pair of bucket seats, or one of those charming two-seater bodies of woven wicker that looked for all the world as if it had been stolen off of somebody's front porch. (Did they have front porches in Europe in 1909?)

It was easy to convert a chain-drive machine like a Mercedes to sporting use since it was fairly easy to raise the rear-end ratio for high speed by merely changing the size of the sprocket. But not only Mercedes' were turned to sporting purposes. In Germany, Benz and Horch were also so used by the sabre-scarred young sons of the aristocracy. And in France, Belgium, and England, many a big-chested Panhard, Metallurgique, or Napier found new speed as it was stripped of heavy carriagework and let loose with only a pair of flimsy racing seats as its burden.

But it was from the trials for which Prince Henry

Road racing at Alexandria Bay, New York, in 1937 (above), a Willys-engined special, an Amilcar, and a TA M.G. leave the starting line in an A.R.C.A.-sponsored contest. At right, an Ultra-Sporting Briton: the low-chassis "100 mph" Invicta, capable of some 95 mph. This car had a six-cylinder, push-rod, twin-carburetor truck engine and a disconcerting habit of spinning like a top. Aside from this annoying peculiarity, the Invicta was a most pleasurable vehicle to drive.

CMF 824

One of the more popular British sports cars is the Austin Healey 3,000 (below). Built by BMC, the huge English manufacturing combine, the Healey has a 3-liter, six-cylinder, push-rod engine and gives remarkably good performance. Its top speed is over 110 mph and it can reach 60 mph from rest in just under ten seconds. It has disc brakes forward and drum brakes on its non-independently sprung rear axle. The Porsche Type 356B-1600 coupe (bottom) is but one model of the various Porsches which were originally based on Volkswagen. They range from "cooking" versions like this, to the extremely potent road-racing types. Although its opposed-four engine is only 1,582 cc and has a compression ratio of 7.5:1, it develops 70 bhp and is capable of very nearly 100 mph. The Triumph TR-3 (right) has been phenomenally successful in this country. Small and light, it can reach 110 mph from its push-rod, 100 bhp, four-cylinder, 2-liter, 8.5:1-compression engine. Most recent of the line which introduced the sports car to the postwar United States is the MGA "1600" (bottom, right).

of Prussia offered a trophy in the years from 1908 to 1911 that there emerged a type of machine which was the direct ancestor of the sports car of today. From 1908 to 1911, the Prince offered a trophy for a motoring "Tour" that was not a race nor, in our sense, a rally, although part of it at least consisted of a speed trial. The winner was chosen by means of a complex formula that pleased no one. And each year all the losers swore that they'd never have anything to do with such a ridiculous event again. What irked the losers mostly was that instead of a "Tour," the "Prince Henry" became a pretty rough race, in spite of the fact that the cars were required to be touring machines, complete with fenders, lights, and enough room for four passengers.

The participants didn't know it but they were engaging, for what was probably the first time, in sports-car racing.

At least two of the machines arising from these "Tours," the Austro-Daimler and the Vauxhall, were direct links to the sports cars of our time. They were neither stodgy touring cars nor were they racing cars. They were, perhaps, the first genuine sports cars.

The "Prince Henry" Austro-Daimler, built in Vienna and designed by Ferdinand Porsche, won the speed trials in 1910—which, by the way, was the most important of the tours; in 1911 they degenerated into a mere procession—and also won the entire event by placing second and third with duplicates of the winning machine.

These 27/80 Austro-Daimlers had four-cylinder engines of 5.7 liters with immense valves inclined at forty-five degrees in hemispherical combustion chambers. The valves, in cages, were operated by a single overhead camshaft driven by a vertical shaft from the crankshaft. Its twin magnetos were driven from the lower end of the shaft. This engine has never ceased to amaze me, for it is almost identical in design to that in the 1907 Welch I drive, even to the archaic, total-loss oiling system. However, with its light steel pistons, oversize valves, and better carburetion, the Austro-Daimler developed some 95 bhp, nearly twice that of the Welch, although their cubic capacity was almost identical.

The chassis of the Austro-Daimler was quite ordinary, the rear wheels chain-driven. It was very high-geared and the gearbox had close ratios, another sports-car virtue that still has not been learned by some manufacturers in our time. Top speed was over 80 mph.

Unorthodox Lancia "Lambdas" (below and right) had independent front suspension, integral body-cum-chassis construction, and V-4 engines as early as the Twenties. Although not fast (rarely being able to exceed 85 mph), they had fine road manners. Note how the body-chassis frame extends upward to the car's waistline. The "Competition" Delahaye (far right) won the "Fastest Road Car" race at Brooklands in England in 1939. This 1936 model had a 3½-liter engine adapted from that used in Delahaye trucks. It could better 110 mph. A Lagonda similar to this 1937 Lagonda "Rapide" (lower right) won at Le Mans in 1935. The "Rapide" used the same Meadows commercial engine which had earlier powered the Invicta. Although heavier than the Invicta, the "Rapide" was slightly faster, since it developed almost 150 bhp as against the Invicta's 115—due partly to the fact that W. O. Bentley had breathed upon it. Mr. Bentley had joined Lagonda after leaving Rolls-Royce (for whom he had worked for a short time after Rolls absorbed the Bentley name). It was W. O. Bentley who later designed the complex, expensive, and highly desirable V-12 Lagonda.

The "Prince Henry" Vauxhall was a rather different beast. It had a far simpler engine, a 3-liter L-head of notably unexciting specifications, but with the ability to turn up 2,500 rpm, which was a high speed in 1910. It developed 52 bhp, the later 4-liter versions 75. Although these were capable of only 75 mph (really nothing to be sneezed at in 1914), it was the manner of their progression that gave them their charm and made their fame. With a very low unsprung-to-sprung weight ratio — the "unsprung weight" is that not borne by the springs, such as wheels, brake drums, differential—it had a lightness and delicacy of handling such as we cannot know in the heavier cars of today. During the visit of a British team at an Anglo-American Rally, I watched Laurence Pomeroy, a famed motoring journalist and a first-class driver, take his Edwardian Vauxhall around the track at Thompson, Connecticut. Not only were its lap times quite as fast as cars fifteen years its junior, but its road holding and the precision of its steering were easily their equal, too.

But the "Prince Henry" Vauxhall's claim to greatness lies in the fact that it was the direct ancestor of the 30/98 Vauxhall, with the Bentley one of the more notable English sports cars of the Twenties.

Obviously there were machines besides the Austro-Daimler and the Vauxhall emerging as true sports cars: Bugatti, Hispano-Suiza, Mercedes, Aston Martin. Their names would grow greater after the war. Sadly, the names of the great American sporting machines—Mercer, Stutz, Simplex—were doomed to wither away, almost to be forgotten until their resurrection by the antique-car enthusiasts of our time.

The dozen or so years between the end of Kaiser Wilhelm's war and the onset of the cold chill of the Great Depression were, at least to those who love the spidery starkness and near brutality of the vintage sports car, the great days of sporting machinery. Each country's sports cars bore the stamp of its national characteristics, its geography, its economics.

England, in contrast to the countries of continental Europe, had not only a wealthy upper class, but also a large, educated middle class with a sporting tradition. Therefore, in addition to the expensive, hand-fitted, large and powerful machines such as the Bentley, Britain also produced a host of small, comparatively cheap sports cars for the middle-income enthusiast. Also, since few English sports cars were built for export they were well-suited to the English road, which was billiard-table smooth, incredibly twisty

Cecil Kimber, in 1923, modified a Morris Cowley and called it an M.G. (for Morris Garages). It was so successful in rallies and hill climbs that the Morris organization went into the production of M.G. sports cars similar to the 1927-28 model at left. In 1929 the first M.G. "Midget" appeared. A later version of this—the TC (above, right)—took America by storm in 1946. The TC had a four-cylinder, 1,250 cc engine, which gave 55 bhp and approached 70 mph. Its precise steering and good road holding were a revelation to American drivers.

and narrow, and seldom climbed mountains. Typical pre-World War II English sporting machinery were the Invicta, Riley, H.R.G., Lagonda, Vauxhall, Sunbeam, Frazer-Nash, A.C., Alvis, Squire, and, of course, the M.G. Although I am sorely tempted, I can deal with but a few of these here.

Of all these cars, I believe I know best the Invicta, specifically the "100 mph," 4½-liter, low-chassis model. I owned one for seven mostly happy years, starting in 1943. The car I had was built in 1934 and was one of the last of its type—chassis No. S-155. It had a six-cylinder push-rod engine, with twin S.U. carburetors, developing some 115 bhp at 4,000 rpm. Approaching 4,000, these engines begin to feel pretty rough, and I still recollect with horror the time I found No. 3 main bearing lying in the crankcase when I undid it for cleaning. But otherwise the Invicta was a charmer. It was fast (about 95 mph—0 to 60 in 14½ seconds), wonderful looking, with its plated out-

side exhaust pipes, and honestly and ruggedly built. Although its steering was impeccable, its strong, elliptically sprung chassis had a built-in vice. Because too much of its weight was up front and because of its ultra-low underslung frame, it had the maddening habit of swapping ends. For very little cause it would spin around and I'd find myself facing the way I had come. In spite of these peccadillos, Donald Healey won the 1931 Monte Carlo Rally outright on a similar car, and in 1933 an Invicta driven by A. C. Lace on the Ards Circuit in Ireland put in a faster lap than Sir Henry Birkin's 4½-liter Bentley. If the Invicta, which cost some $6,000, could have weathered the Depression, its bugs could have been designed out and Buick would have had to call one of its models by another name.

If any car was built with one end in view—to give its driver all the wild excitement of driving a spirited motorcycle—it was the untamed and highly original

chain-drive Frazer-Nash. From 1924 on, many models were brought out—the "Colmore," "Boulogne," "Exeter," "T.T. Replica" and more—and they were fitted with almost every type of sports engine that came into their maker's ken. It's difficult to find two Frazer-Nashes that are alike. The manufacturers would bolt together almost any combination you wanted. But no matter what the model, all Frazer-Nashes had a delightful and archaic system of chains to drive the back wheels—not unlike that in the James Steam Carriage of 1833. From a head-snapping clutch, power was transmitted through bevel gears and then by a rattling rat's-nest of chains and sprockets to the rear axle. (Sprockets could be quickly changed so that you could have any gear ratios you fancied.) Sliding dog clutches locked the desired sprocket to a cross-shaft and made lightning gear changes a cinch. The solid rear axle, without differential, made corners feel funny, the hard quarter-elliptic springs discouraged lady passengers, and the quick-as-a-wish steering required the conductor to watch where he was going every minute, but driven with verve and zeal no sports car was ever more fun.

In 1935 the factory, to the dismay of dedicated "chain-gangsters," dropped the wonderfully stark models, although they'd still make you one to order until 1938 or so, and brought out a British version of the German B.M.W. A pity, that!

For the impecunious young sports-car Englishmen of the Thirties, there was a fair number of low-priced, low-powered, albeit pleasingly sporting little machines from which he could choose. The Singer, the M.G. "Midget," and the Austin "Nippy" were typical. Of these the M.G. Midget became the most popular and had more to do with spreading the cult of the sports car than any other machine ever built. Although the M.G. Midget did not appear on the scene until 1929, the M.G. (for Morris Garages) had been around since 1923 when Cecil Kimber modified a Morris Cowley for competing in trials and rallies. Until 1929, the M.G.'s had been quite successful, medium-sized sporting machines of about 2 liters. But the first Midget had an engine of only 847 cc, which put out some 20 bhp. This engine and the chassis, too, was based on that in the popular Morris "Minor," but with modified manifolding for better breathing. An overhead camshaft operated the valves and was itself driven from the crankshaft by a vertically mounted generator, which odd arrangement persisted for years in spite of the trouble people sometimes had with oil from the valve gear dripping into the generator.

This tiny M.G. was immediately, joyfully embraced by the young sports motorists as the ideal machine for trials, club racing, and fun on the road. For in spite of its measly 20 horsepower it was a lively little devil. With its light wood and fabric bodywork it weighed only a bit over a thousand pounds. They loved its jaunty look, too, for it was low-built, with cutaway sides and a saucy, pointed tail.

It wasn't long before people were hotting up these little machines and racing them in spite of their having fabric universals and gas tanks over the driver's knees. The factory wasn't far behind them and produced a super-sports version known as the "Montlhéry" Midget. These had their engines reduced in size to fit into the 750 cc racing class. With improved chassis, bigger engine bearings, downdraft carburetors, and such, they developed over 30 bhp while a few with 9 to 1 compression put out 45 bhp, and in supercharged form no less than 60 bhp at 6,300 rpm.

Luckily, this 1923 U.S.-built Kissel (right) couldn't go very fast, its two-wheel brakes being what they were. In spite of its rakishly sporting look, it was breathing hard at 70 mph, for its six-cylinder engine developed only 65 bhp. The chain-driven Frazer-Nash of 1935 (below) has a 2-liter, twin-overhead-camshaft Blackburne engine and does 85 mph. This car looks as if it has a rear seat, but that after-compartment is largely taken up by chains and sprockets. Bottom: This 3-liter Sunbeam of 1926 had the first twin-overhead-camshaft engine to be offered to the public in a non-racing machine. It had the high compression ratio of 6:1 and produced 90 bhp—good for its day. It was capable also of almost 90 mph. Note that its front fenders fitted the wheels very closely and steered with them. A friend who owned one of these cars was often annoyed by largish stones insinuating themselves between wheel and fender—and sometimes tearing off said fender. Bottom right: The Sunbeam's engine. A 1936 "Competition" Delage like the one at far right won the English Tourist Trophy in 1938. It had a six-cylinder, 3-liter engine.

It was away back in 1932 that the typical M.G. Midget, with its long sweeping fenders and the slab gas-tank, first appeared. This was the J2, and it was from these J2's that all the subsequent M.G.'s that have appeared down the years were developed: the P Types, the TA's and finally, after World War II, the TC's which made this country sports-car conscious.

The Briton enjoyed his sports car. He entered rallies (the rally of those days was still a form of motor sport instead of a numbers game for electronic engineers) and he entered trials. These trials, which still are a part of the sports-motoring scene in England, although nowadays the cars entered in them have evolved into weirdly specialized mechanisms, consisted of a number of slimy, muddy, hog wallows set on a steep angle. With their flair for understatement, the British called these rock-strewn mud holes "trials hills." The idea was to rush along with hundreds of other mud-plastered entrants from one of these obstacles to the other and climb each one non-stop against the clock, often at night and in the rain. If you got stuck in a morass, you not only lost points, but suffered the indignity of being dragged to the top by a traction engine.

Until the war, the English sporting driver's mecca was Brooklands. This motor-racing track, irregular in shape, several miles around, and complete with steep bankings, was built as early as 1907. Here, the Briton could not only watch Grand Prix types competing on week ends, but also join in sports-car racing. One of the favorite events sent masses of sports cars of every complexion charging off in a one-hour "blind" to see who could go farthest in that time.

Moreover, for a small fee it was possible on quiet weekdays to take your sports car out on the track and have a high old time going as fast as you liked.

Alas, Brooklands is no more. During Hitler's war,

the military wrecked the track and after the war its board of directors sold it off for industrial sites.

France during the 'tween-war years was the only other car-building European country where enough middle-class young men existed to support the manufacture of sports cars other than Bugattis, Hispano-Suizas, Delages, and Delahayes. The Salmson, Lombard, Senechal, Amilcar, and Chenard-Walcker, among others, were all comparatively low-powered, medium-priced cars with a character that was almost uniformly Gallic.

As much in the French idiom as any of them, and the most famous as well, was the Amilcar—not, you remember, Hamilcar. That Amilcar I used to gawk at was, most likely, the 1923 Grand Sport. These early "Amils" had such incredibly narrow bodies that the seats were staggered to give the passenger a little elbow room. These 1923 cars were known as the Type C.G.S. and had four-cylinder, L-head engines developing 40 bhp. The light and fragile-looking chassis sat on half-elliptic springs in front and quarter elliptics aft, and even then had four-wheel brakes, although about as big as hockey pucks. These Amilcars looked as if they might turn over while standing still. A view under the hoods at their puny, crudely finished engines was a dismal prospect.

But looks were deceiving. The Amilcar was an amazingly potent little creature. It won hill climbs right and left. One of them won the twenty-four-hour Bol d'Or; another came in fourteenth at Le Mans in 1924, qualifying for the Rudge-Whitworth Cup. As for lasting power, you still see them around after almost forty years. One of them was offered to me not long ago for $1,500—more than it cost new.

An entirely different kind of Amilcar with a six-cylinder, supercharged, twin-overhead-camshaft engine appeared in 1926—the G6. This expensive and

Lushly curvacious is the 3-liter, 1946 Delage (above). The body is by Figoni et Falaschi. The Disco Volante Alfa Romeo (right) created a short-lived sensation in 1953. Built in two engine sizes, a six-cylinder 3-liter, and a four-cylinder 2-liter, it had a tubular chassis — an early example of "birdcage" automotive architecture. The 3-liter car weighed only 1,600 pounds, and Carlo Dusio, who built the Cisitalia on the opposite page, claimed to have driven one at 140 mph. Unfortunately, these "Dischi" never went into serious production. A German "Sportwagen," the type 328 B.M.W. of 1937 (bottom), had a tubular chassis, rack-and-pinion steering and independent front suspension.

In road races of the early
Fifties, the Cadillac-engined
English Allard (left) cleaned up.
Farina's taut and functional
body styling for the Fiat-powered
Cisitalias of the late Forties
(below) started a fashion
that still persists. Their Fiat
engines were usually 1,100 cc, push-
rod, four-cylinder types, which
developed about 60 bhp. The cars had
tubular chassis and could do better
than 90. Figoni and Falaschi
built the opulent body (bottom) for
the twelve-cylinder, 1939 Delahaye.

desirable road version of an Amilcar racer was guaranteed to do better than 100 mph, but unfortunately only a few were ever built.

I cannot resist mentioning one other French sports car, the Delahaye. Although most Delahayes were lush and flamboyant machines for the rapid transport of French millionaires and their curvaceous mannequins who posed beside the cars in *Concours d'Elegance*, Delahaye in 1936 produced as lean and purposeful a sports car as anyone could desire.

This "Competition" model had a push-rod, 3½-liter, three-carburetor engine which was said to be a hotted-up version of the engine used in Delahaye trucks. Although it was no beauty to look at, it was a tough and durable power plant. In sports form it produced a very creditable 160 bhp at 4,200 rpm and pushed the light two-seater along at better than 110 mph, enough to win the "Fastest Road Car" race at Brooklands in 1939. This much-talked-of competition was organized by a group of Englishmen, each of whom was confident that he had the speediest machine on the road. Even though it caught fire just before the start, the Delahaye, driven by Arthur Dobson, got out in front and was never overtaken by the other racers—including two Alfa Romeos (a 2.6 and a 2.9), a Talbot-Lago, and a very potent, competition Delage. I recently drove the 2.6 Alfa which was, in 1939, driven by G.E. Templar but now belongs to Ed Bond of Saybrook, Connecticut. That Delahaye must have been a very *puissant* machine indeed to have bested it.

Germany, after World War I, did not have the economic climate to support the sale of quantities of sports cars to middle-class young men; there were too few of them. Although the Germans were quite successful between the wars in international sports-car competition, the cars were mostly Mercedes-Benz's entered by the factory.

Domestic sports-car events after Hitler's rise were quasi-military affairs, the be-swastikaed cars driven by S.S. types through rivers and over rocky fields. A Jeep would have beaten the *lederhosen* off of them.

The only notable pre-war sports car besides the Mercedes-Benz was the Type 328 B.M.W. made by the Bayerische Motoren Werke, which also makes the B.M.W. motorcycle and which, during the war, made the engines for the deadly Focke-Wulf 190 airplane.

The 328 B.M.W., which superseded an earlier push-rod engined sports car, the Type 55, was in 1937 far more like the sports cars of today than its contemporaries. Light (1,800 pounds), tubular chassised, independently sprung in front, with rack-and-pinion steering and hydraulic brakes, it had an astounding performance for a comparatively low-priced ($3,000), moderately powered machine. It had an 80 bhp, 2-liter engine with three carburetors. In fact, the current English Bristol engine is a modernized version of the same power plant, using the same complex push-rod system to operate its overhead valves in hemispherical combustion chambers.

The 328 was capable of almost 100 mph and a racing version whose engine developed 135 bhp won the shortened, wartime *Mille Miglia* at an average of over 103 mph.

Italy is the birthplace of the violent automobile. Ferrari, Alfa Romeo, Maserati, Lancia, call Italy their home. Ettore Bugatti was born in Italy. Only

A throwback to the vintage years, the British H.R.G. (above) was made until 1955. It had stiff, underslung, half-elliptic springs aft and quarter-elliptics forward. Available with either 1,100 or 1,500 cc, four-cylinder, single-overhead-camshaft engines, it was usually seen in the 1,500 form in this country and could approach 90 mph with impeccable road holding. The engines were bought from Singer and reworked. The RS-60 Porsche sports racer (left) has its overhead-camshaft engine mounted forward of the rear axle; its 135 bhp produces almost 150 mph. A similar "Spyder" won the 1,500 cc class at Le Mans in 1957. The Maserati 3500 GT (below) has a six-cylinder, twin-overhead-cam engine, approaches 130 mph.

there is motor racing a national sport as important as cricket in England or baseball in the United States. Ninety-nine out of a hundred youthful Italian males have no hope of ever acquiring enough lire to buy a Ferrari. But let some moneyed young Signore dive out of an Appenine hairpin corner in a Ferrari and scream through the narrow, cobblestoned street of a mountain village and every boy flattened in a doorway to give the screeching *maccina* room feels that *he* is mashing the throttle to the floor, that *his* hands are on the steering wheel to guide the car around the next impossible hairpin.

The handling qualities of Italian sports cars owe much to Italy's terrain and the temperament of her

drivers. Her cars must have magnificent steering and brakes and unburstable engines to cope with steep Alpine roads, dead-straight, engine-killing autostrada and, above all, zealous, lead-footed drivers, each of whom thinks himself a Tazio Nuvolari.

After Alfa Romeo and Ferrari, Lancia and Maserati are the great names among Italian sports cars. Between the wars the Maserati brothers built Grand Prix machines, upon rare occasions fitting fenders and lights to one of them for a sports-car race. Such Maserati sports cars as existed were models like these, de-tuned by their owners for road use. It was not until after World War II that sports Maseratis were offered for sale by the new owners of the Maserati name. The

In 1951, this Type C, XK-120 Jaguar (left) won the 24-hour race at Le Mans. A speed of 140 mph is claimed for the Type 507 BMW sports coupe (lower left). Its 3.2-liter, V-8 engine, which develops 178 bhp, is made almost entirely of aluminum. Just before World War II a few examples of the A.C. Ace (below) appeared in this country. Pleasant sports tourers with no pretensions to high performance, their six-cylinder engines were designed in the 1920's. (The same engines are still available in the latest model A.C.'s.) They had aluminum blocks with wet liners and a single-overhead camshaft; 80 bhp was developed. The Aceca coupe (bottom) is descended from these machines. It handles beautifully, and its Bristol engine is capable of 105 mph.

cars the Maserati brothers were to build, post-war, would be known by a new name—Osca.

Lancia, however, was a big name even before the Kaiser war, although the cars of that period made little pretense of being sporting machines. In 1922, Lancia brought out the Lambda, a touring car of unusual design, but the idea that it might be considered a sports car never entered the makers' heads. Over the years, however, as drivers experienced the Lancia's superb road holding and steering, and discovered that due to these uncommon virtues it could usually make better time over twisting, difficult roads than many breathless and screaming sports cars, it endeared itself more and more.

The early Lancia Lambdas were long, flat, plank-like touring cars of an early type of integral construction. The four-cylinder, 2-liter engine was the first of the narrow "V's" which have since become a Lancia trademark. A single overhead camshaft worked the valves. The carburetor was mounted, of all places, at the rear of the engine and fed the cylinders by way of a passage running through the center of the head. Early models had three-speed gearboxes, later ones four-speed. But even the latest Lambdas were hard put to better 80 mph.

It was the Lambda's unique front suspension that gave it such lovely road manners. Its springs were long coils inside big vertical tubes which served as kingpins. These tubes also contained the hydraulic shock absorbers, and the whole front end was knitted together by a formidable bridgework of tubing and braces, part of which continued rearward to form a cradle for the engine. The vertical tubes containing the springs ended in little round plates in the front fenders, and the same kind of people who talked about sealed engines in Rolls-Royces warned that these plates must not be removed lest a spring fly up and drill through your forehead. Never saw it happen to even one mechanic, I'm sorry to say.

After six years of war, the factories of Europe that had been building sports cars were either masses of bombed wreckage or had turned their machines over to the making of the silly hardware of modern war. It appeared that it might be years before anybody would build sports cars again.

It was astounding, naturally, to see the sports-car builders begin almost immediately to make mouth-watering machines for motor sport. But what was even more astounding was the way Americans suddenly, violently, fell in love with the sports car.

It was, of course, the TC M.G. that started it. Cute as a button, lively, its handling was a revelation to Americans resigned to the slow, mushy steering of the barge-like cars they had been used to. For the Detroit automobiles of the late Thirties and Forties were far worse than American cars of today.

Those few of us who had been long involved with machines like Bugattis and Alfas were just a little annoyed at this sudden invasion of our domain by parvenus in checked caps, and by the salesmen with

recently learned British accents who graced the sports-car showrooms springing up everywhere from Passwater, Texas, to Peculiar, Missouri. But there was no denying that the rush was on. At first the new boys bought mostly British cars, for they were more easily available. But in the Fifties, as the factories of the continent swung into production, the now sophisticated American sports-car buyer began lusting after Mercedes-Benz's and Porsches, Cisitalias, Alfa Romeos and Lancias, and even Maseratis.

For the American sports-car enthusiast learned fast. He joined sports-car clubs and avidly read not only the British auto magazines, but the new and excellent American magazines like *Road and Track* and, latterly, *Car and Driver*.

Today, wonder of wonders, there is even a great American-built sports car, the Corvette, made by, of all people, General Motors. (Unfortunately, the beautiful, though high-priced Cunningham is no longer in production.)

But most surprising of all is the way Americans have embraced all types of motoring sport. Before the war sports-car racing was indulged in by a small group of very "in" types who called themselves the Automobile Racing Club of America. They raced a weird agglomeration of everything from G. P. Bugattis to a Ford-engined Amilcar, wherever they could — even, in 1940, through the roads and around the exhibition halls and pavilions of the dormant New York World's Fair grounds.

By European standards such sporting events were as nothing. The Europeans had for years engaged in

A 166 M Ferrari: Built in 1949, its 2-liter, V-12 engine gave 125 mph.

Twin-overhead-cam Maserati engine

Sports-racing Maserati dash

Famous "Birdcage" Maserati

Lotus sports-racing car

Drivers foot-race toward cars in Le Mans start at Sebring.

Lister-Jaguar at speed

Aston Martin—Salvadori up

Alfonso de Portago at Sebring

Sports-racing Ferrari in practice

sports-car racing of such magnitude as to be beyond the imagination of Americans.

Take the Italian *Mille Miglia*, for example. The *Mille Miglia* was not, in its heyday, a mere race. It was a form of national hysteria. The 1,000-mile course itself, a gigantic figure eight starting in Brescia in the North, with its waist at Bologna and its southern loop touching Rome, was a piece of grandiose insanity. It climbed through the often fog-shrouded Futa and Raticosa passes, ran upon long straight stretches burning in the coastal sun, and twisted through cobbled mountain villages. And everywhere were people, millions of hoarsely screaming, wildly keyed-up Italians, gesticulating at the drivers, pointing out the next turn (often wrongly, if he were, say, a German) and encouraging their favorites.

The first race was in 1927. Minoia, driving an O.M., won at under 50 mph, taking over twenty-one hours to run the course. By 1933 the great Tazio Nuvolari had cut the time to sixteen hours. In 1955 Stirling Moss in a Mercedes-Benz did it in slightly over ten hours —at an average of 97.9 mph. Along the straights he got up as high as 170 mph.

Each year the race got wilder—as well as faster. At the beginning only catalogued machines might enter, but toward the end so-called "prototypes"—mainly disguised Grand Prix machines — left the starting ramp at Brescia at one-minute intervals to force their way through the hundreds of sports and Gran Turismo machines in many different handicap classes, which already were screeching south, often in rain and darkness.

It was amazing that only a few spectators and drivers were left dead each year, but in 1957 a spectacular Spaniard, Alfonso, the Marquis de Portago, new to the race, blew a tire after being warned that he needed a tire change and charged into a crowd of spectators. He killed fourteen of them including six children. Since then by government decree the *Mille Miglia* has been toned down to a quite boring event, more like a rally than a race.

Such racing is, of course, impractical in this country, although before the war I tried to interest the authorities in running a race over the perfect road circuit that exists in New York's Central Park.

No sooner had a few sports cars been unloaded here (and sometimes dropped on the dock by Anglophobe longshoremen) than their happy owners slapped numbers on them and went racing. In the East, Watkins Glen and Bridgehampton welcomed the newly revived sport to their streets and country lanes. Towns in California followed suit. But as cars got faster and the richer boys started bringing in Ferrari and Cadillac-engined Allards, the races were moved to airports and to closed circuits, at least one of which — the twelve-hour race at Sebring, Florida—has achieved international recognition.

Although there is still, happily, much racing around the country in smaller machines like Alfa Romeos, Triumphs, and Austin-Healeys, modified to the requirements of the sports-car clubs, much sports-car racing is now in the hands of tough professionals, and even the sports-car magazines are prone to sneer at what they call the "gymkhana, checkered-cap school of motoring enthusiasts."

The sports-car owner can still—if he has a built-in electronic brain—get some fun out of another form of motoring competition, the rally. The American type of rally originally was patterned on the famous European rallies like the Alpine Trial and that great-

granddaddy of all rallies, the *Rallye Monte Carlo*.

Each winter when the gales roar across the Polish plain, when Scotland and the Scandinavian peninsula lie coated in ice, and the wolves howl among the Balkan snows, cars from all these uncomfortable places converge on sunny Monte Carlo.

The "Monte" started in 1911 when twenty-two cars entered. Today, as many as three hundred start from Warsaw, Lisbon, Glasgow, Palermo or almost any large city in Europe, except Russia. No matter where a rally car starts, it will traverse almost 2,000 miles of European road in January, go through controls and time checks, and cross the glacial passes of the Alps. Cars lose points if they are too late or too early at controls, which requires much painful navigation and mathematical calculation, or if they arrive at Monte Carlo clobbered up. The more smashed fenders, the more lost points. And it's mighty easy to smash things up on icy Alpine hairpins at night when the specified average time between controls is about 10 mph faster than any sane driver would attempt on the Fourth of July. Surprisingly, so many cars arrive in Monte Carlo without loss of marks that it has been necessary to hold eliminating trials. Before the war one of the trials was the notorious "Wiggle-woggle" — a complex series of figure eights done against the clock. One year an enterprising Roumanian entrant in some fiendish manner attached his brakes to his steering, so that applying the anchors automatically threw him into a calculated skid, sending him around the wiggles and woggles faster than anyone else.

The rules are different from year to year and nowadays the organizers are like as not to send the tired contestants out for a gay road race at night over a

David Brown's Aston Martin DBR1/300 (left) was one of the most successful British sports cars that ever engaged in international competition. In 1959 it won the Tourist Trophy, Le Mans, and the 1,000-kilometer race at the Nürburgring, thereby gaining the world's sports-car championship, never before won by a British machine. Shown here is Roy Salvadori driving at Le Mans, where, with Carroll Shelby, he won at 112.5 mph. Traditionally, British sports cars have been four-square devices, complete with in-built headwinds. But the English, as evidenced by the Lotus Elite coupe (above) and by a few of their other newer sports cars, are beginning to out-do the Italians. The Lotus, with body and chassis of fiberglass, is powered with a 1,220 cc Coventry Climax, single-overhead-camshaft engine, which delivers 75 bhp. Since the Lotus weighs but 1,750 pounds, these few horses are able to urge it along at almost 115 mph. Yet its acceleration is disappointing. It takes almost 13 seconds from rest to 60 mph. Its admirable sure-footedness, due partly to four-wheel independent suspension, is one of its strong points. This Lotus is but one of a large family of Loti, all of them fathered by the famed designer, Colin Chapman.

mountain circuit, have them engage in a speed hill-climb, or even race around the Grand Prix course at Monaco in their efforts to find the ultimate winners. There is one over-all winner and various class winners, depending on engine size.

Before the war, Athens was a favorite starting point for the more dauntless types. But even they would arrive (if they arrived at all) shaken by their adventures. One cold year, Athenian competitors reported that many high-banked Balkan rivers were difficult to cross because the enterprising natives had removed the plank bridges for firewood. A competitor named Ostaczinski, a member of a Polish crew from the Balkans, once swore to me that the only way they could hold off a pack of ravening wolves that pursued

The term "sports car" is used quite loosely. To some people a sports car is a near-racing machine, to some it is a car used mostly for the fun of driving. But even sedate-looking closed machines like the Lancia Flaminia (left center) can have the attributes of the genuine sports car. This car's 2½-liter, V-6 engine develops 131 hp. It can be handled with such verve and enterprise and can put up such high averages that it surely merits its description as a sports car. Upper left: An English Morgan, stripped for racing, on the course at Marlboro, Maryland. It has a TR-3, four-cylinder engine developing 100 bhp. Above: A British-built, Bristol-powered A.C., also at Marlboro. This car is capable of 110 mph. Bottom left: Italian 1,200 cc Fiat Spider Roadster. Bottom right: English Sunbeam Alpine II. Its 85 bhp engine is capable of 100 mph. Left: On the starting line at Danville, Virginia; Alfa Romeo Giulietta Spider in the foreground.

them was by throwing empty slivovitz bottles at them. But the contestants' tall tales and adventures are not always funny. There are many tragic stories and examples of heroism.

In 1932, for example, a Mrs. Vaughan, a surgeon and an inveterate rally competitor, in company with a young lady medical student, was within a few hours of the finish line in a Triumph when they came upon the grisly wreckage of several cars. They got out of their car and, in imminent danger of having following competitors smash into them, set four broken legs before going on to win the *Coupe des Dames*.

When they arrive in "Monte," the crews, having lived together in their cars for several sleepless nights and hungry days, are barely on speaking terms. However, after some hours of sleep, sunshine, and good food, they start polishing their cars for the *Concours d'Elégance* and the *Concours de Confort*.

And it is in these contests where the big Rolls-Royces and Bentleys do best. Here they can show off their specially fitted coachwork complete with in-built toilets, hot and cold running water, tape recorders, trick road lights on stalks (for poking under fog banks), electric wipers for the headlights. It's a wonder they ever make Monte Carlo at all under the weight of this fascinating junk, in addition to the usual stuff Monte Carlo rallyists carry: shovels clipped to the fenders, unditching apparatus, spare snow tires, bottles of gas for filling tires, plus a dashboard and cockpit-ful of instruments for navigating and calculating the course.

When it comes to calculating instruments, the American rallyist need take second place to no one. If you've ever wondered what it might be like to get inside an electronic brain, just sit down next to the driver of an American rally car. For the American rally depends more on calculating microseconds and hundredths of a mile than it does on brilliant and dangerous driving over impossible roads, which American cops tend to discourage.

Most rallyists, therefore, rally just for the fun of the game — and a chance at the little silver trophy awarded to a winner. This butters no parsnips, but your rallying regular is an intense and dedicated man. Why? I think, mostly, it works something like this. Suppose that after much fancy salesmanship you have finally convinced your wife that a sports car is necessary to your common happiness. You at last own that brazen-voiced little machine of your dreams. Now you see yourself, helmeted and goggled, as the scourge of the racing circuits. Your wife has other views.

"You crazy?" she says. "You with four kids and hardly any insurance. Anyhow, you might break our darling new car. If you're going anywhere in it I'm riding with you."

So you enter a rally. It's fairly safe, you've heard it's fun, and you can take your wife along. And even if you're not racing, you have a nice big racing number on the side of your car.

When you get to the place where the rally starts, you find lots of people just like you and your wife, but you also find quite a few serious looking, two-man teams who seem to be electronic wizards, fooling with enough stop watches, calculating machines, surveyor's odometers, and other navigational gadgetry to take them into orbit around Jupiter instead of just a pleasurable two-day jaunt in the Catskill Mountains. But like them you set your lone watch to the time signals some important-looking officials are bringing in on a portable short-wave radio, while other unsmiling officials test your car for mechanical fitness.

At last it's your turn to leave the starting line. Your wife is rustling a sheaf of instructions and fiddling with a stop watch.

A man says, "Go!" Your wife presses the button on the watch and starts reading the instructions:

First Leg: Average speed 39.8 mph
1. Turn right at airport gate
2. Turn left at Clarke's Store
3. Turn right at Essex Road
4. Bear right at red barn to Rte. 9
Second Leg: Average speed 31.6 mph
1. Turn right at Wharton's Antique Shop
2. Bear left at Sea Horse Cafe
...and so on for page after page.

You get lost in exactly 12 minutes 10 and 2/10 seconds by your stop watch.

The only time I ever tried this I not only got lost, I immediately got mixed up on the average-time business, to the annoyance of the grimly serious timing-officials who hid behind privies and haystacks, their hands full of clipboards and stop watches.

When the day's rallying was over, I joined the contestants in the hotel where they stayed overnight before starting off again in the morning. Here they had a ball arguing calculating machines, tenths of seconds, and lost points.

I started to talk to a white-moustached gentleman at the bar who was wearing a brass-buttoned blazer on which was sewn various sports-car-club insignia. I said something about Bugattis. He moved away.

I never did see the end of that rally, but I read in the papers that an engineer and a tax estimator won the 523-mile run by being only 74 seconds off schedule.

That's what you need to win. Numbers in your head —rocks too, maybe.

European manufacturers have always taken rallying seriously. When one of their cars wins such an event, its success is loudly trumpeted in advertising. Even if a car doesn't get anywhere near first place, it may be publicized as being " . . . first in the class for 150 cc cars driven by left-handed lady pinochle players." The Triumph TR-3 (above) is competing in the Liège-Rome-Liège Rally. American rallyists tend to stuff their cars with displays of glittering instruments (right). This Saab boasts four expensive stop watches, three Curta calculators, and a dandy little widget that counts wheel revolutions. Patriarch of all such games is the "Rallye Monte Carlo" (below). An Austin Healey Sprite enjoys a bit of the lovely Alpine weather normally encountered in January.

LINKS WITH THE PAST

Every time my venerable fifty-four-year-old touring car and I pull into Mr. Wilcox's garage, which has stood opposite the village green since well before my car was built (it was H. A. Wilcox's Bicycle and Automobile Repair Station in those days), we go through the same experience. As I descend from the driver's seat so that Mr. Wilcox can lift the cushion to fill the gas tank, the town loafers — who hang around the gas station now that the general store is no more—give up leaning on the side of the garage building and with elaborate casualness stroll over for the fiftieth time to make a careful examination of the old machine. A few cars stop on U.S. 1, and their drivers join in the rapping of fenders and the fingering of brass. By now a small crowd has gathered, and when Mr. Wilcox lifts the hood to add some oil, three heads join his under the hood in a careful survey of the engine.

"Ay-yuh," they say, "they don't make 'em like *that* no more."

"Please don't touch the brass," I say (fingermarks leave brownish green spots on the painfully polished brasswork).

"Solid brass," they say admiringly.

"Look at all that bronze in the engine."

"You can't get leather like that anymore." (They don't know it was re-upholstered just a year ago.)

The newest, bedizened, 485-horsepower Detroit Wunderbird can drive up to the gas pumps, but none of the crowd bemused by the ancient car will grant it even a glance.

People seem to be infatuated with old cars. Some of us are even so crazy about them that we own them and drive them. Is it because they are working relics of an imaginary, happier past? Is it because people are enchanted by their simple, well-made mechanisms and delightfully archaic look? Are some of the people who own them merely rich show-offs?

People succumb to antique motor cars for all of these reasons and many others, too. There are now over 20,000 members of antique car clubs in this country: The Antique Automobile Club of America, the Horseless Carriage Club, The Veteran Motor Car Club. There are additionally clubs devoted to particular makes, like the Model A Restorers Club and The Rolls-Royce Owners Club, clubs for not-so-old cars like The Classic Car Club, and even a club for middle-aged sports cars—The Vintage Sports Car Club of America.

But don't imagine that this lusting for elderly vehicles is only an American disease. The virus exists all over the world. British Clubs like the Veteran Car Club of Great Britain and the Vintage Sports Car Club are older than their American counterparts. There are antique car clubs in every corner of what used to be called the British Empire, including South Africa, Tasmania, and Canada. Les Teuf-Teuf is a French Club, the Allgemeiner Schnauferl-Club, German. There is even a Classic Car Club of Japan and an outfit called the Ustredni Automotoklub of the Czechoslovak Soviet Republic.

Although most of the members of these clubs own at least one ancient motorized chariot, and a few of the richer ones with highly developed pack-rat instincts own many more (I know one man who owns over two hundred), a few do not. This group may only want to receive the excellent magazines some clubs publish, or they may be interested in one of the more exotic offshoots of the hobby. Some collect brass headlights and bulb horns or old catalogues and instruction books, which they pursue with all the zeal of an archeologist hunting the Dead Sea Scrolls.

The excitement of the chase—the tracking down and dragging home of an hoary and derelict machine—is one of the great, nerve-wracking pleasures of the game. Before I found my own gray-beard of a car, I went out on safari with the man I mentioned, the one who owns the two-hundred-odd ancient vehicles. He's diffident about people knowing that he owns hundreds of cars, so we'll call him Spencer.

Spencer, a millionaire, arrived at my place to pick me up wearing a tattered pair of coveralls.

"No sense in letting the characters who might be willing to sell an old car think I'm rich," he explained. We climbed into a decrepit truck to which was hitched a trailer built for hauling cars.

"Once you buy an old car," Spencer said, "it's a good idea to drag it right home. Some of the types who've hung on to old wrecks for years are oddballs who change their minds. That's why it's a good idea to pay cash and get a receipt. If you give them a check, they sometimes refuse to cash it and the deal is off." Spencer had a definite series of stops in mind for this day's hunt, places where he had spotted old cars whose owners had refused to sell. "A man might throw you off his farm when you try to buy his old Ford in May, but be happy to sell it to you in December. You've got to keep coming back." He told me about one old bird and his Ford.

One day Spencer, who seems to have an extra eye in the side of his head which sees old cars in the dim darkness of archaic garages, spotted an ancient Ford in a garage as he drove past. He stopped and approached the elderly gentleman who appeared to be running the establishment.

"That's a nice Model T Ford you have in there.

Preceding pages: Huge antique car meet at
Hershey, Pennsylvania. The 1907 Welch which appears in
the frontispiece is seen (top left) as it looked
when it was first discovered. Right: The dismantled
engine of the Welch sits on the floor of Ralph
Buckley's Antique Auto Shop during restoration. Mr. and
Mrs. Warren S. Weiant (top right) sit in their
1899 Locomobile Steamer which was the official
American entry in the 1959 Brighton Run in England.
Note the mirror covering part of Weiant's left leg. This
mirror was not for viewing the road, but for taking
a look at the water gauge on the side of the car. The famous
Twin-Six Packard (above) first came out in
1915. This car with its twelve-cylinder, 6½-liter engine
was as flexible and smooth-running as a modern
machine. Its only disadvantage was its two-wheel brakes.

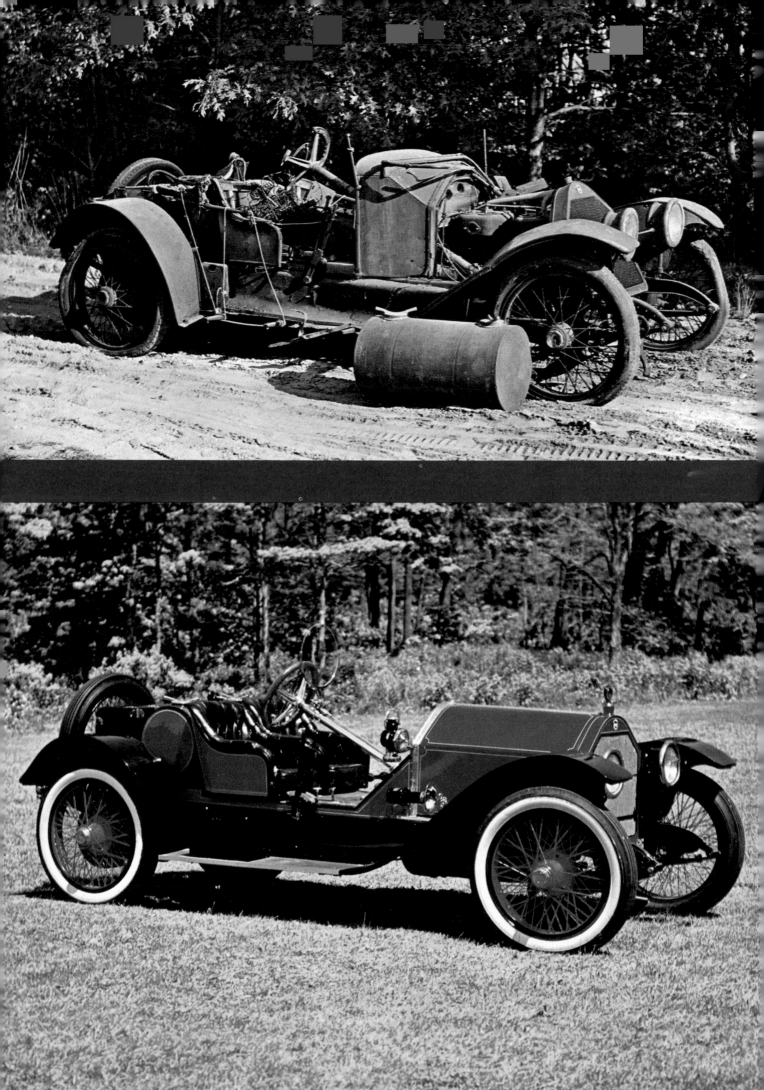

May I look at it, sir?" (Spencer is very polite, especially where old cars are concerned.)

"You may, son, you may." Spencer examined the car and, trying to hide his excitement, asked if he might buy the machine.

"That car serves a very special purpose, son. You see, it sets over a hole in the floor and if we moved the car, how'd we keep people from falling in?"

"Perhaps I could pay for filling in the hole, and then you'd sell me the car."

"Better look at the hole first, son." Spencer looked and changed his mind. It was a gigantic old greasing pit and the cost of filling it would have bought not one, but three flivvers. Looking around the old garage, Spencer noticed a very rare type of Model T cylinder block, serving as a step between the front part of the garage and a room on a higher level in the rear. He tried again.

"Would you care to sell me that cylinder block, sir?"

"And what would I use for a step?" Spencer offered to have a carpenter come and build a proper step.

"Used to this block, son."

"But it's all shiny and slippery," Spencer pointed out. "You might break your neck, sir."

"That's right, son. I dern near did the other day."

"Tell you what I'll do," offered Spencer. "I'll trade you another block exactly the same size with the top all roughed up to take off the slipperiness, if you let me have this old one."

"It's a deal, son."

Spencer rushed back to his garage, but in all that welter of ancient car parts, he could find no spare Ford block. The only one in the place was operating under the hood of a nicely restored car. Spencer did the only thing any antique-car man could do. He ripped apart the more modern engine to trade its block for an older one. After all, he might have use for it some day.

"There is no such thing as a likely or an unlikely place to find an old car," Spencer said as we drove along. "I bought a one-cylinder Cadillac from a man on a pig farm in New Jersey who never signed his name to anything, and an air-cooled Chevrolet in the smoking room of the *Mauretania*. I found an International Harvester car on the third floor of

a toilet-paper factory in Brooklyn, and a Locomobile which had been walled up in a basement, so that I had to hire house wreckers to disentomb it. I bought an engine for a 1902 Prescott Steamer from the belongings of the late Collyer brothers. Lifting collapsed barns off old cars seems almost normal to me."

We stopped at a junk yard.

"There's a wonderful 1913 Isotta-Fraschini in here that I've been trying to buy for a long time," explained Spencer.

He pointed out a rusty little mess, half-sunken into the ground, with the lower halves of its wooden-spoked wheels rotted away. The part of its wooden body that still remained was weathered to a silvery grayness, and pathetic little tatters of once-red leather upholstery stirred in the breeze. The steering wheel was gone, the hood had vanished, and the engine, exposed to years of snow and sun, was a small pile of corroded aluminum, blackened brass, and rusty iron.

"Very nice," I muttered politely.

The junkman bustled over. "Hello, Mr. Spencer. Looking over my little beauty again?"

Spencer nodded and a murmured conversation started. I moved out of earshot so as not to hinder any delicate negotiations. But there were no negotiations, and Spencer and I climbed back into the truck.

"I've been offering that guy a lot more than that little car is worth, just because it will fit into a spot in my collection. It would cost thousands to restore, but that junkie is just sentimental and won't sell. He knew that car when they were both young and to him it's still new and whole and shiny. In the meantime, he just lets it rot away so that in a few years it will unfortunately be beyond restoration."

Not all antique cars are found in such deplorable condition, Spencer explained. Sometimes cars are found in almost the same condition as they were when new. These are often the well-cared-for but never-used pets of wealthy families, who keep them warm and dry and full of oil in memory of dear old grandpa.

With thousands of collectors avidly hunting down early cars, it is becoming harder, although not entirely impossible, to find pre-World War I machines. Many people are settling for automobiles of the Twenties and even the Thirties. Certainly, many cars of this period were important classics; however, some of the vehicles on which much labor and money is being lavished actually are no more than mass-produced Detroit iron.

Many people have an exaggerated idea of what an antique car is worth. Hearing that a collector has paid $7,000 for, say, a gem of a 1911 Lozier, they will demand thousands for the ruin of Uncle George's

Miraculous metamorphosis: This unrestored 1916 Stutz Bearcat looked a little rough before year of labor by Kenneth Rohl and William Hoffman. Note the anachronistic cowl which had to be stripped off. Rohl and Hoffman, who are not professionals, did all the restoration except the painting and upholstering.

The old-car fancier prepares his car with fanatical care, laboriously polishes paintwork and brass to dazzle the judges. But meets are fun, too. There are contests to determine who can crank his ancient darling into life fastest, to see whose car runs slowest in high gear. There are also blindfold driving tests and balloon-spearing games. Best of all, the antiquer loves to examine other vintage cars. If his wife lets him, he'll drive home laden with brass lamps, old license plates, and other treasures members have offered for sale.

1911 Metz that he left to rot in the barn in 1912. They don't realize that perhaps $6,500 of the Lozier's value lies in its wonderful restoration. Further, the Lozier was a high-quality car to begin with. The Metz, as Uncle George would have sadly told you, was a dog when it was new. Fifty dollars might be too much to pay for the Metz.

An antique bought from another collector who has already gone through the pangs of restoration may be a heartbreaking disappointment, since some so-called "restorations" by ham-handed collector-mechanics can practically ruin a car.

Some people are not satisfied with bringing a car back to its original condition; they try to improve it. They chrome-plate parts which were originally nickel-plated. They install the latest Kalifornia Kustom plastic upholstery, revolting even in a Los Angeles hot rod, upon the seats of an elderly landaulet. They paint the undersides of fenders white. They fake the ages of cars by building early-style bodies on later chassis, etc. These are minor crimes. But they also replace tired parts, like gearboxes and differentials, with recent types from junk yards, and hide modern self-starters under the floorboards. To a meticulous restorer, these crudities are reprehensible.

Amateur restorers are sometimes indifferent mechanics who can ruin irreplaceable parts beyond repair. You'll note I said "sometimes." Many a bookkeeper or dentist who rushes toward his disassembled darling in the garage every night for five years does as painstaking and correct a restoration job as anyone could hope for.

If a man has the time and the ability *and* the burning desire, home restoration is the cheapest way. Professional restoration can be costly. The greatest expense, by far, is for labor, at, say, $4.00 an hour. Since it can take as many as 2,000 man-hours to bring a car back to life, commercial restorations are out of the question for many people.

Purists use as much as possible of the original car in their restorations, even tracking down things like the original spark plugs for their engines. The advertising columns of the antique-car-club magazines are filled with piteous pleas from such seekers after parts for their cars. It is possible, however, to buy new spark plugs and archaic sizes of tires for most old machines. New parts for really ancient vehicles are non-existent, and it is necessary either to fabricate them or to cannibalize a non-restorable car of the same type. Collectors purchase so-called "parts-cars" for this purpose.

After Spencer—his trailer still empty—had dropped me off at my house, I began to think about an old car a friend of mine had mentioned to me. He said it was a Welch of about 1905, that it lay in a carriage house on an estate that was about to be sold, and that he thought it could be bought.

I began reading everything I could on Welch's,

which wasn't much, but I discovered that the Welch had been a high-quality car with one of the first overhead-camshaft, hemispherical-combustion-chambered engines and a fascinating multiple-clutch transmission. This was enough. By the time the caretaker of the moldy old estate let me in to look at the car, I was feverish with desire.

The Welch was a shocking sight. It was vast, its rear disappearing into the gloom of the coach house it shared with some ancient carriages (one of which had been Secretary of State Seward's). It stood there like a weird prehistoric monster under its huge, rafter-scraping top. Its colors were indistinguishable; paintwork, woodwork, leather, brass were all the color of thirty-one years of dust. But one look under its hood at that crazy engine and I had to have it. I haggled not. I bought it.

When a friend of mine came up with his trailer to disentomb it and haul it home for me, we found that the carriage-house door in front of the car had not been opened for thirty-one years either. A crowbar helped that. The tires, which had been held off the floor, looked fine—round and plump; the Welch had slept on jacks. But when we tried to pump them up, the air just wheezed dismally out of unseen lesions; the tires had petrified to wood-like hardness. Later they had to be sawed and chiseled off the rims. Surprisingly, they supported the Welch as we towed it, creaking, out of its resting place and aboard the

trailer. The brass acetylene headlamps, though dented, were complete, but one of the kerosene sidelamps was missing. We questioned the caretaker—he knew nothing about it. My friend nudged me and rubbed thumb against forefinger. I pulled out a ten dollar bill, and miraculously the sidelamp materialized. (A sidelamp like that is worth fifty dollars.)

When we finally got the Welch into my garage (the tires were like broken-up papier-mâché from bouncing on the trailer) and had a good chance to examine it closely and soberly, I was overcome with remorse and foreboding at the enormity of the crime I had committed against the economic fortunes of my wife and kids, at the impossibility of ever making a car out of that horrifying mass of junk.

The Welch was a horror. It resembled pictures of 1907 Welch's but slightly. (We quickly discovered it was an '07, not an '05.) It had been "modernized" in the style of 1915. Its one-man top was a gruesome anachronism, as was its windshield. Some unfeeling wretch had added front doors and 1915-style mud-

233

guards. Its *derrière* had a rounded, decidedly un-1907-ish vulgarity.

"Isn't she beautiful?" I asked my wife.

"Very," she answered.

I set to. I threw away the top, tore off that infuriating windshield and those front doors. I started to investigate the car's internals, unscrewed things, lost nuts in the distant fastnesses of its mysterious gearbox, barked my knuckles, covered myself in half-century-old grease. I gave up.

Luckily, Ralph Buckley (whom I mentioned earlier in connection with Mercers) was willing to take it into his Antique Auto Shop in Pleasantville, New Jersey, and restore it for me. He and his helpers took the Welch to bits; if anything was unscrewable from any other part it was unscrewed. Then they started to build a new Welch from the old parts. First they sandblasted the chassis frame to remove the paint and crud of half a century. Then they erected upon it the engine, the transmission, the front and rear axles. If any part was worn or broken it was rebuilt as new.

When it came time to replace the bodywork, pictures of old Welch's were studied and measured and replicas of the original fenders were fabricated. That odd, rounded rear of the body was found to be but superimposed tinwork and was peeled off to reveal the original coachwork beneath.

A year went by. One day Buckley phoned me to come and get my car. I had, of course, been down to Pleasantville a few times in the interim. The first time I couldn't even find the car, it was in so many small bits and so dispersed about the shop. The second time I had seen the engine, all polished brass and shining steel, being set into the frame. This time I couldn't quite believe my eyes, for as I rounded the corner and drove up to Buckley's shop, there, shining in sparkling paint, its brasswork shimmering in the sunlight, was a brand new 1907 Welch, just like the wonderful pictures in those old, old copies of "The Horseless Age."

But what do you do with an ancient car once you've found it and brought it back to life? You can drive it,

of course, as I do my other car. But there are some disadvantages to such use, due mostly to people in modern machines. Their drivers gawk at you instead of at the road, and it's horrifying to watch the number of near accidents you cause by being a visual attraction. Another nerve-wracking habit of the modern driver comes from his determination to have a good look at your radiator in order to prove to his carload of relatives that your car is a Pierce-Arrow (They *always* think any big old car is a Pierce). To this end he dives in front of you and slams on his four-wheel, stop-o-matic power brakes. Since you have two-wheel brakes and thin tires with but a tenuous grip on the road, a lively few moments ensue.

Most ancient cars are used largely in connection with the events organized by the antique car clubs: meets, parades, and rallies.

Don't for a moment imagine that an antique-car meet is approached in any attitude of levity. To the participant in a big meet, such as the giant conclave of old cars held in Hershey, Pennsylvania, each fall, it is a deadly serious and heartburning business. For weeks before a meet he tries to divine the attitudes and foibles of the judges who will be examining the cars grouped in the same class as his (there are some nineteen different classes separating the steamers from the gas cars, the 1905 cars from the classics, etc.). Will the judges be impressed with a robin's-egg-blue cylinder block? Should he paint the wheels or leave them natural.

But mostly, he—and his wife—and his children—clean the car. Cleaning the car doesn't mean just cleaning the car—not to the trophy-hungry antique-car club member. After he gets it much cleaner and shinier than you would dream possible, he *really* starts cleaning. He attacks crevices with toothbrushes, even pipe cleaners, and not just on the bodywork, either. He delves into the dark recesses of the engine, he waxes and polishes the drive shaft, he anoints the muffler with secret cosmetics. The sacred brasswork is a career in itself, requiring hour after hour of dedicated rubbing with the owner's favorite

"Commemoration Run" from London to Brighton each November attracts hundreds of pre-1905 vehicles and millions of spectators. Far left: A group of competitors leaves Hyde Park. In the foreground is the famed motoring journalist, S.C.H. Davis on his Bollée Tri-car. An iron-tired 1895 Panhard and Levassor (above) leads the procession through London streets. At left, a competitor stops, en route, to adjust his 1902 Panhard.

235

A 1934, 1,100 cc Lagonda Rapier (left) leads a 1928 front-drive Alvis at a vintage sports-car race in England. Mr. and Mrs. Henry Austin Clark Jr. appear (below) in their 1916 Pierce-Arrow Model 66 Raceabout during the first Anglo-American Vintage Car Rally in England in 1955. Right: C.C. Clutton on the 1908 Hutton. Entered in the 1957 Anglo-American Vintage Car Rally, the Hutton had been built by Napier for the Isle of Man Tourist Trophy Race.

brass polish, selected from among the many kinds whose merits have been seriously discussed between his fellow brass polishers.

He doesn't often grease his darling's underpinnings. Heaven forbid that some tiny gobbet of grease near the left kingpin offend the judges and cost a demerit.

The richer antiquers avoid this labor. They have squads—nay battalions—of flunkies to prepare their machines for meets. I know of one such gentleman, a far-western oil tycoon, who boasts even a "Chief Curator" for his vast collection of beautifully restored cars. (This is *not* the man who has so many antiques he piles them on end to save room.)

It's delightful to drive toward a meet in your nicely tuned and polished antique car, waving happily to other antiques on their way to the meet, but you and the other people on the road are taking the grave risk of not winning a trophy that day. The smart and experienced cup hunter brings his machine, swathed in protective coverings, aboard a specially built trailer. Not for him an engine spotted with oil from actually being run, or a chassis defiled with the dust of the road.

At the meet the cars of each class are lined up in groups to await the judgment. Sometimes it takes hours of waiting for the judges to get to your car, but this period is one of the pleasanter aspects of the day. You talk to the people around you, discussing cars and other meets where the unspeakable judges had not the perception to give your beloved machine even an honorable mention.

Suddenly, the moment of truth. The judges, grim-faced, clip-boards in hand, surround your car. Each carries a marking chart for your car which rigidly allots (or subtracts) points for condition of brass, of upholstery, of paintwork, cleanliness of engine, etc. They even ask you to start the engine, noting how readily it commences, how it sounds (after this the trailer-the-car-to-the-meet boys feverishly polish away any specks of oil that may have sullied their lavender engine blocks).

As the day wears on, some people enter their cars in gymkhana-like events: jousting at balloons, teetering on giant seesaws, blindfold races, and the like. There are even contests for people who dress up in

236

costumes that they fondly imagine are of the same period as their cars.

This dressing up in funny clothes and false moustaches is dying out somewhat in the more sophisticated eastern meets, but in the Far West it is still de rigueur for women to wear plumed hats and lace dresses, while the men appear in top hats (to which are affixed goggles), string ties, violently checked tail coats, and spats. If you showed up at a British meet looking like that, they'd chuck you into the Thames.

The big British meet is the Commemoration Run from London to Brighton each November. This event celebrates the Emancipation Run of 1896 which marked the end of the notorious Red Flag Law. Limited to "veteran" cars,—under the rules of the Veteran Car Club of Great Britain, only machines built in 1904 or earlier are "veterans"—hundreds of such early cars leave Hyde Park, usually on a miserable, rainy morning, bound for Brighton on the south coast. More spectators show up along the way to cheer on the snuffling machines than at any motoring event—over 3,000,000 in 1960—and there is no

nonsense with trailers. You get your car to Brighton under its own power or you don't get a plaque.

Another thriving British organization, The Vintage Sports Car Club, looks back to the great past of sports and racing machines. They concern themselves with such sports cars as existed before 1931. But they don't just polish them and look at them; they race them and they hurl them up hills in rigorous climbing contests.

In 1954, Cecil Clutton, the president of this vigorous outfit, organized a contest between the Veteran Motor Car Club of America and his Vintage Sports Car Club; the Anglo-American Vintage Car Rally. Early American sporting vehicles sailed for England to engage in a contest with ten pre-1931 British sports cars. After eight days of rallying, hill climbing, and bending races (a race in and out of artificial obstacles), the British won. Two years later the British came over here and the Americans won.

Now there is a Vintage Sports Car Club of America. Maybe that old Stutz vs. Mercer argument can be settled once and for all.

". . . the scientists thinking up these machines seem to be trying to make them as un-car-like as possible."

Ask a Detroit automobile executive about the kind of car his company might build in the next two years, or even five years, and his mouth clamps tightly shut, perspiration appears on his brow, he takes a furtive look over his shoulder.

For, although every manufacturer's new model looks like the kissin' cousin of every other manufacturer's new model, the bigwigs of Detroit are always darkly reticent about their plans for the future. The near future, that is. They'll talk readily and happily about the cars of twenty years hence.

The big companies all spend great pots of money on the huge, beautifully designed research laboratories in which they are designing the distant future's passenger-carrying vehicles. You'll notice we didn't say cars, because the scientists thinking up these machines seem to be trying to make them as un-car-like as possible.

One outfit is trying to eliminate wheels, others are ready to ditch the piston-powered gasoline engine. Still another laboratory wants to eliminate the road. Most laudable of all, perhaps, is one company's efforts to get rid of the driver, or at least take the steering wheel away from him.

Before examining Detroit's chromium-encrusted crystal ball, however, let's try to foretell the characteristics of the car of just a few years hence.

The passenger car of tomorrow will almost certainly borrow heavily from the sports car of today. The channel-framed chassis is almost done for right now. The unitized-body chassis has taken its place, at least in the cheaper cars. For the more expensive machine, the tubular space frame covered with an aluminum skin is almost certainly in the offing.

Since the early Twenties, aluminum engines have been common in Europe. Hispano-Suiza and A.C., for example, had aluminum blocks with ferrous cylinder liners some forty years ago. Recently, Buick and Oldsmobile, and even staid Rolls-Royce, have gone over to light alloy engines. Within a very few years the cast-iron engine will be as rare as the horse collar.

The disc brake will become universal in a very few years, even on the cheapest Detroit automobile.

Will the engine stay up front in most cars? Yes, but there will be an increase in the number of rear-engined designs, as engines grow lighter in relation to the power they produce. Owing to the use of aluminum alloys it will become more practical to use more powerful engines in the rear without making cars unmanageably tail-heavy.

Transmissions, both automatic and manual, will also move rearward, and what Detroit calls a "transaxle" (gearbox and differential in one unit) will be commonplace. Nor is this anything new. Stutz, Packard, and A.C. used rear axles incorporating gearboxes generations ago; Lancia and the Pontiac Tempest use such an arrangement today, although unlike the machines of fifty years ago, they have swing-axled, independent rear suspensions.

Inspired by the spectacular success of the tiny rear-powered British Formula I machines, like the Cooper and the Lotus, Ferrari and Maserati are already

Preceding pages: Cars in Detroit's crystal
ball are General Motors' turbine-driven Firebird III,
Ford's "Volante"—an inoperable model of a fan-
flown "Aero-car"—and Plymouth's conception of a sports
car—the XNR. Chrysler's gas-turbine engine (below)
has been successfully tested in a Plymouth.
English Rover Company's 1956 "T-3" gas-turbine car
(center) had 110 bhp, 52,000 rpm engine, four-wheel drive.
"L'Étoile Filante" (bottom) is Renault turbo-car.

building racing sports cars with rear engines in tubular space frames. Sports two-seaters with similar
chassis-engine arrangements, but with a bit of weather
protection and a modicum of luggage space are almost
a certainty in the near future.

But what about the Wild Blue Future? What about
gas turbines, for example?

Ever since the last war and the development of the
jet engine, fantastic amounts of money have been
poured into experimentation with the jet engine's
near relative, the gas turbine, not only by Detroit's
big three, but also by Rover and Renault abroad.

You can't blame them, for the gas turbine has many
advantages:

1. It is light and small for the power it produces.
Chrysler's latest turbine weighs but 450 pounds (a
conventional V-8 weighs about 800) and delivers 140
hp to the drive shaft, giving a performance comparable to a 200 bhp piston engine. Yet it measures only
27 x 27 x 25 inches.

2. It is much simpler, having about a fifth as many
moving parts as a piston engine.

3. It needs no radiator or liquid cooling system.

4. Its electrical system is simpler. No ignition system is needed, aside from one spark plug for starting.

5. A turbine is vibration free.

6. It starts easier in winter and needs no warm-up.

7. A turbine will run on almost anything from bourbon whiskey to whale oil.

The gas-turbine car for Everyman is almost, but
not quite, here. The problems of early turbines—high

fuel consumption, especially at low speeds and part loads, lack of engine braking abilities, and slow speed response to pressure on the accelerator—have just about been licked. In mass production a turbine can eventually be built more cheaply than a reciprocating engine of equal power.

As far back as 1956, a turbine-engined Chrysler made a successful 3,020-mile trip across the continent. In 1959, a Plymouth sedan averaged 19.39 miles per gallon at an average speed of 38.3 mph for 576 miles. In 1956, George J. Huebner, Jr., executive engineer in charge of Chrysler research, predicted that the turbo-car would be a reality in ten years' time. He still hasn't changed his mind.

Why then the foot-dragging? As Mr. Huebner pointed out to me recently, the turbine isn't just a new kind of engine to be slapped under the hood of next year's Plymouth as it moves down the assembly line. It is an entirely new kind of power, as different from the reciprocating gas engine as the gas engine was from the slow-turning steam engine sixty years ago. It will eventually require an entirely new concept of automotive design, new methods of production, a retraining of workers and service personnel, even a new technique of driving.

Nor are the big manufacturers about to dump the billions they have invested in plants for producing the perfectly usable—and continually improving—piston-engined cars of today.

The electric car, because of its silence and simplicity, always has fascinated automotive dreamers. But, as we have seen, the electric of the past was far too slow and much too limited in range. "If only someone would invent an ultra-light, powerful, quickly rechargeable battery," they say. No one has, and it doesn't look as if anyone will in the near future. But

Fuel cells installed in Allis-Chalmers tractor (top) provide enough electricity to power 20 hp, D.C. electric motor, which develops 3,000 pounds of drawbar pull. The German NSU-Wankel engine (above) is believed, in some quarters, to be the next step in automotive power. Unlike either piston engines or gas turbines, the combustion cycle takes place in constantly moving, banana-shaped chambers which grow larger and smaller as eccentrically mounted, "trochoid" rotor revolves in its casing. Water is pumped through concentric outer casing for cooling purposes. The engine runs with turbine-like smoothness due to absence of reciprocating parts. An experimental engine weighing 35 pounds, developed 40 bhp at 8,000 rpm and was said to be capable of 15,000 rpm with a considerable increase in power. Experiments mounting four engines on a single shaft are in progress. Curtiss-Wright holds American manufacturing license.

an electrically driven car, powered by an entirely different kind of battery, may be coming.

This battery is the fuel cell. Unlike the storage battery, it is not merely a crude reservoir for the electricity with which it is supplied, but actually *produces* current. A fuel cell utilizes the phenomenon whereby oxygen and hydrogen form water when combining. In the fuel cell these two gases are fed through metal tubes into a caustic solution. As they combine, they make not just H_2O, but also a small, one-and-a-half volt electric current. The cells can be tiny—an experimental Allis Chalmers tractor recently had its hood stuffed with no less than 1,008 of them; about 1,500 volts worth—but they delivered enough moxie for the tractor to plow up a golf course in a demonstration.

The cells can deliver their current directly to a small electric motor at each wheel hub, thereby eliminating in one fell swoop drive shafts, transmissions, clutches—even the kind of brakes we have been used to, since the motors can be instantly reversible.

Thus far, however, most fuel cells have been used in space projects for powering the gadgetry in satellites and such. So you'll have to wait.

You'd think that the people who put America on wheels with the Model T Ford would have some special respect for wheels. Far from it, Ford for some years now has been doing its best to figure out a means of doing in the poor old wheel. Ford calls its wheelless wonder a Levacar: levitation-car. It is quite unlike vehicles supported by reaction to air jets, such as the British Hovercraft and its American counterparts built by Curtiss-Wright. Those are, I hope, flying machines. This book is, I think, about cars.

Instead of wheels, the Levacar is supported on discs several feet in diameter and flush with the flat bottom of the vehicle. These discs, called Levapods, are perforated with holes through which compressed air is forced downward. This raises them very slightly above the road surface on a thin cushion of air. It is this frictionless cushion, only a small fraction of an inch deep, upon which the Levacar rides.

The Levapods do not propel the car. They only provide the air cushion. The car itself can be propelled horizontally by means of ducted fans, jets, propellers. The Ford people talk about 300 to 500 mph speeds. The power required to make the compressed air is very slight and can be produced by a small auxiliary to the main horizontal power source.

To demonstrate the amazing lack of friction when riding on a thin cushion of air, the Ford researchers built a lovely little device called the Levascooter, which looks like a kid's scooter without wheels. It makes just enough air to raise itself a few thousandths of an inch off the floor. Its forward movement is provided by your strong right leg—if you can get on the blasted thing. For it slides around the floor as if it were on ice. A sidewalk outdoors would be too rough for the scooter, just as present-day highways would be too rough for a car-sized Levacar. Therefore, the current idea at Ford is to run bus-sized Levacars on smooth, monorail tracks, embraced top and sides by frictionless Levapods. But, again, these are railroads, not automobiles.

For some time now, General Motors has inclined toward the belief that you should not be trusted with a steering wheel in your hands. You may remember that during the past few years they have turned out various turbine-powered, super-dream-cars that actually could run. These are the Firebirds I, II, and III. The steering-wheel thing started with a publicity movie on Firebird II, which showed an advertising man's dream of the all-American family, all shiny

"The gas-turbine car for Everyman is almost, but not quite, here."

teeth and ruddy good looks, setting off on a trip. All of a sudden Pop folds up the steering handles (it wasn't a wheel, even away back in 1956) and turns on a radio transmitter. In clipped tones, he tells a guy in a tower something about going into "auto-control," meaning that this special Buick, or whatever it was, would from then on head for Cincinnati, or wherever, with nobody steering. The car would get there by following an electric wire sunk in the road. After a few "Rogers" and "Overs," Pop relaxes with a drink and the car sets off into the sunset and eternal happiness.

Although I believed it implicitly at the time, Firebird II couldn't *really* follow its nose along an electric cable buried in the road. But a couple of engineers at G.M.—Joe Bidwell and Roy Cataldo—thought they could actually make this no-hands pipe dream work. By 1958 they had a car with two electronic probes down under the front license plate sniffing its way along a magnetic cable buried in a piece of highway. The probes sent signals back to an electronic analog computer in the glove compartment. The computer then translated the signals and "commanded" the power-steering system to turn right or left.

Since then, G.M. has refined this system. Bidwell and Cataldo's first rig could only steer. It couldn't put on the brakes if the car got close to an obstacle ahead. Nor could it gradually reduce engine speed as it approached a car traveling in the same lane. Now, by means of a multiple wire cable buried in the road, a block system like a railroad's, and a small control-box in the trunk, G.M.'s "Auto-Control" system can do all of these things. They haven't built a full-sized road like this yet, as far as I know, but I have seen a scale model work. Perfectly horrifying.

G.M. has another device that still lets you control your car, but it's not a steering wheel. This thing looks like the short and stubby gear lever surmounted by a ball that is beloved by pukka sports-car drivers. After you start the engine and set the transmission in "drive," you control the car entirely by manipulating this ball-on-a-stick. Push it ahead and the car accelerates in a straight line forward. Pull it back and the engine slows down while the brakes go on. Move it to the left and the car turns left. Move it right and you turn right. (I forget how you reverse.) The limits of movement are short; about two inches. Oddly, you still have the "feel" of steering and braking; it's easy to get used to. This "unicontrol" stick has no mechanical connection to the engine, brakes, or steering. Its movements control rheostats which signal computers which, in turn, signal the various hydraulic mechanisms doing the work. Control is steady, regardless of your speed. A quick movement of the stick at high speed won't send you into a wild skid.

"A friend of mine . . .
told me the other day of a fine
new method of automatic
propulsion he had dreamed up."

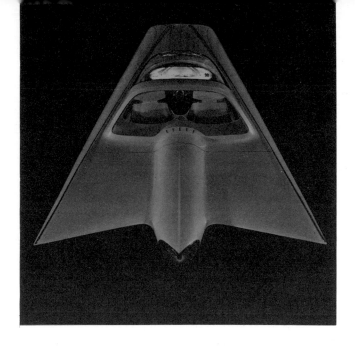

One of the engineers at the tech center told me about a Chevrolet sedan they had fitted with "unicontrol." He drove it into a gas station to fill the tank. The gas-station attendant was fascinated. He looked the car over thoroughly, ooh-ing and ah-ing, because it was a brand-new model not yet in the showrooms. He never even noticed that it had no steering wheel.

But don't tear your steering wheel and column out by the roots. Not yet. G.M. has no intention of building cars without steering wheels for quite a while. Maybe never.

A friend of mine, a low, beatnik-type fellow, who, I suspect, hates cars, told me the other day of a fine new method of automatic propulsion he had dreamed up. "As you know," he said, "we are, all of us, just an agglomeration of magnetic particles that make up the atoms which compose us."

Knowing nothing of the nuclear sciences, I agreed.

"Since we're all just a lot of magnetic impulses," he went on "why couldn't you just break a fellow down into his electronic components and put him on tape? Then all you have to do is send the stuff on the tape, by radio, to wherever the guy wants to go. There they reconstitute him. Or if he isn't in a hurry, you could even mail the tape."

"That's a *real* compact idea," I said, "I'll take it right over to American Motors."

Nonoperative, two-wheeled Ford "Gyron" (top) is a typical example of styling-department doodling. General Motors Unicontrol (above), fitted to experimental, turbine-engined Firebird III, eliminates the steering wheel, the brake pedal, and the accelerator. Moved forward, it speeds up the car in a straight line; rearward, it throttles the engine and applies the brakes. Moved at an angle, it steers the car. Control actuates electrical devices that signal hydraulic mechanisms which steer and brake the car.

PICTURE CREDITS

ALBERT MECHAM COLLECTION OF THE LONG ISLAND AUTOMOTIVE MUSEUM: 46-47, 52, 56, 62 (upper), 64 (upper left) 70 (lower), 72, 75 (center).

ALBERT SQUILLACE: right-front endsheet, 217 (second and third rows; bottom right), 230 (right; upper left), 231 (upper right, center left, lower left).

ALLIS-CHALMERS MFG. CO.: 242 (upper).

ANTIQUE AUTOMOBILE: 100 (upper), 101 (lower), 163 (lower).

A. MAGGIO, PARIS: 184 (upper).

A. TRAVERSO, CANNES: 187 (lower).

ASTON MARTIN LAGONDA LTD: 218.

AUTOSPORT, ENGLAND: 163 (upper), 232 (left), 234, 235 (upper; lower), 236 (upper; lower).

AUTO-UNION, GERMANY: 185 (lower left and right).

BRITISH CROWN COPYRIGHT, SCIENCE MUSEUM, LONDON: 19 (bottom).

BRITISH TRAVEL ASSOCIATION: 67 (lower right), 111 (lower), 159 (right), 166 (upper), 197 (upper), 208 (lower left), 237.

BROWN BROTHERS: 88 (both).

CAR AND DRIVER: 170 (except top), 205 (lower), 242 (lower).

CHARLES DOLLFUS: 14-15, 17 (upper right, center left, lower right), 18, 20 (upper left), 22, 23 (lower right), 28-29 (right), 34 (lower), 35 (lower), 36 (lower), 43 (lower right), 78, 85 (three photos bottom right), 108, 109 (bottom), 126 (lower).

CHRYSLER CORPORATION: 238 (bottom left), 238-239 (bottom right), 241 (upper).

DAIMLER-BENZ, GERMANY: 32-33, 33 (upper right), 92, 93, 123.

DAVID CHAMPION SPINDLER: 148-149 (right).

FIAT PHOTO: 220 (bottom left).

FORD MOTOR COMPANY: 164-165, 166 (lower), 167, 238-239 (center), 245 (upper).

FUMAGALLI, MILANO: 187 (upper).

GENERAL MOTORS CORPORATION: 198 (top), 238-239 (top), 245 (lower).

GÜNTHER MOLTER: 242 (lower).

HENRY N. MANNEY III: 223 (bottom).

HOFFMAN MOTORS CORPORATION: 149 (right), 220 (center).

INDIANAPOLIS MOTOR SPEEDWAY CORPORATION: 178-179 (upper), 190 (lower right).

IRVING DOLIN: 132-133, 223 (center), 249.

JAGUAR CARS INC.: 136-137, 138, 139, 140-141, 141, 198-199 (bottom).

KIRKPATRICK COLLECTION OF THE LONG ISLAND AUTOMOTIVE MUSEUM: 183 (upper).

LESLIE SAALBURG: 150-151.

LONG ISLAND AUTOMOTIVE MUSEUM: 37 (lower), 40-41, 48 (lower), 55, 57, 58 (upper; lower), 62 (lower), 65 (upper right), 66-67 (upper), 68 (lower left), 70 (upper), 74-75 (lower), 100-101 (upper), 130-131, 158-159 (center), 160-161, 174 (left), 196, 208 (upper), 210 (upper left), 211 (center), 227 (center), 228 (upper; lower), 233.

LOUIS KLEMENTASKI, ENGLAND: 158 (left), 192, 205 (upper right), 206 (lower), 209.

LUIGI CHINETTI MOTORS, INC.: 199 (upper).

MARCUS W. TAYLOR: 215 (upper).

MENCH PUBLISHING COMPANY, RIDGEFIELD, CONN.: 202-203 (lower).

MUSÉE DE LA VOITURE ET DU TOURISME, COMPIÈGNE: 76-77, 80-81.

OWNED BY THE HENRY FORD MUSEUM: 102.

PATRICK BENJAFIELD, ENGLAND: 157.

PHOTOGRAPHIE DU CONSERVATOIRE NATIONAL DES ARTS ET MÉTIERS: 17 (upper left), 25, 33 (lower right), 34 (lower right), 36 (lower left).

PORSCHE OF AMERICA: 213 (center).

PUBLIFOTO-PIX: 210 (right).

RADIO TIMES HULTON PICTURE LIBRARY: 17 (center right), 20-21 (center), 21, 23 (lower), 28 (left), 39, 42-43 (lower left), 53 (upper), 63, 64-65 (lower), 66 (lower left), 71, 74 (upper), 75 (upper), 79, 82 (upper), 85 (upper), 98-99.

RALLYE MOTORS, INC.: 217 (top row).

RALPH STEIN: 18-19, 30 (lower left), 35 (upper), 54 (lower right), 74 (upper), 104-105, 107, 120 (upper left and right), 134 (bottom), 186 (upper), 208-209 (center), 208 (lower right), 211 (upper), 214 (upper), 227 (upper left), 227 (bottom).

RENAULT OF FRANCE: 241 (bottom).

ROAD & TRACK: 119 (lower right), 134 (third from top), 144, 145, 149 (left), 184 (lower), 186 (lower), 188-189, 190 (upper left, center, and right), 191, 193, 197 (lower), 201, 205 (upper left), 206-207, 210 (lower), 210-211 (bottom), 212, 212-213 (lower), 213 (upper), 214 (lower), 216, 219.

ROBERT S. GRIER: 134 (second from top), 152 (both), 200.

ROGER HALLE: 126 (upper left).

ROLLS-ROYCE: 115, 118, 119 (upper right and left), 121 (lower).

ROVER CO., LTD.: 241 (center).

R. M. GROSSMAN, INC.: 215 (lower).

ROOTES MOTORS: 179, 220 (bottom right).

SMITHSONIAN INSTITUTION: 24, 26, 27, 30-31 (right), 38 (lower), 43 (upper left and right), 53 (lower), 60, 110.

STANDARD-TRIUMPH MOTOR COMPANY, INC.: 203 (upper), 223 (upper).

STEAM AUTOMOBILE CLUB OF AMERICA: 111 (upper).

TECHNISCHES MUSEUM FÜR INDUSTRIE UND GEWERBE: 30 (upper left).

THE AUTOCAR, LONDON: 38 (upper), 49, 50 (lower), 68-69 (lower), 82 (center; lower), 83, 84 (upper right), 96, 126 (upper right).

THE MOTOR, ENGLAND: 134 (top), 170 (top), 183 (lower), 204, 206 (upper).

THOMAS H. BURNSIDE: jacket, left-front endsheet, 37 (upper), 44-45, 48 (upper), 50 (upper), 51, 54 (upper), 59, 73, 86-87, 90-91, 94, 94-95, 109 (upper), 112-113, 116-117, 120 (lower), 121 (upper), 124-125, 128-129, 142-143, 146-147, 148, 154-155, 156, 169, 172-173, 174 (right), 176-177, 180, 194-195, 217 (bottom left), 220-221 (top left), 221 (upper right; lower), 224-225, 230 (bottom), 231 (upper left, lower right), right- and left-rear endsheets.

THOMPSON PRODUCTS AUTO MUSEUM: 68-69 (upper).

TONY BIRT (FOR HAMBRO AUTOMOTIVE CORP.): 202 (top), 203 (bottom).

UNDERWOOD & UNDERWOOD: 106.

WARREN S. WEIANT: 227 (upper right).

BIBLIOGRAPHY

A PICTURE HISTORY OF MOTORING L. T. C. Rolt, London, 1956.
A RECORD OF MOTOR RACING Gerald Rose, London, 1909.
ASTON MARTIN Compiled by Dudley Coram, London, 1958.
BUGATTI—A BIOGRAPHY W. F. Bradley, London, 1948.
CHRONIK DER MERCEDES-BENZ FAHRZEUGE UND MOTOREN, Stuttgart-Bad Canstatt, 1956.
COMBUSTION ON WHEELS David L. Cohn, Boston, 1944.
DUESENBERG J. C. Elbert, Arcadia, California, 1951.
ÉLÉMENTS D'AUTOMOBILE L. Baudry de Saunier, Paris, 1906.
FILL 'ER UP! Bellamy Partridge, New York, 1952.
FROM VETERAN TO VINTAGE Karslake and Pomeroy, London, 1956.
GRAND PRIX Barré Lyndon, London, 1935.
HISTOIRE DE LA LOCOMOTION TERRESTRE L'Illustration, Paris, 1936.
HORSELESS CARRIAGE DAYS Hiram Percy Maxim, New York, 1937.
LA LOCOMOTION Octave Uzanne, Paris, 1900.
LA VOITURE DE DEMAIN John Grand-Carteret, Paris, 1898.
LES 24 HEURES DU MANS Roger Labric, Le Mans, 1949.
MAINTAINING THE BREED J. W. Thornley, London, 1956.
MONTE CARLO RALLY Russell Lowry, London, undated.
MOTORS AND MOTOR DRIVING Badminton Library, London, 1902.
MOTOR VEHICLES AND MOTORS W. Worby Beaumont, London, 1902.
RACING HISTORY OF THE BENTLEY Darell Berthon, London, 1956.
RACING VOITURETTES Kent Karslake, London, 1950.
RALLYING TO MONTE CARLO Mike Couper, London, 1956.
TECHNICAL FACTS OF THE VINTAGE BENTLEY Bentley Drivers Club, London, 1956.
TEN YEARS OF MOTORS AND MOTOR RACING Charles Jarrott, London, 1906.
THE ANTIQUE AUTOMOBILE St. John Nixon, London, 1956.
THE BENTLEYS AT LE MANS J. D. Benjafield, London, 1948.
THE BUGATTI BOOK Compiled by Eaglesfield and Hampton, 3rd edition, London, 1958.
THE COMPLETE MOTORIST A. B. Filson Young, London, 1906.
THE FERRARI Hans Tanner, Boston, 1960.
THE GRAND PRIX CAR Laurence Pomeroy, London, 1949.
THE MAGIC OF A NAME Harold Nockolds, London, 1949.
THE RACING CAR Clutton, Posthumus, Jenkinson, London, 1956.
"W. O."—THE AUTOBIOGRAPHY OF W. O. BENTLEY London, 1958.

AUTHOR AND HIS 1935 PHANTOM II CONTINENTAL ROLLS-ROYCE.